STRING'S CROSS

A NOVEL BY

Guri P Essen

Copyright © 2015 by Guri P Essen

Library of Congress Control Number: 2015906113

HeronDrivePress
San Ramon, California

Copyeditor Joyce Gunn
Cover design by Brianna Stuart

ISBN-10: 069242086X
ISBN-13: 978-0692420867

To Joan,
To our incredible kids Leah Thalia and Peter Alan.

To my copyeditor and treasured mate Joyce.

"What would you consider the best intellectual training for the would-be writer?"
George Plimpton, The Paris Review

"Let's say that he should go out and hang himself because he finds that writing well is impossibly difficult. Then he should be cut down without mercy and forced by his own self to write as well as he can for the rest of his life. At least he will have the story of the hanging to commence with"
Ernest Hemingway

"Every novel is some kind of higher autobiography."
Saul Bellow quoting Alberto Moravia

Prologue

IN the beginning God created the heaven and the earth.
Gen. 1:1

You may have noted the stock disclaimer following the title page which reads: This is a work of fiction. Names, characters, businesses, places, events and incidents are either the products of the author's imagination or used in a fictitious manner. Any resemblance to actual persons, living or dead, or actual events is purely coincidental.

That legal caution attended to, you should be told that almost everything ever written is fiction. Each day that the stock market is open, the nightly news will give you numbers for its major indices - the Dow, the Nasdaq, and the S&P500. Facts! After that, they'll tell you why these numbers have gone up or down. Fiction!

Write a page telling exactly what went on with you and a child, a parent, or a close friend on one particular, very special day for the two of you. Ask that person to do the same. Now read them back to one another. Which is fact, which is fiction?

Names of well-known people, like names of well-known places, set a novel's stage, lend it color, significance. What is said of these landmarks, these people or places, will vary. Mt. Rushmore will be called, by some, a tribute to human genius, by others, the desecration of nature's beauty.

In this story nothing is said of the big mountains that hasn't already been said. Of the hills and valleys, they speak for themselves as they were heard or imagined, with names they did or did not use, and with no intent to slander or present them in any unfavorable way.

Part I

The Virgin Birth

Chapter 1

Excerpts From the Five Books of
Moses - and Elsewhere

It might not be fair to begin here with the statement that Rosa Maria Ambuehl was decidedly anti-Semitic. Unfair, first, because Rosa was *anti* almost everyone not white Anglo-Saxon Protestant. Lutherans, though hardly Anglo, were acceptable. She herself was Lutheran. Second, the grandfathers of Rosa's boyfriend Irving, himself an avowed atheist, were both rabbis.

> *These are the families of the Levites: the family of ...*
> Ex. 6:18-20; Num. 3:19; 26:58-59; I Chr. 6:2-3,18; 23:12-13;
> 24:20; Luke 3:23-28

Born in the Bronx in the last year of the nineteenth century, World War I was responsible for Irving's relocation to the west and to Rosa. His enlistment to serve in that great European conflict met with one of those war department curiosities resulting in his being assigned as company bugler to Hawaii's Scoffield Barracks. This at a time when Hawaii's National Guard was called into federal service to replace the troops being transferred back to the U.S. and on to Europe. At war's end, Irv's contingent joined Camp Kearny's 40th Division in San Diego for demobilization. There, with fellow Scoffield soldier Archie Miehls, he began his west coast existence.

With a population under 75,000, less than a seventeenth of his hometown, Irving was created for the little beach city of

San Diego. He was a natural athlete and an indefatigable swimmer, having gained that skill chasing ferries across the Spuyten Duyvil and Harlem rivers between the Bronx and Manhattan. He stood at just over five-foot-ten-inches tall, square-framed, the perfect mesomorph. With curly hair, a slightly aquiline nose and an eye contact grin, he had the requisite flapper magnetism. Some called him a Spencer Tracy look-alike.

And Irving wasn't all body. He had a quick uneducated brain that almost matched. He had learned the usual before dropping out of school halfway through his ninth year. He could name the capitals of each of the forty-eight states and his gift for numbers, second only to his swimming, was strengthened during his adolescence by verifying the liquor sales in his uncle's tavern. The "kleiner schmok," as the bartenders called him, would mark liquid levels on the bottles and report to Uncle Josh any anomalies between the diminishing spirits and the cash register tallies.

Irv had been hanging around "the store" for as long as he could remember. The long dark counter, the stairs leading to the tiny upstairs office, the hugs from the regular lady drinkers were all part of his childhood. Later, he would think often of two particular events: the death of the Rabbi, his father's father, and the day his own father left and didn't return.

The early years of the twentieth century were exciting ones in the big city and life in uptown Harlem was no exception. Between 110th and 150th Street, from Manhattan to Third Avenue, lived the third largest community of Jews in the world. It was here that the Rabbi taught and where his oldest son, Josh, served his refreshments. It was here that young Irv watched the horse-drawn carts morph into those powered by gasoline - a first attempt at transportation ecology - cleaner streets, less pollution, no more horse shit.

Longevity was a part of the paternal genome. Irving was nine when he saw his grandfather start down the tavern's ladder-like stairs from the office above, a nearly full pitcher of beer in his right hand. The Rabbi uttered a kind of grunt, then cascaded down to the foot of the bar. He was ninety-nine; he was dead. Josh put a couple of nickels into the kid's hand and guided him out onto the street. Irv bought himself an often-favored combination: a pickle and an ice cream cone.

Less than two years later, seated on his favorite stool near the stairs, he listened to shouting from the office. Ruthie, on the stool next to his, tickled the scalp beneath his curly hair with her finger tips. "Don't pay any attention," she whispered, "Brothers are always at it." But his father stomped down the stairs and out the front door. It would be sixty-four years until Irving saw him again.

Abraham begat Isaac: and Isaac begat ... begat ...
begat and begat ... begat Rosa
almost Matt. 1:1-17

Rosa's early years were as pastoral as Irving's were urban. Her father, Peter August, born in Davos, Switzerland in the middle of the nineteenth century, was one of thousands to heed the advice of their Swiss leaders and emigrate to America. The once-fertile Swiss soil could no longer support its small sustenance farmers, and winter sports had yet to take root in the highlands. Illinois was, at that time, the agricultural capital of the United States.

Peter left Davos in 1886 with his only child, a four-year-old son, August; childbirth had claimed the boy's mother. Peter's destination was Highland, Illinois. His plan was that once settled in the U.S., he would probe the German speaking world for August's new mother. But the Prairie State with its unending views of a land given over to a single crop - maize, oats, hay, wheat, potatoes or barley - drained the alpine native of his spirit. If not for August, he would have jumped at Horace Greeley's admonition of twenty years before and taken off running for the West.

1889 became Peter's year of salvation. A younger man, also from Switzerland's Graubunden Canton, arrived with newspapers and two photographs of what the papers called the "City of Dreams." Port Townsend, Washington would become, the articles said, the largest harbor on the west coast of the United States. Beyond the bay, one of the photographs revealed an irresistible forest of evergreens. The deciding shove came from a single storyline his friend helped translate, " ... and young women are arriving from the east and from a number of places in Europe to help balance the city's shortage."

Work came easily in Port Townsend where Peter found himself in demand as landscaper or gardener for many of the ornate new Victorian homes cropping up along the waterfront. More importantly, his quest for a wife became obsessive. The bride brokers he had heard of couldn't be found. It was difficult: a matter of finding the right foreign newspapers and of communicating by ship and by rail. But in a little over a year he had found her, Caroline Gesell. He had her picture, he had a letter in her own handwriting. He had saved enough money to pay for her passage. He danced with nine-year-old August. Life was something to love.

There was still the question of how to book that passage. Getting Caroline from her home in Dinkelsbuhl, Bavaria to his in Port Townsend, Washington took a bit of planning. Someone had told him that Washington University's president, Asa Mercer, had brought a group of young ladies from Boston to Seattle in the mid-sixties to be Seattle's new teachers. Asa had them take a train to New York City, a ship to Panama, a train across the isthmus, and another ship to San Francisco and on to Seattle. But that was before completion of the transcontinental railway. In 1887, just a couple of years ago, Seattle had become Northern Pacific Railroad's western terminus.

Northern Pacific Rail had reneged on its promise to Port Townsend to run a line there from Tacoma. Instead, it had stopped short in Seattle. If Caroline was to cross America by rail, Seattle was where the ride would end. Peter made the final arrangements. It would be rail to Le Havre, ship's steerage to New York, rail across the country and a short sail up Puget Sound to his home.

Caroline arrived in Port Townsend, along with the beginning of a U.S. economic downturn. The city was now at the summit of its growth, population seven thousand. It was mid-September 1891. Nine-year-old August, staring down at his feet just past the dock end of the gangway, held the sign, "Willkommen in Amerika, Caroline Gesell." As she stood before the sign, Peter shouted his encore welcome, including a reference to open arms, *"Ja, wir begrüßen Sie mit offenen Armen, Caroline."*

Smiling didn't come easily to Caroline. She looked back and forth from the child to the man. The tall, straight farmer with his tanned skin, wavy deep brown hair and a full, just short of handlebar length mustache, was far handsomer than she had anticipated; and the boy, well, he looked healthy.

Peter also hid his reactions. She was smaller than expected and sterner looking than in her photo. Yet he couldn't miss the nice warm curves apparent even through her heavy clothing. Maybe it was the way her hair was styled, tied tightly back and bunched up to cover her forehead, that kept that warmth from softening her face.

Besides his skill with plants, Peter had one other gift: a crazy knack for corrupting words. His English was gathered word-by-word from newspapers and a dictionary, and he was now a bilingual punster, mixing his native *Switzerdeutsch* and poorly-understood and poorly-spoken English into a montage of bewildering verbal expressions. It was a talent, to both their pleasure and embarrassment, he would pass along to his children and to his children's children. Today it was a game saver with his welcome: "From the blue see to our fertile blossoming new motherland shore, we see come the round blossoms of our welcome new mother." Her newly-creased forehead made it clear to August that Caroline spoke no English, or if she did, this English was beyond her. He translated his father's words dutifully and verbatim into German. After which all three looked at one another in amazement, and the laughter began.

Peter and Caroline were married on October 11, 1891. He gave her a family treasure: a necklace made of sixty-one flat gold links terminating in a hollow, decorated, five-sided object cradling what he assumed had to be a ruby. Six additional links were attached to the base of the pentagon, three on either side. Rosa Maria was born ten months later, August 19, 1892.

The "City of Dreams," the site destined to become the city with the largest harbor on the west coast, was dying. Northern Pacific's deception had sealed its fate. There was to be no rail connecting it with the outside world, and the national slowdown, predicting the U.S. depression destined to arrive the following year, was hastening the town's demise.

While work became increasingly difficult to find, word was coming from both Germany and Switzerland that water and land for farming could be had not far inland from the southern California coast. This promised land, they were told, was like the rocky soil of Peter's youth. Rosa was two months old when the family followed the sun south to settle amid the fledging orange groves of Ontario, California. For as long as she lived, Rosa would insist she was a native Californian.

Chapter 2

The Exodus - and the
Welcome of the Land

*into the land of the Canaanites, and the Hittites, and
... , a land flowing with milk and honey*
Ex. 13:5

Once a scrawny kid, taken from school at thirteen because of his frailty and precociousness; now a great hulk of a man, a man with surprisingly delicate features countered by piercing eyes and a beard completely hiding his neck. At twenty-nine, he is a successful man, a self-taught engineer and a celebrated designer of ships. He has enjoyed most of his life in Canada's Kingston, Ontario, where the lake by that name, Ontario - an Iroquois word for 'sparkling water' - commingles with the Saint Lawrence River. Now he misses his parents, his sister, and two of his brothers who had moved south three years ago. He is also not too pleased with the previous winter's heavy snows, and he is restless. After a conference with his wife, Annette, it is decided. They will pack up their two sons, Andrew and Ben, and visit his family in dry, sunny Riverside, California. George Chaffey, Jr. will never return.

His father, George, Sr., once owner of a profitable Kingston ship building enterprise, had retired to twenty acres of what he referred to as an irrigation community, a place where he could purchase water as well as farmland, water to tease his dry land into agricultural productivity. The younger George and his family arrived there to find fields of healthy young fruit trees, pretty and green. These first orchards were the proud accomplishment of the family botanist, his younger brother William, then twenty-five. The years of separation had strengthened the bond between the two men, William respecting the brilliant, intellectual George and George marveling at his down-to-earth, get-it-done brother. It didn't take them long to plot and to explore.

With their youngest brother, twenty-year-old Charles, they rode about the countryside. They would gather up some food for lunch, saddle the horses, and spend the day riding and looking, George always amazed at the great desert expanse. It was in the early fall of 1881 that they ambled along for twenty-five miles or so northwest over the Santa Ana River to the stark vast deserts below the San Gabriel Mountains and its crown, old Mount Baldy. Below the mountains and as far as one could see, all was a rocky, sandy ocean of land, dotted here and there with wild mustard, sagebrush, chamisal, and an occasional cottonwood or willow hugging a dry stream bed. All George Chaffey could see was row after row of green trees, broken up into neat square parcels.

George and William were to discover that seven years earlier a single house had been built in that unlikely place. On November 24 of that year, Thanksgiving Day, they met with its owner, Captain Joseph Garcia, and his wife, Elizabeth. The Portuguese-born Captain, after a life of adventure on the high seas and a short stint at winemaking in the Cucamonga hills to the north, had dropped his anchor to retire in this barren, isolated outpost. He owned the house, the surrounding five hundred and sixty acres, and the water rights to Day Canyon and the creek on the property's eastern border. The importance of these rights was not lost on the men from the land whose name meant "sparkling water." A deal was struck. The Chaffeys would buy the entire holdings. The price was set at $30,000.

The Chaffeys named the place Etiwanda in honor of an Algonquin chief, a First Nation friend from Canada. They were ecstatic. They dreamed of Etiwanda, the Etiwanda Colony, becoming an agricultural Mecca. They formed a mutual water company, an innovative notion, to ensure future settlers that no farm would die of thirst. Each and every parcel would be entitled to life giving water. Then, other areas came onto the market and they could not contain their energy, their hunger to transform the land. With financial aid from their parents, Charles, and another brother Elswood, they first bought up another 6,218 acres of the desert. For this land, a two and a half hour walk to the south and west, they paid nine dollars and sixty-five cents an acre. Soon it was again expanded, south to the Southern Pacific Railroad tracks and north to the Kincaid Ranch. This new domain took its name from their home province, and within one short year of the Etiwanda purchase, became the Ontario Colony.

The brothers laid out the new colony as a large grid. Avenues ran north and south, streets east and west. A central avenue showcased the beauty of the development. It was to be two hundred feet wide, divided, with a grassy, pepper tree shaded parkway along its center. George named that street Euclid after the celebrated geometer he had revered as a child. An agricultural lot was set at ten acres. Each would border a frontage road. Cement pipes, new to farming, were cast and buried to bring water down from the hills. And, not naive to marketing, the brothers built a fountain by the railway station which spouted water when a train passed by, but was otherwise turned off. At 1790 North Euclid Avenue, Captain Garcia built and moved into the first home in the colony of Ontario.

It was to this Chaffey fairyland, on its tenth anniversary, that the Ambuehls came. There they added to the membership of what was becoming San Bernardino County's large German-Swiss community. They settled not far from another group, orchardists and laborers from the other side of the world, the southwest of China. These disparate partners would bring George Chaffey's dream to life, transforming the desert into a beautiful green valley of oranges and lemons, olives, sugar beets, and celery.

> *And he sat her on the third step of the altar. And the*
> *Lord gave her grace and she danced with her feet and*
> *all the house of the Lord loved her*
> The Apocryphal Gospel of James

Peter, Caroline, August, and little Rosa were welcome additions to the young Ontario colony. The strapping, outgoing Peter, always there to lend his back to a problem, became an instant friend to everyone. He was in great demand as a farm laborer. Caroline, too, adjusted quickly to the harsh life of a farmhand's wife, but neighbors were more circumspect with her. They were thrown off by her seeming impassiveness. How could a German, from the prim and manicured old walled city of Dinkelsbuhl, be so comfortable here in the ever present dirt of this new world. And she didn't speak much of her past, and only vaguely of farming. If asked why she'd come to America, her stock response was, "I didn't want to eat any more brown bread." She was an anomaly.

The children created their own kind of stir. August, even more than his father, was the family clown. One day he would grow into the Lincolnesque stature of his father, but at ten he was simply tall and gangly. He had bonded quickly with his stepmother, and Rosa's birth was a great wonder to him. As she grew, his awe never waned. He would feign sleep and watch between barely opened eyes as Caroline breastfed her by the crib across the small room from his bed. Later he became Rosa's protector, her confidant, and her entertainer. In the family's first Ontario sanctuary, a two room, six hundred and twenty foot cottage at the rear of the Puehler farm where his father worked, August would keep her laughing with his imitations of the sounds of both animals and people. While she was still tiny, he would sneak up to her crib and wake her with the growling and barking of a dogfight. Before she started school, but when she was old enough to wander onto Euclid Avenue and watch the traffic, his Chinese parodies became her favorites.

She would sit on the glider at midpoint of the great front porch of the Puehler's spacious Victorian and stare wide-eyed at the activity. The trolley, always a delight, labored by across from the street's two northbound lanes. At the time of these outings, it was powered by electricity; not so for the first three years the Ambuehls were in Ontario. Back then, when the car came from the left on its northern, uphill run, it had been pulled by two mules. It passed the Puehler house about two-and-a-half miles north of its origin near the railway station. At Twenty-fourth Street, the trolley's northern terminus and about four miles farther north of the Puehlers, the mules were loaded onto a pull-out trailer for a gravity fed coast back down to the station.

Rosa gazed lazily at the comings and goings of the farm laborers, the farmers, and the trudging school kids, then snapped to attention at the passing of either a bicycle or a Chinaman. The latter fascinated her most. They were her first encounter with the strangeness of human diversity, elements which for her entire life would bring her both anxiety and delight. Most often she saw small groups of Chinese men - two, three, four, or more - walking together and making loud unintelligible sounds to one another. More rarely she would see a couple, the woman following a few steps behind her companion, or still less frequently a school-aged child. All were dressed in drab baggy clothing; the women often wearing large cone shaped hats of woven grass for protection from the sun, the men and boys sometimes with their hair shaved except for a single long braid, some with round caps pulled tight against their heads. She would laugh, thinking of "hungla munga," and her brother's other gibberish imitations.

She was only four when she began these solo excursions from the family's tiny home. It was about a quarter-mile slog through the Puehler's twenty-acre orange grove from there, the dwelling her dad, as ranch foreman, was entitled to share with his family. Her route between the trees and over the clumps of brown earth required all her attention. A greeting or a laugh from a ranch hand, peering down from high on his spindly three-footed ladder, could end in a twisted ankle or even a complete hands-down sprawl onto the lumps below.

Rosa was neither awkward nor graceful, but she inspired a kind of amused respect. Slim, like the men in her family, she walked or danced, even over this uneven ground, with quick decisive steps. And she would sing or hum, often off-key, the popular songs of the times; this year's favorites were: "A Hot Time in the Old Town," "Mother Was a Lady," and "Sweet Rosie O'Grady." She, of course, identified with "Sweet Rosie." She was also very fond of the now ten year old "Rock-a-Bye Baby." And no child could resist "Ta-Ra-Ra Boom-De-Ay," ever popular from the year before she was born. Like the rest of the community she had learned the music she knew from the weekly, sometimes semi-weekly, bandstand concerts.

The bandstand was another of the thoughtful amenities the Chaffeys had given to Ontario. It was located a couple of blocks north of the railroad station about a forty-five minute walk from the farm - an hour for a grouchy Rosa when she wasn't riding on her father's shoulders.

Most of the town showed up for the concerts. For the outgoing Peter there was an additional attraction. He had learned to play the *Schwyzerergeli* as a child. Not well, but with enough practice to read a score and keep up with the other performers. Here in America, where it was called a Swiss Accordion and not too well thought of musically, he relied on his popularity and persuasive humor to be granted a seat in the local band.

The instrument itself had been acquired quite by accident at a gathering of the congregation of the then five year old First Presbyterian Church of Ontario, formerly the Euclid Avenue Presbyterian Church. The event was to raise funds for a new building. Ironically, the original structure with its towering one hundred foot spire had been completely destroyed by a Santa Ana windstorm shortly after its final mortgage payment had been made. Friends of the church were there to donate any valuables they could spare. All proceeds would go toward the construction of a new church.

Peter was overcome by the find. It wasn't a *Schwyzerergeli*, but it was close. The bass keys on the left were controlled by a row of brass levers, not the buttons he had known. At first glance it seemed to be one of those funny single-keyed things that would later be made famous by the Creoles, the Zydeco musicians of Louisiana. A closer look proved him wrong. On the right hand side the melody keys were in three rows: the familiar B flat, E flat, and the mixed A, D and G he had grown up with. He would be able to play woodwind scores without transposing.

Could he buy this luxury? They had been in Ontario only a few weeks. Of course it would help the church! He found Caroline going through an assortment of tools and cooking utensils. She held up a small crosscut saw. "Could you use this?" she asked; "it looks better than the one in the shed." Peter looked down, reddened slightly, and shifted his weight back and forth from one foot to the other. Caroline, he knew, was working hard to steer them to a richer life. Richer in every sense of the word. From the first she had spoken of a home, even a farm of their own. Here they were just getting started and frivolity was winning over practicality. She could sense his unease. "What is it, Peter?" Without speaking he reached for the saw and placed it back on the table. He took her hand, led her to the accordion, picked it up and with great care squeezed out the latest popular tune, the sappy new waltz, "After the Ball." Their donations netted them an eight-inch iron skillet, a small crosscut saw, a rather large monkey wrench, and an accordion of unknown origin.

More than anything, Peter wanted to please Caroline, but he liked things. He liked his new accordion. He treasured his tools, his long ripsaw, his wood plane, his new crosscut saw and monkey wrench. Carefully, and with a flourish to the script, he carved his initials, *P.A.A.*, onto each tool's wooden handle. Even the handle of his pocket knife was branded *P.A.A.*.

Technological innovations were also capturing his imagination. A new kind of bicycle had been invented. The high wheelers with pedals attached directly to the front wheel hub, perching their riders five feet above the ground, had given way to a machine with two wheels of equal size, the rear one connected to pedals with a fine chain turning small light sprockets. Called the Rover by its inventor, it came to be known as the "safety bicycle." Peter wanted one. He rationalized that it was a real need, not like buying the accordion. But in the end, his sturdy Swiss character and his thoughts of Caroline prevailed. There would be no more frivolity.

Peter's resolve bore fruit. Over the four years following their arrival, both his family and the community of North Ontario prospered. Due largely to this prosperity and to the attendant bickering it engendered between rival business leaders, landowners north of the railroad tracks called their locale North Ontario. They elected not to annex with Ontario, the city of their southern brothers. For the Ambuehls the time was a revolving cycle of work, save, invest. They made a down payment on ten acres near North Palm and Fourteenth Street, a little over a mile northwest of the Puehlers, and they invested in North Ontario Packing. Caroline seemed able to keep an attractive living space and serve up hardy German dishes without spending a cent. She became, as well, an adroit observer of how money was made and lost. Peter, for his part, earned much admiration for his management of Rudolph Puehler's ranch.

Rudolph, an early real estate customer of the Chaffeys, had been one of the first to plant. His twenty acre Valencia orange grove was laid out by Chinese laborers brought from their camp in Cucamonga by a white contractor, himself recently arrived from Canada. The contractor's appointed foreman, sixty-three year old Ah Quong, had been in California since the gold rush. Quong, a product of generations of Cantonese farmers with a command of English much greater than that of his Swiss employer, worked his charges well. After first tapping into the new irrigation pipes, his Chinese crew set out the Valencia saplings, leaving proper space between each row for two-horse teams to pull soil cultivators and to load the boxed produce at harvest time. Each acre was planted with around a hundred and thirty-five trees.

For ten years revenue grew as the trees matured and yield increased to around five boxes per tree. Also growing was an American resentment against the Chinese. It was particularly virulent in California. Initially, welcomed for their industry during periods of great labor demand: the gold rush, the building of the railroads, and the establishment of farms. Now, ten years after the passing of the Exclusion Act which denied all Chinese the right to immigrate for the ensuing decade, non-Asian laborers and labor leaders were calling for their ouster. There were boycotts and riots. The ugliness in California, mainly in the rural areas, caused many San Bernardino Valley Chinese to vacate the farms and find refuge in the Los Angeles Chinatown ghetto. Ah Quong, in his early seventies, twice hit by rocks and once beaten on his way to work, was one of them.

Rudolph Puehler felt helpless. He had trusted and respected his orchard manager. Even had a kind of difficult to acknowledge younger brother affection for him. A pretty good farmer himself, Puehler couldn't even tell his men the time of day without old Quong. Sitting on a hard pew while awaiting Sunday service at the Methodist Church, these musings at first prevented him from noticing the new arrivals sliding in on his right. Young August sat down next to him followed by Caroline holding baby Rosa. Next came Peter. Rudolph could hear August singing during the processional. Most of his words were correct English, while Caroline only hummed and Peter sang a strange sounding Germanized English - or was it English-ized German.

Rudolph stopped the young family after the service, introducing them to his wife Emma, his five daughters, and little Rudy, Jr., not much older than Rosa. There was an immediate affinity between the older experienced landowner and Peter, the strong ambitious newcomer. Rudolph shared his troubles: the bigotry against the Chinese, the impending turndown in the economy, the particular problems he was having with his trees. Peter listened. Peter told of his life in Washington, of the work he had done in the short time since his arrival, and of his disappointment in not finding a Lutheran church. Rudolph listened, and it was perhaps this last revelation more than anything else that cemented their relationship.

From that day on it was an extended family; the older Puehler girls, Alice and Katherine, teasing and flirting with August, babysitting Rosa and Rudy, and admonishing their younger sisters, Helen, Micky and Ann, to behave in this or that proper manner. The bonding between Emma and Caroline grew as well, becoming as strong as that of their husbands. It was only a few weeks before Peter the newly-hired ranch hand became Peter the foreman.

It was easy in the worsening economy for Peter to replace the diminishing, then non-existent, Chinese labor force with German and English speaking help. But it was an often frustrating transition. Oranges were torn and spoiled by pickers pulling them from the tree, and boxes were packed sloppily with fruit varying in size. Slowly, by example or by harangue, the men were taught. Scissors, not yanks, must part the oranges from their limbs. Stems must be cut close to the fruit to prevent them from jabbing and injuring the skin of a packing box neighbor. Boxes must be filled to the maximum by selecting produce of a similar size. It could take time and patience for the techniques so common in the Orient to become ingrained. Peter had the patience, but not the time. To keep the ranch profitable he had to be tough with his crew. He led by

Chapter 3

Coming of Age in the Land of
The Canaanites

*And the children of Israel dwelt among the
Canaanites, Hittites, and Amorites,
... and gave their daughters to their sons ...*
Judg. 3:5-6

In 1826, the Frenchman Joseph Niepce, without employing an artist, recorded the view outside an upstairs window of his country home. That rendering is believed to have been the first "photograph." Photography would undergo many transformations before becoming, four years before Rosa's birth, available to anyone. The final stages in this development have all been attributed to George Eastman, a former bank clerk from upstate New York. Eastman's early camera, marketed with the admonition, "You press the button, we do the rest," would forever alter the recording of family histories. For millions of Americans those sanctified, "happy," years between the first child's birth and the last child's high school graduation would be encapsulated in the family album. Peter, although it would be too late for him to capture all of his children's years, had been a fan of the KODAK since its introduction in 1888, and shared that goal, a simple goal; a wish to hold dear, to remember. He thought often of the crude painting of his parents hanging on a wall of their Swiss home, regretted its loss to him and the scarcity of such treasures.

What Peter never anticipated were the glimpses of painful change interlaced with the recording of his family's triumphs.

Even less, did he intend to show how his children would develop. How much they would be like him or his wife, or how much they were to be shaped by the times. What could an album actually reveal? Not so long before, Francis Galton, Charles Darwin's half-cousin, had weighed into a part of that endlessly debated Nature or Nurture controversy with the first written discussion of the subject, his *Inquiries into Human Faculty and its Development*. The mother of one of Rosa's little friends, Helen Maurer, had spoken to Peter about the book at a church social. "Isn't it fascinating," she had queried. "Do you think heredity really plays any part in determining a child's future?" Peter's single "Ja" brought the conversation to an unresolved conclusion. But could one see in photographs attributes other than simple appearance? Did they show talents passed along, leadership skills copied, common frailties displayed? Could they joggle, even shock, a viewer with the unexpected? How much might a social psychologist fathom, or even guess at, what would become of those reflected in the little images? Would he see the formation of political allegiances, the making of heroes, the despair of limitations?

Rosa, now called Rosie by everyone but her mother, would be ready to start school in the fall. August was to become an Ontario High freshman. The carpenters Peter had hired were putting finishing touches on their Fourteenth Street home. And happily, Eastman was selling its new Folding Pocket KODAK. No longer would one have to send the camera across the country to Rochester, New York for a film reload. For the first time, film could be bought in rolls and processed into convenient 2¼ by 3¼ inch prints.

The Ambuehl album, typical for its time, was seven inches high and eleven across, with the word Photographs imprinted in large gold, extra frilled Harrington characters across its black cloth-over-cardboard cover. Each of its forty-five thick black pages, held between the book's covers by a bow-tied shoe lace running through two holes punched a half inch in from the left edge, would eventually hold between two and six randomly placed photos. A handful of pages displayed photos on either side. Aside from chronology there was no order to picture placement. Even chronology was questionable, as no one kept track of which was taken first, and often prints from a roll or two of film would be left lying on some flat surface to be later glued into place by whichever family member felt so inclined. It would usually be Caroline. On occasion, but rarely, a print would have a terse caption - like "the Puehlers" or "1903," hand-penned in white ink against the black page.

The history captured in this volume spans the eleven years between mid 1898 and mid 1909, less than a year after delivery of Ford's first Model T. The photos on page one were pasted more precisely than those on the pages to follow: two verticals at the top and two horizontals below, each representing the photographic effort of a different family member. At the upper left the action began with Rosie's blurry image of *Weissfuchs*, their three year old spitz, jumping toward an unidentifiable outstretched hand. To its right was August's fairly well composed shot of his sister with the dog. The two remaining pictures presented the entire family minus the contributing photographer - Caroline missing on the left and Peter on the right.

Most of the album's pages were interesting only to the participants, the photographers or their subjects. There were a few exceptions. August had managed to get a remarkable shot of his father leading a cow to its pasturing grounds some distance north-east of the Puehler ranch. Just to the rear of the cow's neck sat an intense, focused Rosie, legs pressed tight against gigantic shoulders. She was not holding on, but poised to, if necessary, lean ahead and grab for the tether. By some quirk of physics the primitive camera had stopped all motion, yielding a scene with the detail of a Flemish master. Rosie and the cow, as it came to be known (not Peter, Rosie and the cow), captured the center of one whole album page. To a guest it was, at eight pages in, the first stopping point.

The Puehler girls posed coquettishly for many of the shots. One might guess that August was once again the photographer, but maybe it was just their reaction to a camera. On the other hand, shots of the girl's parents, Rudolph or Emma, were unusual. Of the half-dozen or so scattered throughout the book, the one with Rudolph and Peter shaking hands commanded attention. Rudolph looking up pensively had for some reason drifted into English just before the shutter snapped. "Saht vill vork," he had said; "Ve fends verst sthay, deen da utter." They had been talking of Peter's impending plans. He had already begun planting trees and the new house would be livable in a few more weeks. Peter had become more than another son to the older man, he was indispensable. The first mention of him striking out on his own had elicited an uncontrollable and regrettable outburst. Many subsequent discussions and offers ensued, including profit sharing, the joint ownership of some land, and the building of a larger and finer house for the ranch foreman. The handshake in this photograph cemented their final agreement. For the next three years, while training his successor, Peter would split his time between his and his friend's farm. And yes, the new foreman would speak German.

Everyone wanted to take pictures in the summer and early fall of that year. It was 1898: toward the end of June the Ambuehls would be moving into their new home; in mid-August, Peter would celebrate his forty-fifth birthday; and in September, August and Rosie would both be in school. The move was without major incident, and the album shows an attractive house, though not as ornate as many of the buildings in the neighborhood, including the school which Rosie was to attend. That twelve year old structure, the first school in what was then called the San Antonio District, was caught on film by proud father, Peter. The school was L-shaped, with an elegant gazebo-like edifice springing from its roof at the juncture of its two wings. Windows rose from about five feet high to just below the tall building's eaves. At the time of the snap a number of kids peered out of those openings, and in the yard outside others wandered about. Most of the children were blurred or fuzzy from motion unstopped by the camera. All of the boys wore two-piece wool suits with long stockings leading to knickers terminating below the knee. The girls, most in white, had on calf-length cotton dresses, some with two or three frilly ruffles. Rosie, not in this picture, had a similar two-ruffle model created by her mother, and would wear it, or one not much different, on her just over one-and-a-quarter mile walks to the school.

Another school would open that year, the first high school in the Ontario Colony. It was to share resources and some faculty with Chaffey Junior College, the college idolized by August for its sound beating of the USC Trojans in a football game played the year of their arrival. Unfortunately, last year on their only rematch, they lost 38 to 0. USC actually administered Chaffey Junior College and High School until 1901. Created as another of the Chaffey brothers' dreams for an ideal farming community and built on land they gave and with funds largely from an endowment they had established, it was initially called the Chaffey College of Agriculture of the University of Southern California. Despite the team's recent loss, August's chest expanded at thoughts of becoming a student there.

His picture seemed to contradict this pride. Taken from quite a distance and from the side with a mix of palm and firs obscuring its northeast corner, it made the three-story structure look much smaller than it was. What it didn't hide was a unique third floor where a steep tiled roof opened to large dormer windows, the only exterior clue to that floor's existence. The school was right on Euclid Avenue and about two-and-a-half miles from the new house. One of the Puehler girls would be part of the thirteen freshmen to attend Chaffey, and August would be walking right past her front porch on his way.

In its right upper corner, a few pages further along in the album, is a nicely framed shot of Peter and Caroline standing on either side of the garden shed built behind, and just after completion of, their new house. She is on the right holding the shed's door as far open as it will go. Peter on the opposite side looks in. The photograph cannot capture his surprise. Scrawled below in white ink is one of the book's rare captions: *"Dads bd - Aug. 13, 89."*

Not usually treated as a big event, Peter's birthday this year seems to have been enthusiastically anticipated by everyone but him. Helping the carpenters finish, moving and managing two farms, Peter was tired. He would be up before dawn and into bed with Caroline late in the night, later even than his energetic sixteen year old son. His family's behavior - their secrecy, occasional shushing, even their unprovoked giggling - escaped him. The pattern persisted in town as well, where an assisting clerk might look aside and nod to another passing patron, or one of his frequent contacts might query, "Anything new going on for you, Peter?"

What had been hidden in the shed and now revealed by Caroline is an object that brought a squeal of happiness from her husband. Not seen in the photo, of course, are their children: August with the camera, and behind him and his sister many from the neighborhood, all applauding, yelling, and expressing their goodwill. The dark green machine inside - green with a thin yellow decorative stripe around its front tube and yellow wheel rims, like its manufacturer's other products - will be the subject of many future photographs. It is John Deere's new "Moline Special," a bicycle with 28 x 1½ inch pneumatic tires on wooden rims, and a fixed rear hub - when the wheels go around, the pedals go around. There are no brakes, other than stopping the pedals. Caroline, saving and stashing small change for several years, had purchased it a month earlier at E.V. Caldwell's for $42.50.

A few pages later in the album, we see a smiling, jubilant Peter leaning against the bike. He's wearing denim overalls held tightly around his ankles with metal clips. His arms stretch out to either side, each hand holding a dark green Bordeaux-shaped bottle obscuring an equally dark red liquid. Peter has broken a Chaffey brothers' rule against bringing alcohol into the Ontario Colony. The thought amuses him. He doesn't drink much and knows that a glass or two to offer and to drink will not diminish him in the eyes of other Colony members.

The five-mile bike ride to Cucamonga was an easy one. Cucamonga, later becoming with Anaheim and Azusa a stock joke of comedian Jack Benny, was at the time home to the world's largest wine maker, Brookside Winery, then known as the Italian Vineyard Co. Founded by Secondo Guasti in the 1880s, its grape plantings, largely zinfandels, would eventually extend to over five thousand acres. Nearby in the same town, the Thomas Bros. Winery could make a rightful claim to being the first commercial wine producer in California.

Riding back to the ranch with his ten bottles, almost two gallons of wine with a combined weight of about twenty pounds, challenged Peter's new cycling skills. He had gotten a few burlap gunnysacks from the vintner and wrapped and packed the bottles so that they would hang over the bike's top-tube between his legs. This arrangement left him with a kind of bowlegged riding posture which he could not sustain.

A number of short rides, each followed by repacking efforts, ended with five bottles hanging just inboard of his hands on either side of the handlebars. As long as his road was straight all was fine, but cornering without being pulled over too far, tipping and breaking his cargo, required much concentration. He comments as he holds one bottle in each hand for the photograph: "Next time ve get a barrel and roll it home."

In the many bicycle pictures that follow, one of Rosie riding the bike by herself is notably absent. Of course she wanted to climb aboard from her first sight of the machine. And climb it would have been, since the top of her head was only a little more than a foot above the bike's horizontal 'top-tube.' Years later when tall enough to manage the ascent, her first ride ended abruptly at the foot of a tall eucalyptus, a native of Australia and one of many surrounding and helping protect Peter's oranges from the wind. The tree suffered no damage, and thanks to its wooden rims neither did the bike - except for a few scratches to its green paint. Rosie's scratches were also minor, and embarrassment did not overrule her explanation of the crash: "How else was I supposed to stop?" This question was not entirely without logic. One could only pedal so fast. When going downhill, if you held your feet to the side and let the pedals fly, you would actually pick up speed. So then, how did you stop?

A face previously unseen suddenly appears and takes up several album pages. It is not an unattractive face, but it is a face fuller than any member or friend of the Ambuehl family. It is a face that could be called rotund, or provocatively, even corpulent. And in those views of its owner that extend to the waist or below, the sense of size is undiminished. The Puehler girls have been forgotten. Bessie now commands all of August's attention, both fancifully and photographically.

They found one another at a track practice soon after the beginning of the spring semester. Of course they had known each other and were in classes together. How could it be otherwise in a class of thirteen? From the first there had been that raw animal beckoning - the invitingly fleshy female and the tall skinny male. Was it simply geometric, the subconscious recognition of two components that would fit together like Legos? Or was it more primitive, some function of a pre-human hypothalamus? Whatever the reason, Bessie froze as she watched August trot around the dirt oval that Friday afternoon in late March. He was wearing knee-length shorts and an unbuttoned white cotton shirt damp from his exertion. His teammates were all leaving. When he stopped, she was there looking up at him. No one else was present. She reached out, took his hand, and they walked in silence to a grassy opening in a tight cluster of firs behind the school. There, at the foot of the trees, they melted together in a total body wrap.

It was all unfamiliar to August. Sex, he knew, was a part of life. He had witnessed his step-mother change and soften toward his father after their first few months together, but it had all been covert. The stories he had heard, stories of indecent goings-on in the town, were just that, stories. Affection, desire, lust, they were not proper emotions for talk or for display, either at home or anywhere else he might have frequented. Here, with Bessie, he dissolved. He rubbed his face into her cheeks and into her breasts. His hands caressed every pore on her body as that body enveloped him like a bath of honey. Both her body and his own urged him to go on, but his upbringing wouldn't allow it. Marriage was the only option.

Rosie had a hard time dealing with Bessie, both in reality and in the abstract. In her soon-to-be seven year old imagination, a fairy princess - someone much like herself - would be the suitable companion for her brother. "She's not very pretty, is she?" was the first direct appraisal of Bessie she shared with him. It began a rift between the protector and his charge that would take years to bridge.

At Chaffey High, Bessie and August became items of respect, envy, and ridicule. Their devotion to one another amused, jarred and touched, evoking giggles, jokes, blushes and raised eyebrows from all eleven fellow classmates. Even the six faculty members were not immune. Chaffey High was not an easy place for farm teens and the couple brought a kind of awkward unity to the new school.

The new faculty, most sharing work time with the Junior College, were all academics, instructors with multiple teaching roles: science and mathematics - English and botany - English, German and history - Latin and history - Spanish and drawing. If not for Roy Dickerson, who took his obligation to teach Science and Mathematics in its broadest sense, August would not have stayed on as a student as long as he did. Roy saw in the boy someone attracted to science, but without the deep interest or drive to pursue it with passion. August was almost his father's clone. He looked the country squire, or bumpkin - depending on perspective - but lacked a number of the older man's attributes, shrewdness among them. Also, August had no interest in farming. He would wince the following year when he saw his father listed on the Twelfth United States Census as a farm laborer, and he would feel none of that man's joy when ten years later, in the population count of 1910, boxes labeled "Occupation" were filled in for "Ambuehl, Peter A." with "Farmer, Fruit."

Bessie's attempt at a picture of August operating a telegraph key in Dickerson's science lab was only partially successful. Although she took the photograph around noon on a sunny day in late May, the lab, a third-floor room on the building's north side, got little light through its one dormer window. The resulting underexposed print showed off two of the teacher's props, a Stanley Transformer and a Tesla Coil, with greater clarity than its intended subject. Dickerson had observed that August involved himself in lessons requiring physical activity and had guided him toward telegraphy. During his Sophomore year, his last at Chaffey, August spent hours in the lab learning a little transmission theory while developing an exceptional key-hand.

He took a summer telegraph operator job at the Ontario rail station soon after the end of the spring semester. He was fast, dependable, and often praised. It didn't require much management persuasion to get him to remain when school re-opened in the fall. Bessie returned as a Junior feeling like a ghost, empty and vacuous.

The following year, near the end of summer when both were eighteen, they took off together for San Bernardino. August had been offered a salary increase and a post as switchman-trainee with the California Southern Railroad, a subsidiary of the Atchison, Topeka and Santa Fe. They married soon after arriving, with a Justice of the Peace officiating and two railway employees acting as witnesses. Neither August nor Bessie thought of the adventure as an elopement. Everyone else did. A year later, nine of their previous classmates, six girls and three boys, received high school diplomas, the first graduates of Chaffey High.

In that same year, 1902, Rosie appears in three photos; one by herself and two with her father. Both father and daughter are smiling and holding musical instruments. Rosie's smile is timid, even a bit self-conscious, while Peter's is a full, face-contorting beam. Rosie has just received a zither. An itinerant musician has made his way through Ontario selling a fixed-price zither-lesson combination. You buy the instrument and he will come to your house and give a one-hour lesson twice a week for the next six months. In photo one, Rosie stares down at the stringed device which rests on her knees. In the other two Peter stands behind her, his arms, and the accordion between them, a blur. She looks up at him in one and toward the photographer in the other. In both she appears to be plucking at the strings. Sadly, the anticipated musical joy suggested by these images will not prevail; no one in Ontario will ever see the wandering minstrel again.

Caroline's dealings with the vanished huckster was one of two financial transactions she would always regret. The other was for the stock she bought in North Ontario Packing, the recently gone-belly-up company once touted most promising in the county. But the stock deal was the cost of learning about the investment market, while the zither fiasco just hurt. Caroline had none of her husband's musical ability, imperfect as it was. The sounds on the zither that scoundrel created the day he made his pitch had almost brought her to tears. How good it would have been for her little Rosie to have absorbed even a tiny bit of that. She understood the self-reproach she felt at her own gullibility added to the hurt, but it didn't help.

> *Behold, Mary has reached the age of twelve years in*
> *the temple of the Lord. What then shall we do with*
> *her, lest perchance she defile the sanctuary of the Lord?*
> The Apocryphal Gospel of James

After August left, a new kind of bond surfaced between Rosie and her dad. She thrashed about for the lost security her brother once offered. No one would ever say or do a mean thing to her if he was around, but ask her now if she missed him and you'd likely hear, "Hope he's happy with his fat wife." More and more she turned to Peter over Caroline for answers to everyday issues: bedtime, homework, transportation, maybe even what to wear. So it wasn't surprising when she went to him about First Communion. It seemed natural enough to Caroline; Peter was more into church than she. Peter was thrilled. Rosie might be younger than correct for a proper church; there was still no regular Lutheran service in Ontario, but the Methodists he reasoned wouldn't know one way or the other. He met with Pastor Miller, agreed to what kind of instruction she would receive and set a date. He'd been warned to allow time for dress making.

Peter scheduled Rosie to meet with Deaconess Corkhill four times, Saturday at two-thirty and Friday after school for the two weeks beginning August 6th. The news brought a head lowering sigh to his daughter, moisture blocking her vision. How could he of all people have forgotten that the last planned meeting, Friday, August 19th, would be her twelfth birthday? Peter reacted appropriately to this rare display of sensitivity; consoling her at the time and arranging for the final teaching to be moved a week to the following Friday.

It was two days after her birthday. There was no warning. Nothing had ever been said to prepare her for this. She was in a toilet stall in the Methodist Church ladies room. The morning service was to begin in about ten minutes. She heard water running. "Is that you Emma?" she cried, hoping for her friend Emma Wilme, whom she had seen outside earlier. She was lucky. "Yes," came the reply. **"Get my mother!"** It was not a request, it was an order, an order delivered with an urgency not to be ignored. For this crisis there was no thought of her father.

Caroline's ministerings were efficient, but totally unfulfilling. Rosie was cleaned, provided with something to absorb her bleeding, and seated in the pew between her parents all before the choir began the opening hymn: "O Come, O Come, Emmanuel."

O come, thou Wisdom from on high,
and order all things far and nigh;
to us the path of knowledge show
and cause us in her ways to go.

Caroline's feat was remarkable considering that disposable pads were not much used, having been introduced in the United States only a few years before, and that it would be thirty years before women wore snug-fitting underwear.

A picture taken three weeks later occupies an entire page. It is dead center, only one of three in the album so displayed. There is no legend. A radiant, unsmiling Rosie stands before an altar. This shot like all the others is black and white, but to an observer the colors are clear. She wears an immaculate white cotton gown that falls to calves covered in long black stockings. Her shoes are black and shiny. Her left hand hangs at her side and in her right is a book held parallel to the ground. Long brown hair spills out from beneath a waist-length veil of the same white cloth as her dress, held in place with a wreath of pink roses.

Gangly, awkward teenager describes her, as adolescence adds inch after inch to Rosie's height but nothing to her width. Seemingly ignorant of that knowledge, she delights in putting on costumes: men's clothes, women's clothes, fashionable or outlandish clothes, and it pleases her even more if she's the subject of someone's camera. It's an activity that will last through her early adulthood. In several shots, she wears wool knickers and jacket borrowed from a classmate; with his cap over her hair, she could pass for her brother. Dressed this way she likes to imitate her father, both his mannerisms and his carriage. Much of his demeanor is already natural to her: an easygoing openness in interactions with a large and ever-increasing number of friends and acquaintances, and a casual warmth extended to most others. She shows signs, as well, of his bizarre humor with its strange allusions and contorted puns which no one but he understands.

Peter, too, is undergoing changes. A year before Rosie begins high school we see him amid his fruit trees holding a cane. He's not really supporting himself with it, but his legs have been acting funny for awhile. He's been stubbing his toes a lot, bumping into things and the soles of his feet have lost some feeling. Occasionally those legs don't want to support him at all and he has to sit down and "take the weight off" them. He's been to see Dr. Bedford right near home in North Ontario, and Dr. Tyler, when Tyler made a visit from Redlands. The two physicians made sure his urine didn't contain too much sugar, but were otherwise noncommittal. Not because they were hiding anything, but because they had no idea what caused his complaints. They solemnly concurred the best advice was 'rest.'

There's a four by six-and-one-half inch print, the second centered on a full album page and the only in the book not taken by a Pocket Kodak. It is the work of Schwichtenberg, a commercial photographer from Pomona, for inclusion in *The Fasti*, Ontario High's yearbook. This year, 1908, two years after North Ontario has become Upland, the school is correctly known as Ontario High. When August attended, it was Chaffey High, and three years from now it will be Chaffey once again. Several other changes set it apart from the ten previous years. First, although Schwichtenberg's picture shows thirty-three students, eighteen girls and fifteen boys, the Freshman Class size reported in *The Fasti* has grown to fifty. Second, of the original faculty only principal Jefferson Taylor remains. Total faculty number has increased by two, and none now share teaching responsibilities with the junior college. Third, a new, beautiful building is under construction which will replace old Chaffey J.C. during the high-schoolers' next academic year.

A glance at the freshmen posed on the front steps of the old brick building would seem to reveal few deviations in apparel; half the girls are in long, white, cotton gowns, the others either in flowered dresses or white blouses with dark skirts to the ankle and, except for a natty young man in tan trousers and another wearing a vest, all the boys are in heavy, gray, two-piece wool suits. Inspected closely, however, some detail in each costume lends it uniqueness: a dark scarf, a bow tie, a lace collar, or the bloused sleeves gathered just below the elbows of Rosie's white frock. Rosie's image is unique in another way. Seated at the far left in the second row up - the girls are in rows at the foot of the stairs with the boys above - her left arm is bent at the elbow bringing her hand to forehead level, and in that hand she holds a thin stick, a stick at least four feet long. She wears a self-satisfied smile.

The album's last pictures are mostly of Rosie, either by herself or with her friends, in one of their many attempted comic guises: housepainters, witches, minstrels, ..., cowboys. In one Rosie is sitting in a bucket, 'rowing' it with two brooms. "Laugh at us," the shots seem to plead. In contrast, the remaining three of her father - two with his cane, the last on crutches - show a man seemingly attempting to minimize himself, to disappear. In the book's final picture, and the third to be centered, Rosie and five of her friends are bending forward with their hands on their knees. It's not possible to tell who's who, since they face away from the camera.

Chapter 4

Contradictions in Canaan

You have given us, just as You swore to our fathers,
"a land flowing with milk and honey."
Deut. 26:15

She guided Jack's hand under two layers of cloth until his open palm rested comfortably against her bare left breast, then looked at him questioningly. She wanted to laugh at the awkwardness of it all, while simultaneously wondering and feeling: wondering if he understood the uniqueness of her nipple, feeling the sensation of sweetness between her legs.

Only a few continued to call her Rosie or Rosa and describing twenty-four-year-old Rose Ambuehl is difficult. Rose's face was lovely but not beautiful, her features nicely shaped but with nose and ears a bit too big. There was a sexual charm about her, a natural animal attractiveness, a provocativeness to her breasts, hips and buttocks, but she could not be called "sexy."

Rose had grown to five feet seven, still thin, and carrying her body's height with the kind of virile grace her father had once carried his, and she knew well how that body worked. There would be no more menstrual surprises. Talking with friends about intimacies, body parts, the unmentionables of the time, had become a major part of the curriculum in her last years of school. The girls, most often it would be girls, usually two, occasionally three, would find some quiet place, an empty classroom, a grassy patch between orchard trees, and share their findings. It wasn't always just talk. Sharing a look-at or feel of an anatomical part could work its way into a conversation. Humor was their protection. Giggling their shield. "No, mine looks more like ... ." "Let me see." Giggle giggle.

At that time Rosie had been fixated on her nipples. Her breasts, never large, grew to be shaped with textbook correctness: rounded at their base with no sag, curving down with no swoop. Her nipples, however, were different. Why didn't any of her friends have nipples like hers? They were fat buttons. Big as a quarter and fat, like a ball that had been squeezed together. You couldn't even see much of an areola, hidden as it was behind the nipple.

The Ambuehls moved to San Diego shortly after Rose's twenty-first birthday. Peter's lower body had become too much of a challenge for the local doctors; feelings diminished in both feet, while his overall leg strength declined. It wasn't a steady, uniform thing. He'd seem almost normal one day and, while trying hard not to be seen in it, might require a wheelchair the next. Then there was the balance thing. He'd lose his surefootedness. Sometimes one leg would act like it was shorter than the other, or he would just take an awkward step, like he was stumbling on uneven ground.

Dr. Bedford agreed with Ambrose Tyler, his colleague from Redlands, the problem was either neurological or the popular farmer suffered from some type of mental imbalance. The case piqued Dr. Tyler's interest while simultaneously offering further justification for him to contact fellow physicians with his new toy, California Interstate Telephone Company's new long-distance service. His calls pleased him. It wouldn't matter if the observed symptoms were physical or mental, as little distinction was made between neurology and psychiatry in the early years of the twentieth century. A great many patients of those practices were, in fact, veterans of the 1898 four-month war with Spain.

Tyler's calls resulted in a collaboration of sorts with Professor Henry G. Brainerd, M.D., Chairman of the Department of Neurology at UCLA. Tyler was in awe of Brainerd, a man whose papers included studies in cerebral anatomy, brain tumors, neurosyphilis, post-traumatic Jacksonian epilepsy, and criminal insanity. The collaboration was short-lived. Brainerd had Tyler send him a copy of Peter's medical records and, once received, took no further phone calls from his Redlands associate. Instead, he mailed the records to the medical office, near San Diego's Saint Joseph's Hospital, of his friend, Herman Probst. After reviewing the records, Probst, who then served as the Hospital's single neuropsychiatrist, called Bedford requesting that Peter be sent to see him as soon as possible.

It wasn't an easy sell for Bedford. Peter balked at the very word, neuropsychiatrist. "They think I'm not right in the head," is a fair translation of the impression he shared with Caroline. Her response: "Hear what the man has to say" was followed up with the more persuasive, "I'll come with you. We'll stop in Colton for a visit." The route of the Atchison, Topeka and Santa Fe from Ontario to San Diego was most direct by way of San Bernardino, and would give them the opportunity to spend some time in the small adjacent town of Colton with August, Bessie and their granddaughter Margaret, now almost fifteen. August had done well. But for a seven-day work week, and Bessie's crazy religious belief as one of the local "Shellites," life was fine. The home they owned in Colton was pleasant and a tolerable walking distance from the signal tower where he pushed and pulled levers controlling all the routing switches in the big San Bernardino railway yard.

Peter felt uncharacteristically relaxed before the impending doctor visit as they entered Probst's office in San Diego's Hillcrest district. His son's concern had buoyed him, and while he was again retelling Caroline of his observation that August treated his own daughter, Margaret, much as he used to treat his half-sister, Rosa, both were startled by a loud raspy German greeting. The speaker's drawn out 'U' as he pronounced Ambuehl, identified him as having come from somewhere in Germany's east central region. It appealed to Peter's humor; German here would be in three flavors - Swiss, Bavarian, and Upper Saxon. The voice could be identified as coming from just this side of a door to another room. Its owner was a stocky, unkempt looking man wearing an un-pressed, knee-length white lab coat. Both his beard, maybe a month or two old, and his full head of graying hair appeared uncombed. It was impossible to tell his age. After the formal Herr and Frau greeting, he yelled a follow up, "Caroline, Peter, come on into this office. I'm Herman."

Now Peter tensed up. This man didn't look or sound like any doctor he had ever known. He reached out, took Caroline's hand, and squeezed it as he followed Dr. Probst into the small inner office. The office was sparse, containing one plain modest oak desk, three identical armless oak chairs, and a three-drawer oak filing cabinet. It was much tidier than its owner. Probst lost no time in small talk. "I've gone over your records and think I know what may be your problem." It was an unfortunate choice of words. To Peter it meant, he thinks I have a problem, not a disease. Probst went on, "I'd like to ask you a few questions and would like you to answer only yes or no. Is that all right?" Peter's hesitation seemed embarrassingly long. He didn't want to be asked questions about his private thoughts, about sex, about his parents, about his fears. He especially didn't want to be asked those things in front of Caroline. "I don't know," was all he could muster. Probst, not clear as to Peter's caution, responded simply, "Well, let's give it a try. If I ask you something you don't want me to ask, then let's talk about it." He didn't wait for an answer.

"Do you sometimes lose your balance without any reason?" was the first query. Peter experienced great relief, he was not being asked about his state of mind, his thoughts, his fears, he was being asked about a physical thing. "Yes," he almost shouted. And so it went. "Do your legs sometimes feel weak? Have you lost feeling in your feet? Do you bump into things? ... Do you ..." "Yes, Yes, Yes, --- Yes, .." "Now, Peter," Dr. Probst added, "something puzzles me. I would expect that your leg muscles cramp up sometimes, but there's no mention of it in your chart. Do they?" "Yes." "It's alright now to say more than yes or no. Why do you think this information's not in your chart?" Peter's lame response was slow and quiet. "I don't know. Maybe Dr. Bedford or Tyler never asked me."

Herman Probst began what appeared to be a rehearsed narrative, and he began it with a disconcerting enthusiasm. He had been a friend and student of a man he referenced as, "that great German physician." "I knew Adolph Strumpell when he was a professor at the University of Leipzig." It turns out that thirty years ago in Heidelberg, Strumpell had treated two brothers and their father for symptoms exactly like Peter's, later discovering a degeneration of their spinal cord nerve fibers. The condition, first called Strumpell's Disease, was now know as Hereditary Spastic Paraplegia. The rarity of the disorder provided a partial excuse for Herman's excitement. Here, in his office, was a man who suffered from causes he maybe knew more about than anyone else in the United States.

Probst's narrative did not go uninterrupted. Caroline, lulled into comfort by the familiar German accent, the one spoken so widely to the north and east of her birthplace, asked all the relevant questions. She asked about therapies, about life-expectancy, about pain. Peter simply stared at her. The wonder he felt for his wife often underwent these periodic reminders. He raised no questions of his own. Probst would solicit help from Reed College in Oregon which had just begun a physical therapy program, the first in the world. He would look into ways to reduce the spasms; both quinine and curare had been tried. There might be some danger. They would talk about it. But most urgently they needed to be closer, needed to be where they could see one another often, where they could work together.

Rose was employed by 'The Misses Gerry Millinery' at 237 2nd Avenue in Upland, a half hour's walk from home, when she learned of her parent's decision to sell the ranch and move to San Diego. The news was a shock. The Chaffey brother's Ontario dream had become her Eden. She loved her job, and her social life also pleased her. She had many girl friends and several boy friends - not boyfriends, but boy friends.

She had quit school four years earlier. Like her brother, academics never came naturally and, like him, she left after her sophomore year. Peter was mildly upset; no Ambuehl had yet received a diploma. A failure in first-year German, her native language, was the insult triggering the decision. Of the original faculty, only Principal Taylor remained. Vice-principal Ulysses G. Durfee, A.B., Stanford, taught Physics, Chemistry and German. Either because of an incapacity to understand it or an intolerance of the way *Switzerdeutsch* sounded, Durfee awarded the 'F' without comment. Taylor kindly suggested Rosa appeal and stay in school, but the grade may have provided a wanted incentive. Dressing up, posing, and learning all she could about clothes, from inside out - undies, hose, frocks, hats and shoes - had become her passion, her occupation. Professional modeling had never occurred to her, but a model she was.

Upland, a city with a then population of around two thousand, had three millineries: The Misses Gerry Millinery, M. A. BRIDGE - "Great Reductions during the Summer Months," and E. Grace Gribben - "Ladies' Hatter." (The quoted expressions are taken from ads in Ontario High's 1910 Annual, *The Fasti.*) In the summer, a few days after her last semester at school, Rose visited every apparel shop within walking distance of home. The hat shops were her favorites. They spoke of chic, the garment district, New York fashion, and of what women were wearing in Paris. While none had been looking for help, she received an offer from each. She liked them all. How could one not like a hat store owner?

Of the three, only Abby Gerry's enthusiasm matched her own. Abby, maybe a little older than Rose's mother, knew everything about fashion, and would talk about it for as long as she had a listener. It was difficult for Rose to accept Abby, so much like a peer to her, as a contemporary of the reserved Caroline. During their first interview, which lasted most of the afternoon - and interrupted only by an occasional hat seeker - she was subjected to an extensive history of garment creation and style. "Do you know why black was so popular when you were a little girl?" she asked, and without waiting for an answer, launched into the death of poor old Prince Albert at only forty-two and its effect on his wife, upright old Queen Victoria who wore black, and only black, until she died eight years ago. "Why you were only nine when she died, Rose, and she'd been wearing black for forty years, and - oh my gosh - her mother was German, just like yours."

Rose, never a fan of history, was enthralled. That first afternoon Abby must have conveyed a semester's worth of Fashion 101. She rattled on about how clothes were handmade not too long ago and how that all had changed when southern plantation owners found it cheaper to have their slave's clothes made in New York rather than have the slaves make them. "And later, when the war broke out, those same manufacturers had a field day making army clothes for the Yanks. Today," she went on, "clothes are the biggest business in New York. Not that New York's really much into style. Style's all Paris." Looking down with a hint of confidentiality, she teased, "There's a rumor there'll be a week-long fashion show in Paris next year."

The session with Probst galvanized Caroline. Economically, 1913 was a good year. Henry Ford had just initiated the first moving assembly line and the Ambuehl ranch was profiting from record navel orange sales. Offers for the ranch arrived soon after its listing - two at Caroline's asking price. It didn't trouble her that she hadn't asked for more; her priority was to find a suitable home near Saint Joseph's, and find it quickly.

An attractive place, large for the times, had recently been built at 3776 10th Ave. It was less than a quarter-mile from the hospital, but it required compromise. Built as a three bedroom, two bath. multi-family dwelling, it had attracted no potential buyers. Caroline made a deal. The realtor would negotiate for a price reduction and find them a proper tenant. If Caroline had any fear they might not get the house, it was never apparent. Peter would stay with her in Chula Vista as guests of old friends, the Nachtbauers, until the transaction completed.

As it turned out, Loretta Carvel, a bookkeeper in the hospital's record department, would rent the extra bed and bathroom, and their escrow would be expedited. They could move in almost immediately. Caroline liked Loretta on sight. She was a plain and pleasant young woman, substantial in character while tiny in size, and only a few years older than Rose. For Peter there were doubts, prompting his rhetorical observation, "She's Catholic, isn't she?" Caroline's quick, uncharacteristic retort, "Peter, everyone here is Catholic. Dr. Probst is Catholic. The hospital is Catholic. Is there anyone in the neighborhood who's not Catholic?" scuttled further discussion.

When Rose arrived, only survival furniture occupied The Tenth Avenue House, as it came to be known. The move caused her less trauma than anticipated. Abby, although conflicted over losing a valuable employee and her most ardent listener, had pumped her up with big city stories. "After all," she rambled, "San Diego has a population maybe twenty to thirty times Upland's, and right now they're building a pier in the bay that will let big boats dock there, even boats from New York when the canal's finished. Have you ever been downtown there? Some great stores, maybe not like New York or L.A. but, hey ... ."

Get settled and get a job were the two priorities Rose set for herself. Abby had told her about Marston's, San Diego's premier department store, and she found an old ad showing it to be somewhere nearby in their own Hillcrest neighborhood. Not so, she learned from her house-mate, Loretta. The store had moved a number of times and just last year to downtown as a five-story superstore. "It's still pretty close, about two-and-a-half miles, and you can always take a streetcar straight down Fifth. Oh, and it's got an elevator, the only one in town. I'd never ridden one before." Loretta seemed to know everything about San Diego, and shared what she knew in a quiet, unpretentious way. Rose, like her mother, was immediately attracted to her new acquaintance, but shared her father's misgivings, feeling obligated to disclose Loretta's religion to all mutual acquaintances.

"Striking" best describes Rose as she strode into Marston's main lobby off C Street between 5th and 6th. She was all in white. A moderately brimmed hat, pulled down over her right ear allowed brunette curls to spill over her left temple. The skirt of her gown rested against pointy-toed shoes covering all but a hint of hose. An unbuttoned masculine-cut jacket hung to just above her knees, exposing a simple bodice pushed into full shape by an underlying corset. In her right hand she clutched an envelope - in it a recommendation from The Misses Gerry Millinery.

Convincing the floor manager she was not a patron, but in search of employment, took time - but once properly identified, all went well - or as close to well as could reasonably be expected. The millinery department was staffed to capacity - expert or not, no additional millinery personnel were needed. They did, however, need help in stationery and, if she would be willing, could hire her on a trial basis. Her appearance could be an asset.

Probst lost no time acquainting Peter with the hospital and its staff. He walked him around the four-story main building, through the corridor to a two-story annex, and pointed out the home for nurses about a half block down the street. "They've been training nurses here for about nine years," he offered. "Why do they dress like that?" Peter ventured, raising his chin and shifting his sight toward a woman in a somber black robe, her young face circled in a wimple of white linen extending over her shoulders and crowned with a waist-length black veil. "They don't always; when they're nursing they're usually wearing a white gown and a little cap." "But why, ... ?" Peter began again. "They're nuns, Peter, sisters," Probst interrupted. "Why do you need sisters in a hospital?" Peter shot back. Amusement damping his temper, Probst put a hand on his patient's shoulder. "They're the Sisters of Mercy, Peter. They started this whole thing. If they weren't here, neither would the hospital ... ."

Probst's treatment plan was simple enough. He would use quinine in his first attempt to treat the cramping. Curare would be riskier. Quinine also required caution. Too much and the kidneys were in trouble. He'd keep to himself the other dangerous side effects. The kidneys he'd monitor with the 'phenolsulphonephtalein test' Rowntree and Geraghty had reported in the *Journal of Pharmacy and Experimental Therapy* back in July of 1910. Reed College, the school in Portland he had told Peter and Caroline about, would be graduating its first 'Reconstruction Aides' next year. They knew Dr. Probst as an outspoken advocate and consequently sent him much of their training material. It may not have pleased them to learn he used it to teach Sister Anne Dougherty some specific manipulation techniques. Sister Anne agreed to work with Peter for an hour every Monday, Wednesday and Friday afternoon.

Rose had become a minor celebrity among her Marston co-workers. After two years in stationery, "they," as she put it, "moved me up in the company." The move was literally up, up on the elevator from the first to the fourth floor to her much sought millinery department. It was a move management would like to have avoided. Her popularity in stationery with several of San Diego's aspiring first citizens had to be balanced against frequent hints of her search for more fashion-related work. What management never heard were her stories, the much circulated performances Rose gave her fellow clerks in the lady employees' powder-room. They often followed an important sale. After a big sale of business cards to a naval officer's wife, for example, and when her rest-room audience was sufficient, she rolled back her shoulders, looked toward the ceiling, fluttered her eyes, raised her arms in a gesture of complete exasperation and began, "I just don't know what to have you put on my cards. You know Hubby's an Admiral, a Rear Admiral. He's also a doctor. He has a PhD you know. Should it be Mrs. Dr. Weatworth, ... Mrs. Admiral Weatworth, ... Mrs. Rear Admiral ... ? Oh god, rear sounds so tacky. What do you suggest, dearie, what would you do? Can it be Mrs. Dr. Weatworth, Admiral Weatworth's wife?"

Moving to millinery didn't change Rose's after-sale theater, but an occurrence during her first week on the floor added to her legend - first shocking, then delighting her fellow milliners. She had been working with a very difficult client for over two hours. The woman had tried on almost every available hat and seemed to favor only one. It was a size or so too small. "We have a stretching machine in back," she announced, loud enough for all nearby to hear. The woman acquiesced; if the hat fit, she would buy. After watching Rose enter the storage room and giving her a few minutes alone, two of her associates followed. They found her seated with her left foot resting on an adjacent chair. Her bent left knee appeared to be wearing the hat, while her hands, turned up under its brim, pulled - with much of her strength - in alternate directions against it. "I borrowed the machine from my old boss in Upland," she whispered.

San Diego glittered and Rose, the farm girl, reveled in the treats her new grazing ground revealed - but her one-dimensional embrace hid all views of its difficult growth. Loretta, once having walked with the suffragettes, reminded her how lucky she was to be able to vote now that she'd turned twenty-one. "Men slaves could vote after the Civil War, but we women won that right in California just last year," she pronounced, as if reading from the script of one of her marches. "Last year was good for women, but hard on workers here in San Diego," she went on. "There was a soap-box set up not far from your store, and a lot of workers tried to make speeches about labor conditions. They were run off by local mobs. A bunch of them beat up really bad. Some horsewhipped. I think a few might have been killed. The fellow that owns your store, George Marston, is running for mayor this year. Why don't you help me support him. The man he's running against is supported by a real mean guy, probably the one responsible for having the laborers beaten. His name is Spreckels."

To Rose, the name Spreckels meant, first of all, the Spreckels Theater, the new movie house at Broadway and First, five blocks from the store. The theater played all the latest silent films - at that time showing *In the Bishop's Carriage* starring House Peters and Mary Pickford. Rose identified strongly with Mary Pickford, sharing with everyone that Miss Pickford's birth preceded her own by only four months and eleven days. An earlier, short film, *The New York Hat* with Pickford, Lionel Barrymore and Lillian Gish remained among her all-time favorites.

Rose did know that John Spreckels, the son of Hawaii's sugar king, owned much of San Diego besides the theater. Friends at the store had told her his holdings included office buildings, hotels, the ferry system, the local newspapers, the streetcars, a steamship company, a railway line, all the land a block from the store to the waterfront, and all of the island adjoining Coronado. Like her father and many others of humble origin, Rose attributed this success to personal industry. If Spreckels wanted to run off rabble rousers it didn't seem mean to her. She'd heard those labor thugs had threatened the city, even its police force. Like the large majority of Californians during the thirty years beginning in 1910, Peter voted with the Lincoln-Roosevelt League of Progressive Republicans, and had shared with his daughter a part of The Party's 1908 platform, the part that read: "... The trend of Democracy is toward socialism, while the Republican party stands for a wise and regulated individualism. Socialism would destroy wealth, Republicanism would prevent its abuse. Socialism would give to each an equal right to take; Republicanism would give to each an equal right to earn. Socialism would offer an equality of possession which would soon leave no one anything to possess, ..." Although essentially apolitical, Rose remained faithful - for her entire life - to the Grand Old Party.

San Diego's population nearly doubled during each of the twentieth century's first three decades and the two men, Marston and Spreckels - in their very different ways - shared some responsibility. Marston, called "Geranium George" in his second failed attempt to become mayor, ran on a ticket of planned growth and city beautification. He supported women and minorities, helped found a library and YMCA, gave generously to parks and to the preservation of historic sites - including Junipero Serra's first mission. While Spreckels' newspapers supported Marston on his second mayoral run, unenthusiastic editorials left readers wondering. Did Spreckels sympathize more with Marston's opponent, a leader in the advocates for heavy industry known as the 'Smokestacks'?

Both men contributed much to the development of Balboa Park, an undertaking spurred on in anticipation of the Panama-California Exposition, the event celebrating completion of the Panama Canal. San Diego, honored as host for being the canal's closest west coast U.S. port, awaited an opening scheduled for New Years Day, 1915. The park gave birth to architect Bertram Goodhue's elaborate Spanish Colonial buildings, the world's largest outdoor organ - a gift in the nearby courtyard from John Spreckels and his brother Adolph, and the Cabrillo Bridge - uniting the entire complex with downtown's stores and businesses. Across Park Boulevard to the south, the largest municipal stadium in the country, Balboa Stadium, also sprang into existence as, unintentionally, did the San Diego Zoo, since animals brought to the exposition were quarantined and not allowed to leave.

Not everything built in San Diego those years broke size records. The Missouri Synod of the Lutheran church erected a lovely, mission-style sanctuary, Grace Evangelical Lutheran Church, at the corner of Park Boulevard and Lincoln - less than a mile from The Tenth Avenue House. Its wooden pews could seat up to only 175. Peter praised God for allowing him to be among the first of its members.

Rose moved with verve in this heady, expanding milieu. She wanted to miss nothing. She learned to pull an oar for a woman's rowing team, explored the beach and the hills with friends, saw every new film the Spreckels played, and even committed Missouri Synod sin by dancing at a couple of local clubs.

Although plagued with a questionable taste in music, dancing moved her to make the first of two major purchases, a record player built into a chest-high oak cabinet, the Victrola VV-XIV. The machine proved both functional and a handsome piece of furniture. When not in use, a wooden cover protected its swinging needle-arm and twelve-inch turntable. A crank powering a wind-up motor projected from a convenient height on its left side. In front near the top a set of small double doors opened to allow the passage of sound between downward facing slats. Below, larger doors led to a space partitioned off for the storage of heavy, 78 rpm records. Here, amid a number of contemporary tunes ("Let Me Call You Sweetheart," "Be My Little Baby Bumblebee," "You Made Me Love You," "Twelfth Street Rag," "When You Wore A Tulip," "St. Louis Blues," "Chicken Reel," "Pretty Baby," and "If You Were The Only Girl In The World") rested a few eclectic choices, including a Victor recording of George Voelker's odd "A Hunt in the Black Forest" and two with the songs of Enrico Caruso. He sings Otello on one and Rodolfo from *La Boheme* on the other.

The other purchase, a Singer 66-1 Oak Treadle Sewing Machine, reflected her ongoing seriousness with fashion and frugality. What couldn't be afforded could be made. The attitude pleased Caroline, as did Rose's willingness to share the machine with her. This Rose, the devoted daughter, remained largely unknown at work, where bosses saw her as 'talented sales clerk' and compatriots as 'company clown'.

At home, no day passed without time for each parent. There were few smiles with her mother. She helped cook, clean the house, and worked at the new chore Caroline had embraced, gardening. With Peter it was different. He was still number one. Her dancing didn't upset, but amused him. Pastor Damschroeder need not know. She played him records and showed him steps: Ballin' the Jack, Castle Foxtrot, Walking the Dog, and the Congo Tango. He'd been fairly responsive to Probst's treatment, but wouldn't try dancing with her. As time went by, she felt him distancing. It distressed her.

August visited on occasion, sometimes alone, sometimes with Bessie or Margaret, sometimes with both. Rose had made trips to Colton over the years, but only once since leaving Upland. With no awareness of why, she felt irritable when alone with August and his daughter. "Margaret is nice enough," she would tell friends, "just uninteresting."

Over time Rose became conscious of August's concern for their father. While her talks with Peter were gay, August's were probing. "He hates those tests Probst gives him," her brother once blurted when they were alone. She stared back vacantly until he went on. "He gets tests to see if his liver's alright. It's a kind of dye they use. They used to just put it under his skin, now they stick it into a muscle." He patted the bicep of his right arm with his left hand "And," he added as an afterthought, "he's been getting sores lately." "Oh," was all she could muster.

Marston's and Rose had negotiated a unique work schedule. They wanted her on weekends, their busiest time. She refused Sundays. Grace Church and 'God rests on the Sabbath' - her father's special day - could not be compromised. The arrangement called for four full days, Sunday excluded, with half days Monday and Wednesday. A pattern for short work days emerged. Off at one p.m., a street-car ride would get her home about half an hour later. Then, a snack of something simple - bread, cheese, fruit - and off to the yard or sewing machine, weather or mood dictating her choice. This Wednesday she had planned to finish a special project.

Two years earlier, on February 12, 1914, New York socialite Mary Phelps Jacob had filed for patent 1,115,674, "brassiere." A few, in various sizes, had recently been added to Marston's inventory. Lingerie was down a floor from Rose, near less expensive apparel sold in the 'Smart Shop' departments. The 'Smart Shop Millinery' adequately excused Rose's periodic third floor excursions, providing her the opportunity to examine what sophisticated women would soon be wearing against their skin. The bra fascinated her. She broke a self-imposed rule, picked one up and studied it. Making one was a must.

Rose sat at her sewing machine. The device itself was not visible but hinged into its case below. A coil of one-inch pink ribbon, together with scraps of white silk and two pieces cut to shape, were strewn across its oak board top. Mathematicians would call the shaped pieces isosceles trapezoids, triangles with their tops cut off. Rose held a silk trapezoid to her left breast. She needed to hem it, sew it together side-to-side with the other, and sew on the ribbon straps. One trapezoid would fit over each breast. To keep them in place a wearer would put an arm through the loops formed by a ribbon attached on each side to its outside corners. Long ribbons from the bottoms of the loops would then be tied at the wearer's back.

Finishing it wouldn't be all that hard. She could pick her mess off the top and open the Singer, or just stitch the bra by hand. Instead, she sat staring at it. The house seemed airless and far too quiet. Why, she couldn't answer. Caroline would have escorted her dad to his session with Sister Anne by now, and Loretta, of course, would be at work. She got up quickly, without thought, and still wearing work clothes - a simple long-sleeved white blouse and skirt - found herself outside pulling weeds from between the fuchsias planted to the left of the front porch stairs. It was too warm for early summer and unusually humid. Grumbling "muggy" and wondering how that might affect the young blossoms, she felt her own body warming and dampening. Drops of moisture formed at the tips of her breasts. She was yanking at a clump of crabgrass when she heard his yell, "Hello, Rose." She froze, trying to compose herself while questioning why him, here, now. As she stood and turned to face the road, a slow half-whispered, "Hi, Jack," slid from her mouth.

"It's hot," was all she could think to say as he walked over the grass to where she stood. He stopped in front of her smiling his big boyish smile. Jack was cute. About a year ago he'd moved, with his parents, into the house diagonally across the street. Rose didn't know much about them. Only that Jack sold shoes somewhere in Hillcrest, and that he liked the movies. She had run into him a few times when walking home from the trolley, and they walked together talking mostly of something he'd seen at the Spreckels. She had especially enjoyed his characterization of *The Great Train Robbery*. "Edison really knows how to make a movie. None of us in the audience could believe it when the outlaw actually fired a gun at us." He gasped as if hit and slapped at his heart with his right hand, "And then when they shot at the guy's feet and made him dance ... ." Here Jack took a complicated little dance step. Jack was cute.

"Why are you home?" he asked. "I'm off this afternoon," came a soft unembellished response, "How about you?" "My boss's doing an inventory, so ..." He stopped abruptly, and no longer smiling stared unblinkingly at the front of her blouse - now marked left and right with small discs of sweat. Stunned by this unique presentation of so feminine a feature he managed to stammer only, "You're ... You're pretty." Rose reacted in a way she could not have predicted. Jack's pronouncement, coupled with discomfort from the weather and the restlessness that had driven her outside, awoke a sudden and strong physical awareness. She felt earthy and powerful. She wanted to move, maybe to dance. Her invitation, "Come on in," was almost a command.

Once inside, she put "Chicken Reel" on the Victor Talking Machine's turntable, wound the motor, set the swing arm needle gently onto an outside track, opened the sound doors, and held out her hand. Jack just stood, smiling slightly, boyish charm beginning to return. It wouldn't do to act the part of a sweet, innocent Mary Pickford, she'd have to be Lillian Gish, the seductress, or even an outrageous Theda Bara. Taking a man's dance lead, she curled her right arm around his waist, grabbed his right hand with her left and to the music began - right-front-foot, left-back-foot, right-front-foot, hop, left-front-foot, right-back-foot, left-front-foot, hop. Jack moved only enough to avoid her feet landing on his. Dancing didn't appear an option. She stopped and pulled him toward her, unsure of what to do next, then felt his right hand pressing against her breast. Between thumb and forefinger, he gently stroked a nipple through still damp cloth.

The camisole beneath her blouse was copied from a waist length vest, Munsingwear style 171. She had made it of identical material, light-weight, plain-ribbed, thread-silk. Now it was in the way. She pulled it and blouse from her skirt and guided Jack's hand under two layers of cloth until his open palm rested comfortably against her bare left breast. She looked into his eyes questioningly. For a short while neither she nor Jack moved, but there was too little time to find out what he thought of her nipple, what he thought of her, what he thought of anything. Someone was coming up the front steps. Luckily, the conclusion of "Chicken Reel" had allowed the interloper to be heard. They scrambled, successfully eluding detection, and with Jack's eviction out the back door, the fledgling tryst ended in its infancy. "Good to see you," Loretta called out. "We're being audited this afternoon."

The work room behind was unlit, as was the shop itself. The shop's glass case, normally filled with German pastries for every season-appropriate occasion, was empty. A front window had been broken out and crudely boarded over with 1-by-12-inch planks. In that work room, around a long, maple baking table, Peter and Caroline sat with four old friends, Freida and Dieter Rudeloff and the store's owners, Karl and Greta Nachtbauer. Karl answered Freida's question, "Twelve years, now. Yeah, twelve years, and no, nothing like this has ever happened before."

It was April 12, 1917. The U.S. had been at war with Germany for less than a week. The small group foundered, at first, in an attempt to comfort one another. Each told a part of his or her story. All but one was a naturalized U.S. citizen, and she, Greta, had been born in Illinois. Why this sharing of what they all knew? If they sought approbation here, it would be like asking their mothers if they had any value, were pretty or smart. Caroline's question, "Have you gone to police yet, Karl?" changed the meeting's tenor. "Yet?" he shot back. "What should I do?"

Switzerland's neutrality didn't soften Peter's anguish over the war. He spoke German, his wife was born German, and he loved America almost as a jingoist. It had been his 'land of opportunity.' The war was simply another hard, almost unbearable, blow added to the pain of the paraplegia. Probst kept him moving slightly and from cramping most of the time, but couldn't stop the sores. With skin dampened by occasional incontinence, the decubitus ulcers - what the nurses called bed sores - formed unrelentingly on his thin legs and on his rear. He could not force movement enough to prevent it.

There is a time, Peter knew, when life is just more than one can handle. He met, when possible, with Grace Church minister, Clarence Damschroeder. It helped some. Together they talked with Jesus. Once after Peter prayed, "Dear God, I'm very tired, please let me die soon," Pastor Clarence suggested he let Caroline know what he was thinking. The notion appealed and terrified. Was there something he couldn't tell her? She was his constant confidant, always pleased with his insight and optimism. Pastor's idea was good. He would talk to her. The difficulty of remaining the always upbeat Peter while saying, "I want to die," hadn't quite penetrated.

He sat on the front porch watching her pull a small ranunculus bulb from the main one she had just unearthed. Always the farmer, it pleased him to see her digging in the soil. He called down, "When you're finished, come sit with me." A breeze blowing off the bay contributed to a near perfect August day. Caroline arranged the bulb next to others in a small pail, wiped her hands on the apron tied around her waist, climbed the steps, and dragged a straight-backed chair from near the front door to alongside Peter's wheelchair.

"I'll miss those blossoms," he began. "They were almost as pretty as you." She started a grin on hearing this first 'vintage Peter' since before the war, and would liked to have said something clever in return. For shy Caroline that wasn't possible. She tucked in her chin and looked down at her feet, a blush coloring her still half-smiling face. Peter had hoped to ease into his carefully constructed monologue. That also didn't happen. With no transitional comments, it just gushed out.

"Remember when Rudolph fell from the tree and broke his elbow and said to Emma, 'I can't stand this pain,' and she said, 'It's better than the alternative, Rudy.' Well, it isn't always!" The almost smile couldn't be maintained as Caroline's forehead knit in puzzlement. "What are you talking about?"

Not quite as planned, he thought, feeling some relief in having at least gotten started. "I'm talking about life, mama, about how sometimes in life when you hurt and you're too tired to fight it, you think you'd do anything to stop it. Well one alternative is ... , well, to die." He went on, not looking over to check her reaction. "Sure, death was no alternative for Rudy, he just had a broken elbow. For me, and I've talked with the three wise men, Probst, Clarence and Jesus," he winced - had he taken the Lord's name in vain? - but quickly continued, "I'd like you to help me do a party, find a headstone, get a plot up in God's country, Ontario, and send me off to my maker." Only then could he look back at her - sitting tall in the straight back chair. Tears streamed down her cheeks while her lips curled up, this time in a complete but tiny grin. He'd done it! Praise God, it was done!

Two months later and six months after America's entry into the war, Peter died. For a short while his daughter, a disconsolate Rose, locked herself in her room, refusing to believe. She had experienced none of the harshness felt by her father over the war. Instead, she thrived in this Navy town, working to organize activities for young sailors with both the YMCA and the Salvation Army. San Diego had banned a type of cabaret dancing that year. With Fleeta Marly Walker, her friend from the clubs, she helped convince those groups that dancing would be a healthy and respectable recreation. "Keep them out of those awful dens of iniquity south of the border in Tijuana, Mexico," had been their defining argument.

The flagellating question - phrased in every possible way: "How could I have been off enjoying myself with you so sick?" - tormented, tortured, persisted. Knocks at her door or the words of comfort shouted through it by her mother went unheard. Finally, Caroline, with a deep understanding of her daughter, resorted to Ephesians 6:1: 'Children obey your parents in the Lord: for this is right.' She yelled, "Rosa, come out, now, I need your help." The door opened and a shaking red-eyed young woman fell wailing into her mother's arms. "Would you like to see him before I call the man who will help us move him back to Ontario?" Caroline asked quietly. She carefully avoided the word mortician.

Peter truly looked at peace. Caroline had covered his body with his favorite quilt, a bright patchwork creation of hers, pulled down his eyelids, and twisted up the corners of his lips until they lay hidden beneath his now all-white mustache. She and her daughter sat in chairs across his body from one another. "Your papa didn't make it to three score and ten, Rosa, but he had a happy, God-filled life and he wanted now to be with his God." Caroline's personal skepticism in no way inhibited her from expressing the beliefs she took to be her late husband's. "He told me that was his wish a while ago, and we made plans together." Rose felt through the quilt for her father's hand and pressed hers against it. "Did it hurt him that I went to dances with the sailors?" she mumbled, almost incomprehensively - drops again building on her lower lashes. "It was one of the things that made him happy in his last months, Rosa. He told me he almost slipped up and told Pastor Damschroeder about your dancing, because it made him feel so good that you were supporting America. He loved America. Of course he also loved the German people."

Even death would not allow Peter to let go unanswered the cruelty of so many fellow Americans toward their German-American brothers. His humor was his sword. "I liked the headstone Emma got for Rudolph when he passed on. Do you remember it, mama?" He didn't wait for her reply. "It was granite, tall enough for Emma's name to be added later, and it had a big 'P' carved at the top. I thought that was nice, a good way to honor the family name. I'd like an 'A' on mine - I mean ours. And oh, you know that symbol the German Gymnasts' League used to kind of celebrate the country's unification?" Caroline nodded. "Well, I'd like two of those, one left and one right of our names." And so it was that the stone carver got instructions to place a male, right handed, and a female, left handed swastika to the left and right above the letters PETER A. AMBUEHL.

It was the funeral, the coming home party, Peter had hoped for - friends, food, and laughter. Afterwards, Rose fell into a simple pattern: work at the store then home and chores. Her world not only slowed, it became indistinct, foggy, one day like another. No more stories sent colleagues chuckling from the ladies room. Her mood seemed to foretell a tragedy about to unfold, a global sickness outstripping the misery of war. In India alone the deaths would be close to the number lost in the fighting, eight million soldiers and twelve million civilians - twenty million altogether. The influenza pandemic, known locally as the 'Spanish Flu,' would kill two to five times that number.

San Diego leaders reacted in diametrical ways. To the power elite it was nothing to cause concern. Not true claimed the Board of Health, a body with no power to enforce. The Board ordered the closure of all public amusements: theaters, dance halls, churches, schools, libraries and movies. Spreckels' paper advised readers to "treat as a bad cold." The Board ordered the wearing of masks when outdoors or in public employment. Masks were to be cut from fine mesh white gauze, 14½ by 14½ inches square, folded into fourths. then tied around the head with exposed corners taped. A Spreckels' editorial claimed that masks were alright for Greek tragedy but "only highwaymen, burglars, and holdup men wear them professionally." It concluded, "We sincerely regret that some of the young women in public employment are compelled to wear these masks. We miss their pretty faces." Rose's face was among those missed. Marston had insisted, not only to comply with Health Department policy, but because the flu had been particularly virulent for young adults.

Servicemen in the city also experienced vacillation by their superiors. Sailors at the Balboa Park training camp and soldiers from Camp Kearny teeter-tottered between quarantine and liberty. Throughout the epidemic Fleeta Marly struggled to keep 'the boys' entertained. It wasn't all altruism anymore, if ever it had been. She had fallen for Corporal Archie Miehls, recently returned from Hawaii's Scoffield Barracks for demo-bilization with Camp Kearny's 40th Division. The role she had created for herself - kind of a troop movement semaphore between service brass, health officials, the YMCA, the Salvation Army, and the city council - kept all informed of who was allowed where and when. With Camp Kearny mesa fourteen miles from downtown, the task required time as well as tact, but did provide opportunity to sneak a few Archie visits during periods of restriction.

Fleeta Marly's secondary mission, to see her best friend organizing and dancing again, had so far failed. "My god, I've talked to her a million times," she complained to Archie. She missed Rose, and she missed Rose's help. Flirting, flattery, bluster or sheer persistence always got pert blonde Fleeta what she wanted. This was irritating. "It's been a year, maybe a year and a half, since her dad passed on," she continued. "She'll just shrivel up if she doesn't get out." Archie chuckled. "You make her sound like a prune. For some people it just takes time to get over stuff." "No, Archie, we have to do something." Archie grunted a quiet, "Okay."

Caroline greeted them with a warmth reserved for Rose's friends. Those she liked and those she didn't. Her strained, "Good to meet you," sounded English enough to be understood by the tall young soldier. "Rose won't be home for two, three hours, come in you like," she managed. "I actually wanted to see you, Rosa's mama," Fleeta exclaimed, striding into the living room past her hostess. Once seated, she spared her friend's mother further word searching difficulties by doing most of the talking. Simply, but in great detail, she presented her plan for a party, a surprise party for Rose.

For the most part the plan met with sympathy. Maybe, thought Caroline, it could help return to her that once bubbly child, now often drab, too often somber. Not on Saturday the 19th though - so what if this soldier's division gets demobilized that weekend, whatever that means - doesn't she know the 19th is Holy Saturday, the day before Christ's resurrection? An agreement was reached. There would be a party for Rose on April 26th, the Saturday following Easter. Fleeta would come in the afternoon and have things ready before Rose got home from work, and yes, Fleeta could bring anyone she liked.

But the stranger that dwelleth with you
shall be unto you as one born among you,
and thou shalt love him as thyself ...
Lev. 19:34

In April, the odds are two to one that San Diego skies will
be cloudy. The closer to May the better the bet on overcast.
Yet in the early evening, April 26, 1919, the temperature remained in the high sixties and there wasn't a cloud in the sky.
Rose, off at six, felt restless. She'd wander around a bit, look
in shop windows before boarding the trolley for home. Mama
would wait with dinner. It had been a surprisingly good day for
hat sales. Hats always did well before Easter, but a week after?
Maybe the weather.

Looking at diamond rings through the glass in front of J
Jessop & Sons Jewelers, she caught her own reflection. What
she saw startled her. Her clothes were neat, she didn't look
tawdry, but neither was there a hint of flair - just plain old
Rose. Shouts on the sidewalk behind stopped her preoccupa-
tion with how old she was. She turned to see only a couple
of boys yelling their "Wows!" in appreciation of a San Diego landmark, Jessop's 22-foot-tall clock. All four faces of the
clock showed the time as almost seven. It was later than she
had thought.

She stood in the dark, having opened the front door of
The Tenth Avenue House just as the sun set behind it. Her
mother sat against a leather cushion in the right corner of
her simple oak-board mission-style sofa, a Stickley Settle look-
alike. At the other end a curly haired young soldier was speaking to her in a language Rose seemed to understand, but didn't
know why. Her mother was smiling, answering in her native
German. Rose had not seen her mother smile that broadly in
a very long time. "Mama," was as much as she could get out
when **"SURPRISE!"** came at her from a half-dozen voices.

Chapter 5

In and Out of Eden

And when the woman saw that the tree was
good for food, and that it was pleasant to the eyes,
and a tree to be desired to make one wise,
she took of the fruit thereof, and did eat ...
Gen. 3:6

The past several months had been great. Getting back again with Irv, so positively, so unexpectedly - it was magical. She'd just confessed to Fleeta Marly how happy she felt, content even. Then why couldn't she get a good nights sleep. She'd never had to go 'toto' at night before, and when time to get up in the morning, she just dragged. Mama was no help. "Go get checked out at the hospital," Caroline had persisted. It wasn't until feeling nauseous before breakfast on a day in mid-October that Rose considered heeding that advice. She walked the little over a mile to where Loretta now lived.

Loretta was breast-feeding her fourteen-month-old son Jimmy when Rose arrived. She had moved out of the Tenth Avenue House shortly after marrying Oscar Morse two years earlier. Rose had marveled at the beauty of their wedding. The music, the color, the grandeur of the event all outdid her experience with Lutheran sacrament. If they had only spoken some intelligible language, like English or German. The service had taken place just outside the sanctuary in St. Joseph's Catholic Church: a grand brick structure at Third Street and Beech - bizarrely looked down on by its adjoining narrow, seven-stories-high bell tower.

Rose had met Irving at a party thrown in her honor almost six-and-a-half years ago. She first saw him talking with her mama, and mama had smiled and answered. From then on her remembrance blurred. Everyone talked to her at once. Everyone seemed to introduce her to the only person there she hadn't known. She didn't even remember who they were, only that she knew them. At some point Fleeta, the most dominant of the partiers, grabbed her hand and pulled her to the sofa. She would never forget Irving's welcoming smile, broad and open like her dad's, but also somehow penetrating, a bit brash, like he saw her stripped naked.

Fleeta asked Caroline for help in the kitchen and almost shoved Rose into the newly vacated corner of the bench. Used to seeing the young soldier all charm and push with girls at the dances, Fleeta perceived here an unexpected shyness in him, a reticence to his usual boldness, a demeanor almost antithetical to the one experienced by Rose.

Irving and Rose arranged to go out the following Saturday. Irving would take Rose to the Spreckels where Gloria Swanson had the lead in a new deMille film about social class differences. Rose had heard it to be kind of light - okay for a first date. He would pick her up in time for the late showing.

Rose assumed they would head downtown on the Fifth Avenue trolley, but at the appointed time, Irving arrived driving a Model T Ford Runabout. Although his unit had demobilized, he was wearing an army uniform: a drab affair of coarse olive wool. The coat with its four symmetrically placed flap-topped pockets, two above and two below the waist, reached to his hips. Its left sleeve bore a yellow 'V', made up of three embroidered segments, stitched between cuff and elbow. The breeches had only a trace of flare and ended just below the knees where wrap-around leggings took over to cover his calves. On his head sat a type of campaign hat now identified with Smokey the Bear. It wasn't a flattering outfit, but did help hide his age. He was nine months short of twenty-one.

When Rose opened the door, Irving's face showed true pleasure. She had made herself a dress of light blue silk. A dress which, in its way, predicted the flapper age to come. It wasn't sleeveless and its skirt fell a few inches short of her ankles, not to just below the knees, but she had infused that skirt with a subtle boldness. It hugged her hips and thighs like it had been painted on. Her chestnut brown hair hung down in long, tightly-twisted curls to below her shoulders. There a white lace collar topped a simple bodice and framed her face between it and a wide blue ribbon tied round her forehead, the same blue as her dress.

Irv stood and stared, clutching at his hat with both hands. "That's quite a hat," Rose blurted, not quite laughing. "I've seen a lot of them around town and keep wondering if it wouldn't be easier to wear one of those little caps. You know the kind you can stick into your belt." Irv recovered with, "Like to, but can't. Only guys that were in Europe can wear them. They're called overseas caps. They had helmets too, so they needed a ... ." Irv couldn't finish; he had to get back to the world around him. "Gee, you look swell." Neither of them knew if those words were born of sentiment or habit.

"Thanks" It was a quick response followed by, "I saw you drive up. I didn't know you had a car. Oh," she stood aside and held open the door, "would you like to come in and say hello to ma?" "I would, but we'll probably be late for the show if I do. I stole that clunker and don't really know how to shift the gears. I've never driven a Ford before." "You stole it!?" That's the kind of thing her joker dad or brother would say, but she really didn't know this man. He laughed. "It belongs to a guy who wants me to work for him. He's rich I guess; has a big car, too."

There was nothing gallant about the way Irv escorted Rose into the car. The little black roadster had but a single door, the one installed on its passenger side. Some owners flaunted their dexterity by jumping from the driver-side running board up and over into the seat. Irv chose to get in first. Once both were in, he did lean over to pull her door shut. All this, of course, after he had cranked the car to a start. It was still a year before Henry Ford would deem it a sales advantage to raise prices for an electric starter, and this Model T was already two years old.

Getting underway also proved challenging. Irv deliberated

on which lever to move or which pedal to push first. There was
a big lever with a squeeze handle on its top coming out of the
floor to his left, two small levers under the steering wheel, and
three pedals at his feet. Rose reacted, "Haven't you driven before?" "Huh! Oh sure. I have an army license. Drove a Dodge
at Scoffield all the time, but this thing ... it doesn't have a gear
shifter like a real car." Finally, he grabbed the floor lever with
his left hand and guided it forward, pushed down with his left
foot on the left pedal, then with his right hand pressed down
on the right lever below the steering wheel. They were off.

It was a short car ride to the Spreckels. There, a line longer
than anticipated had already queued up at the box office. It cha-
grined Rose to discover why. The marquee announced today's
show to be *Broken Blossoms*, sometimes called *The Yellow Man and
the Girl*, not her expected *Male and Female*. Rose had heard much
of *Broken Blossoms* and hated it without seeing it. The much her-
alded film, decades ahead of its time, gave a stark and painful
account of child abuse and interracial romance. Even though
it starred Lillian Gish, Rose did not believe it proper fare for a
movie. Certainly not a first date movie.

"Irving," she began, "they changed the movie ... looks like
there'll be a big crowd. ... Maybe we should go dancing or
something ... ." Irv had already backed the little roadster into
a parking space at the curb in front of the theater - a feat requiring a half depression of the left pedal and a full push on
the one in the center. Its twenty-horsepower engine chunked
on. He had picked up on the tension in his pretty companion's
remark and recalled that during their drive over she appeared
delighted - holding her head most of the way out in the open
space between the two-seater's door and its cloth top - brown
curls flying like the ears of an English Cocker. "There's a lot
of gas in this thing, maybe you'd like to drive around a little."
Who was this guy? she wondered; he couldn't have made a
better suggestion.

San Diegans call the few last weeks of Spring, "May Gray/
June Gloom." It's the time of year when coastal clouds hang
around for most of the day. In the afternoons and early evenings, the sky will often give way to a little hazy sunshine. On
this particular evening, a statistician's nightmare, all was clear
in the heavens and the temperature in the upper sixties, higher

than average. "About all I can find in San Diego is the bay," Irving confided guiding the car down Broadway and onto Harbor Drive. "It's pretty here by the water," she reassured him, "and I know quite a bit about the city if you have any questions." "Okay, hey, you warm enough? There's a blanket in the trunk." "Good for now, thanks." Irv crept the 'T' along Harbor as far as Grape - still only a modest walk from the Spreckels. There he stopped the car, shrugged, wrinkled his forehead and made his appeal, "Okay, what's a New Yorker to see in San Diego?" "There's a neighborhood in the hills a little north of where I live. Mission Hills is what they call it. They put some real swanky places up there. Still building some. It's not far from here, but it is hilly."

They made a U-turn to Ash, and headed east before turning left and north. "Wow, you said it about hills," Irv observed, pushing the left pedal to the floor to continue in low gear. "Glad we've got a lot of gas otherwise we'd have to go up backwards." Her query as to why met with something mumbled about gravity feed or gravity fuel, or maybe gravity feed fuel. It didn't matter, she was enjoying herself, and she was enjoying her companion.

They found parking with a spectacular bay view near the Old Catholic Cemetery on Washington Place. The sliver of a waxing two-day-old new moon stood out in the black sky over the water. "Look, that's where we were." She pointed down at Harbor Drive. "Gosh, the cars look so small." Irv was looking at Rose, not at where she pointed. He ran the back of his right hand down her left cheek to rest on her shoulder, then slid it under her brown curls to the flesh at the rear of her neck. She turned to face his stare. Time lost its momentum. They held that pose, unmoving, for many minutes, studying one another - tense, excited, controlled. Slow and deliberately he pulled her toward him and they kissed - over and over they kissed. Tendrils of lightning ran down her body, warming. moistening, charging her. She knew how it felt to fantasize, to touch herself, to feel erotic pleasure, but to be opened like this by a man. It was new. She was twenty-seven years old and it was new.

Now Irv leaned over her across the small seat. His right hand dropped from her neck to her waist and his left reached and stroked the blue silk between her legs. She didn't want it to stop, but it had to stop. Her whole upbringing shouted, 'My God, this is a first date!' She reached down, cupped his hand in both of hers, brought it to her mouth and kissed it. The young soldier, awed by her act, straightened up, put his hands in his lap, and slid over to sit closely alongside his new friend.

They spoke of many things that night: of the moon, the night sky, the tiny cars on the streets below, and of Irving's new dreams. He didn't want to go home, back to New York. He didn't even think of New York as home anymore. "The guy that loaned me this Lizzie, Morton's his name, he's a mucky-muck with San Diego Consolidated, the gas and electric company." "Mr. Morton?" she wondered out loud. They held hands now, talking while looking through the windshield at the still clear vista ahead. "No, Morton's his first name, don't remember his last. One of his flunkies calls him Mr. F." "I'm pretty sure Mr. Marston wouldn't loan me a car, or let me call him by his first name," she teased, "maybe you did steal it." Both chuckled. "No, I helped him, I guess. Consolidated supplies all the power at the camp and Morton's their main numbers guy. Somehow his boys got all messed up tying to figure out how much to charge Uncle Sam for gas. How many cook stoves do you think we have?" He didn't wait for her answer. "Well there are 238 mess halls out there, really, 238." "You know," she interrupted, "I remember when they first ran gas to the camp a couple of years ago. They tapped into a main at Tenth and University, only two blocks from where I live. It was a real mess."

And so it went on. Two old friends, passions leashed for the night, chatting away until the early hours over the personal, the stirring, and the mundane. Irv did finish his story. He had saved the company's treasurer, Morton as he knew him, embarrassment and grief by devising a scheme for accurately tallying gas usage at the camp. Morton wanted him to work in the company's billing department, and although it sounded kind of dull, Irv was leaning that way. All talk came to a stop with Rose's announcement that she had promised Pastor Damschroeder help in the Sunday School early this day. They kissed cautiously for a bit before Irving cranked start their carriage and drove her down the hills to The Tenth Avenue House.

Before parting, they set date two for the following Friday. Irv had told her of an agreement he had with Morton to meet at the Gas Company's offices late that day. Rose was quick to point out that the Gas and Electric Company offices were at Broadway and Sixth, only a block south of where she worked. Great, he would meet her in front of Marston's when she left work, and they'd take the Hillcrest trolley to her place. There, she promised, she would cook him a special German meal.

The aroma of that special meal met Rose and Irving as they walked up the three steps to the front porch. Irv couldn't help himself, "Been slaving over a hot stove all day I smell." Rose wanted to be annoyed, but found it funny. "Mama's looking forward to seeing you again," was the best she could come back with. And it was true. Caroline scrambled from the kitchen to the parlor when she heard them come in. Immediately, Irv exchanged greetings with her in that language Rose mostly understood but couldn't identify. It had to be some kind of German. "Where does your German come from Irv," she finally blurted. "It's not really German; its Yiddish, kind of German written in Hebrew." "Hebrew?" To Rose it was just a word from church. "Yeah, the Jewish language." Now she was startled. "How do you know the Jewish language?" "Because my parents are Jewish." "You're a Jew?" came out loud and somehow in *Switzerdeutsch*.

"We're having *schwinshaxe*, children," Caroline intervened in an intimidating and louder than normal tone. "We'll have it like in Bavaria with dumplings and cabbage. You sit here, Irving, Rose and I will finish up in the kitchen." She placed an arm on her daughter's waist and guided her out a door beyond the dining room. Irving had no knowledge of what they discussed, but Rose returned a quiet and respectful hostess.

Irving made much of how good the meal was and how much he enjoyed it, and although the Jewish faith did enter their conversation again, he ate heartily making no mention of any imperative against *schwein fleisch*.

Caroline, compelled by a natural, open-minded curiosity, asked the obvious question: "How do you worship as a Jew?" Irving laughed, "Worship, afraid I don't. I really don't ... ," here he hesitated. Might not be a good idea to admit he thought religion was all nonsense. "My mother had a writer friend who lived way downtown in New York," he began again. "He, this writer, wrote a book ten years or so before I was born. Called it *Yekl: A Tale of the New York Ghetto.* Mom made me read it before I quit school. It's the story about a guy from the old country, Latvia I think, who comes here and wants to be like everybody else, but gets treated different because he's a Jew. It gets kind of complicated, with marital problems and all, but eventually this Yekl changes his name to Jake, and just acts like he's, well, an American. I'm kind of like that, like Jake." He felt himself blush as he added, "I'm just an American."

A couple of weeks passed before Irv and Rose saw one another again. Irv had taken the job with San Diego Gas and Electric and had moved from camp into a two-bedroom flat he would share with his friend and ex-army buddy, Archie Miehls. Fleeta Marly had found the place for Archie in Golden Hill, a recently settled San Diego neighborhood just south of Balboa Park. It couldn't have been better for Irving. He could walk to work in fifteen to twenty minutes or jump on a Spreckels streetcar at a stop nearby.

The two men had been lounging around the apartment, enthusiastically assessing their new roles in life when conversation shifted to plans for the day. It was early on Saturday afternoon. Archie expected Fleeta to show up around seven. They were to eat out, then go dancing. "Why don't you come with us, Irv? You can pick up a chick at the dance after we eat." It was a proposal demanding concentration. Unwelcome images of Rose kept intervening. Irv came up, eventually, with a suggestion of his own, "What are you doing until Fleeta gets here?" Archie hunched his shoulders and raised open palms into the air. "Good, let's go buy Fleeta a new hat." Archie's grimace lacked clarity. "Why the scowl, Arch?" "A hat, why would I want to buy her a hat? If I did - anyway - I wouldn't know what she'd want or how to pick one."

Archie found himself, an hour later, on a trolley with Irv heading for Marston's. Archie had vetoed the mile walk. In spite of Irving's assurance that it made no difference since she had a key to the place, he wanted to be certain he'd be back before Fleeta arrived.

As they walked from the elevator, feeling self-conscious between rows of women's apparel, they spotted Rose standing behind a tall, middle-aged blonde. She had just pulled a very high-crowned, rust-colored hat to the woman's ears. "...., kind of like a helmet," they heard as they got close. "It's called cloche. This particular hat with its brim slanted down over your ears is very becoming. And the ribbon - tied that way - up on the left side ... it's just so fashionable." The woman peered into the large hand mirror Rose held for her. "It makes me look awfully tall, doesn't it?" Archie and Irv waited, declining service from other clerks, until the sale completed.

Rose felt almost violated when she saw them approach. How could one feel so annoyed, angry even, and at the same time want to run up and kiss that guy? "I'm working," was the only thing she could think to say. "Great," Irv responded. "Archie wants to buy Fleeta Marly a hat." Rose couldn't help herself. She laughed a loud crazy laugh, a laugh all could hear. "Guess it is kind of obvious?" Irv mumbled to no one in particular.

Although Irv had enlisted when only a boy, the evening became a celebration of his and Archie's return to civilian life. For Rose and Irv, the never-dead ember rekindled. It started at dinner with a little wine and the touching together of legs under the table, and it sizzled on the dance floor. Irv considered himself a good dancer, and except for an over heavy lead, he was. His loose athletic body flowed correctly to every rhythm. Rose, for her part, approached dancing like a scholar. While stiffer than her partner, her mind had choreographed every step and dip. They were a pair to watch - moving to the compelling pop music of the time - Berlin, Jessel, Cobb, Whiting, Porter, ...

The band played many slow waltzes that night - "Beautiful Ohio," "I'm Forever Blowing Bubbles," "Blue Sunshine." By the time, late in the evening, when the notes of "Till We Meet Again" filled the hall, Irving held her tight against him, and as the vocalist sang,

> Smile the while you kiss me sad adieu
> When the clouds roll by I'll come to you,

he waltzed cross-step, rubbing her body close - pelvis against pelvis, thigh brushing thigh.

Rose's rearing would once again triumph over cries of the

flesh. Neither Fleeta Marly's entreaties or characteristic persistence would be of avail. Rose would not go home with them for a nightcap, nor would she go to see their new digs. Irving watched the exchange with a detachment inspired by the inevitable. The trolley trip to Rose's was cozy, warm and initially uneventful. They sat close, held hands and, from time to time, shared a furtive kiss. Irv's remarks concerning his transition from army life were what caused her to think of citizen duties. "You need to register," she offered as a reminder. It met with unexpected puzzlement. "Register?" "Yes, register to vote. There are some very important bond measures coming up in the fall, like bay dredging and water issues - even trash collection." It made her feel important to know this, even if it had all come from Loretta. Far from supporting her experience of intellectual worth, Irving's reply stunned like a blow, shifting all thoughts and moods. He spoke openly, affording no consequence to his message. "Can't register yet, I won't be twenty-one till next January."

Dames, what is it with them, ran through his mind over and over as he made his return trip. He hadn't a clue as to what happened. Was it the Jewish thing again - but out of a clear sky when everything seemed so great? As for Rose, it was the great dichotomy, the rend between head and loin. Her body reached out for him. It had from the outset - but he was all wrong. She spoke about him with everyone - with her mother, with Loretta, with all her fellow milliners, and, of course, with Fleeta. Advice came, presented with great diversity, from Loretta's calm and analytical analysis to Fleeta's strident and urgent appeal, but all surprisingly, remarkably similar:

"City versus country upbringing shouldn't make that much difference."
"A seven year plus age gap may not make that much difference."
"See if religion interferes with how you treat one another."
"See if you're tolerant of one another's beliefs."
"Get to know one another better."
"Take it slow."

And so the courtship proceeded - on again, off again - frustrating and joyful. They had been dating for over seven months when the unexpected occurred. Those months tipped heavily toward the positive. Irv pushed her physically, but with respect. More importantly, and to the amazement of all, he became a part of the Grace Lutheran Church community. He seemed to enjoy attending Sunday services and, even more so, the wonderful German meals Caroline often prepared for Pastor Damschroeder, his wife and infant son. Irv played with the baby like an older brother.

The rift occurred during sex play on a Thursday evening in mid-December. It had been drizzling all day. Irv worked later than usual in order to meet Rose at the end of her six p.m. shift. He found her waiting in front of Marston's, covered her with his open umbrella, escorted her to the trolley and took her to his Golden Hill apartment. Archie and Fleeta Marly were away. The ice box was nearly empty, but Rose managed to put together a small supper, pan frying previously-boiled potatoes and concocting jelly omelets. It didn't take them long to stretch out on Irv's bed where, before much time lapsed, he began fondling both breasts - something he had done before. To her delight he always professed admiration for her nipples, calling them sweet, beautiful or any other endearing adjective he could retrieve. His excitement validated the sincerity of those professions. Tonight, he not only hardened and aroused them with gentle stroking but embraced them with his lips, rolling his tongue and savoring the sensations they brought to them both. Her reaction was nothing short of a purr. When he reached, then, to feel between her legs, he got the expected, "No Irv, not there." As always he accepted that no, sat up, smiled and said, "Well, no one's gotten to those special bubbies before." From her dreamy state, and without thought, she just, in an amused way, kind of mouthed, "Well Jack did have a short touch." Irv's reaction, akin to hers when she learned of his age, hit with no expectation whatever.

"JACK, who's Jack," he shouted. Her response, a simple "What?" began a long, complicated and ineffective dialogue, terminating only when he put her on the Golden Hill trolley, scowled, and walked away. Despite Fleeta Marly's later pleas to them both, it would be more than six years before they spoke again to one another.

Chapter 6

The Voice of Many Angels

*And the angel came in unto her, and said, Hail,
thou that art highly favoured, the Lord is with thee:
blessed art thou among women.*
Luke 1:28

The Roaring Twenties brought few changes to Rose's life. She continued to live with her mother at The Tenth Avenue House, and remained in Marston's millinery department, becoming one of their senior clerks. She missed Irv - at first, painfully so - but not uncontrollably. Not enough to be cajoled by Fleeta into contacting him. She dated casually, attended church functions, and inadvertently became an entrepreneur. That came about because of flapper fashion, and the resultant appeal of the flat chest. The bra she had copied and fabricated in early 1914 did the desired flattening. Its two uncupped breast covers reined in all bounce. People who knew her would stare and ask, "How do you do it?" Word-of-mouth brought her clients from all over the community. It wasn't a lucrative business; she made little more than expenses, but it supported her sense of worth. She was a part of American enterprise, like her heroes, Warren Harding, the man she supported for president, and her papa.

Irving's life, by contrast, changed dramatically. He wore a suit Monday through Friday, carried a green visor to work, and sat at a desk from nine to five. When Archie, now an insurance agent, married Fleeta Marly at City Hall, Irv served as best man. Fleeta, accepting but saddened by Rose's absence, compensated by wearing as 'something new' a hand-made 'Rose bra' - a bra she proudly shared by unbuttoning her blouse at the reception. Few weeks would pass without Fleeta providing Irv some information as to Rose's activity, a cruel, but not maliciously intended, habit.

When Fleeta moved into the Golden Hill apartment as Archie's wife, Irving rented a one-bedroom flat on Park Boulevard, the other side of Balboa Park. The greater distance to work, and the expectation of receiving $500.00, the most to be awarded to non-combat veterans under the World War Adjusted Compensation, or Bonus Act of 1924, were his two rationales for buying a car. His choice, a Chevrolet Superior Utility Coupe; a vehicle widely advertised as the lowest-priced closed car with a Fisher body, cost $640 plus tax and $28.50 for shipping. The horsepower tax had been dropped the previous year and replaced with a flat registration fee of $3. That same year, the first gasoline tax, two cents per gallon, also made its way through California's legislature.

The Chevy boosted Irv's social life in unexpected ways. As a prior trolley rider he had dreamed of driving to Mission Beach, his favorite ocean dipping and wave riding spot. The car's advantage for that purpose proved short lived. Spreckels completed an Electric Railway line to the beach the following year, serving both real estate development and a new amusement center, Belmont Park, home to a massive, wooden-scaffolded roller coaster, The Giant Dipper.

The real changer came about because of the Eighteenth Amendment to the Constitution, Prohibition, and its subsequent Volstead Act enforcement laws - laws put into effect only a month after his last date with Rose. Those laws drastically altered the way San Diego partied. Restaurants, dance halls, bars - no legal establishment could serve liquor, beer, or wine. Alcohol distilling businesses and services closed or some, like Aztec Brewing, moved twenty or so miles south to Mexico, to the then-little town of Tijuana. San Diego nightlife moved with it. Tijuana, home of the legal drink, grew like a teenager on steroids. Bars, nightclubs, hotels, and a complete tourist complex, Agua Caliente, came to life. For Irv, never much of a drinker, women, not booze were his drug of choice. He met them at the grocers, at cafes, and most often at the beach. He took them south of the border in his little car - to dine, to dance, and to drink. His only acknowledged regret - the car was a two-seater - no room to bring an extra friend or two.

One could, of course, still get a hard drink without leaving the country. Illegal bars opened all over the United States. In San Diego, most could be found in the neighborhood once called Stingaree after the dreaded barb-wielding ray-fish occasionally stepped on in shallow waters off one of the beaches. The name fit much of the area's earlier activity - gambling, muggings, and prostitution. Until its 'cleanup' about the time the Ambuehl's moved to San Diego, fines paid to the police kept it open and contained. Now, it was safer and secret.

Fleeta and Archie were particularly fond of two prohibition watering places. One at the edge of the old Stingaree district, the other a short walk north in the beautiful U.S. Grant hotel. The hotel, built by Ulysses S. Grant, Jr., son of the president and named for his father, had its elegant ballroom with its celebrated civil war battle murals transformed into the Plata Real Nightclub, where no restrictions were made on what drinks one could order. Hotel co-owner, Baron Long, also an investor in Agua Caliente, shipped his beverages from Mexico to the bay, then through elaborate underground tunnels straight from the bay to the club.

For a young married couple, money was the Plata Real's drawback. By contrast, the cozy shoe repair shop at Fourth and G served libations at a quarter the cost, had no minimum drink requirement or cover charge, and restricted clientele to the polite and the orderly. It did this in typical speakeasy fashion. One had to, in some roundabout manner, obtain a password, then be lead through a cluttered pseudo-shoe-shop to the bar above. Passwords were altered and redistributed when occasion required.

During these prohibition years, Rose had again started attending and helping organize dances for the men in service - now mostly navy - at both the Salvation Army and the ASYM-CA, San Diego's Armed Services YMCA, newly opened at 500 W. Broadway. When Archie was occupied, checking up on a claim or selling a policy, Fleeta would come along. At the Armed Services 'Y' on a Saturday in mid-November, and before the band leader had tapped out a beat for the first dance, the two were surprised to see a speck of olive drab amid the sea of navy blue. Fleeta, first to identify the apparition, blurted with unnecessary volume. "My god Rose, it's Ed, Ed Kramer, and he's still in his old uniform." With effort, they pushed their way to him through the host of welcoming blue swab-bies.

"Nice to see you, Ed," they called out, almost in unison. He responded with a mournfully uttered, "Is Maude here?" not the,"Wow, it's the Gorgeous Duo!" expected from the upbeat old acquaintance they'd known. Fleeta reacted. She grabbed him by the hand and led him to the band's prep-room behind the stage, simultaneously explaining, "We'll be mobbed here on the floor if the music begins." Rose followed them inside, closed the door, then watched as Fleeta put a hand on his shoulder and answered his earlier question. "I haven't seen Maude in years, probably more than three. How about you, Rose?" Rose moved her head from side to side. "Why are you still in uniform?" she pressed quickly; saw the three chevrons over a diamond on his sleeve and added, again without pause, "How come you're wearing first sergeant stripes?" The ques-tions distracted him, precipitating a spontaneous launch into a gap-filling monologue.

"I am a first sergeant," he began. "I didn't leave the ser-vice with Archie and Irv, I re-upped. I'm stationed at East Field now, you probably know the place, just north of the Mex border, down there in Otay. They use it for training, like for takeoffs and landings. I'm in charge of security … ." He went on with what he considered the past few year's major life landmarks. Right now, he was on leave through Thanksgiv-ing, and staying with an uncle who owned part interest in an East San Diego hardware store. His long, torturous narrative about Maude can be succinctly summarized by its last three sentences, "I thought we were forever until I got a letter from her a couple of months ago saying she didn't want to see me anymore. I've called and looked everywhere. Nobody has any idea where she is."

As always, Fleeta had a plan. "Why don't we entertain our sailors until the dance is over, then meet up with Archie and have a drink or two? It'll do you good, Ed, and Arch would really be happy to see you." "Gee, I don't know," came out one word at a time, "I'm just here to look for Maude." "You know, Archie," she shot back, "If anybody would know how to find Maude, it would be Archie."

Rose, ever amused by her friend's manipulative talent - unless it was used on her - had to find out where this was going. "Where do you get drinks?" she asked. Fleeta's expression morphed quickly from blank, to scowl, to a big open-mouthed smile. "There's a nice little place on 4th and Market we like, and ... " Rose didn't wait for the sentence to finish. "That's down in Stingaree town, Fleeta," she winced. "Rose, Rose, you're talking about a place only a block kitty-corner from City Hall, and decades after Wyatt Earp ran gambling joints down there." Ed's mood altered dramatically after that exchange, possibly by transporting him back to remembered play between the temperaments of these two women. He laughed, "Okay girls, let's hook up with Archie after the dance."

Rose couldn't shake her queasiness as the muscled, mustached bouncer led them through the unkempt shop, but once at a table across from the bar she had to agree with Fleeta, it was a very pleasant place. The two men connected immediately in the way common experience and old acquaintance-ship unites. Once talk of finding Maude was put to rest, Archie shared important news of his own. He would be adding Travelers to the cadre of agencies he represented. Big changes were predicted for auto insurance. Connecticut was already talking of legislating financial responsibility laws for drivers involved in accidents. Sanford Perkins would be coming to see him early next year from Hartford. He was a big shot, Secretary of the Compensation and Liability Department. They'd be working out liability policies for Californians.

At a lull in their chatter Archie overheard Fleeta telling Rose, "Irv seems to be doing nothing but work lately ..." She spoke openly and often to Irving about Rose, but was circumspect the other way around. Now, with both of them a little tipsy, those inhibitions had lifted. Archie, unable to stop himself interrupted, "What do you mean work, seems like play, play, play to me." Ed, unaware of Fleeta's scowl, entered in, "Yea, he stops by to see me every now and then. Stopped at the gate just last Saturday. Had a flooz..." Now he did note the look on the women's faces and began again. "Had a young lady with him. They were heading for T-town."

Fleeta was fascinated. Why hadn't Irv told her about Ed. "Do you ever see Irv when he's by himself?" she questioned. Suddenly subdued, Ed answered, "Only once, I asked him to bring Maude to see me a few months back, and after he took her to where we were staying, he came back to the gate and we talked for awhile." With a slight smile returning, he looked over at Rose. "Talked about you, Rose, and about how he envied the way Maude and me were talking about getting hitched." Once again gloom took possession of his face. Archie cut off Fleeta's attempt to press on, and conversation turned to talk of the coming holidays.

About a week before Christmas an all-excited Fleeta rushed up to Marston's millinery. She had to see Rose and it couldn't wait. She was in luck; Rose wasn't with a customer. "Rose darling," she blurted, "don't make plans for New Year's Eve, you've got to join us at the Grant." In return she received a flat, annoyed, "It's kind of busy here, ... it's the Christmas rush, ... can we talk after six." Fleeta, never cowed by hostility or bad manners, pressed on, "I know, Sweetie, but just listen for a minute. Perkins, that guy that runs Travelers Insurance, the guy Arch told us about - well, he's coming here after Christmas. He's bringing his wife and they're staying at the Grant - and on New Year's Eve, can you believe it, he's going to host a party for us at the Plata Real. You've just got to come!"

Rose tried, but could come up with no acceptable reason not to attend. Christmas had been pleasant and low-key for her and Mama Caroline, centered mostly around activities at Grace Church. At the store, hat sales topped all previous season records. Rose loved the year's large variety, and for herself, delighted at the way flapper caps drew out the charm of her long, slim face.

For the party her hat came first. She choose a skull cap made of black net segments adorned with bright, carmine-red carnival, floral and bugle beads - a fringe of faceted, globe and bugle beads hung to her eyebrows in front and to her shoulders in back. She had intended to make a dress, but when she saw a store mannequin in an eye-grabbing gown, exactly matching the bright carmine of the hat, that option dissolved.

She would justify its cost by invoking her employee discount. The scalloped hem of the dainty, straight-cut dress, decorated in golden, snowflake-patterned embroidery, fell to just below the knees. Each side of the dress, from shoulder to hip, was similarly embroidered. Only the deep, v-necked collar, dropping to between her breasts, caused concern. She'd have to alter one of her bras.

Guests were requested to arrive at eight P.M. that New Year's Eve. Rose had asked permission to bring an escort - hadn't given it a lot of thought, probably one of the Lutheran sailors she and Caroline brought home to feed after Sunday services - but Fleeta demurred. Rose accepted her excuse: "I don't feel comfortable asking Sanford Perkins for anything before Archie gets a contract," as vague but classic Fleeta.

Walking through to the lobby of the U.S Grant Hotel and downstairs into the Plata Real Nightclub was just that, a walk through the lobby and downstairs to the club. No one stopped her, looked her over, or asked for a password. Her second surprise, the enormity and grandeur of the place and the large, round, white-linen manicured table where she spotted Archie and Fleeta. They sat next to another couple - eight chairs remained unoccupied. She wasn't early, but unlike the expected others, on time.

Archie leaned across Fleeta, listening intently to the older man. Getting near, Rose could hear: " ... ahead of Automobile Mutual, it's them, Automobile Insurance of America, we have to keep ahead of." Archie nodded. Then she was seen. "Find your place card, Rose, dear." A place card? It was her third surprise.

After proper introductions, Rose found her name across the table from her hosts. Mrs. Perkins' expression suggested mild disapproval of her neckline and hem length, perhaps brought on by Sanford's unconcealed visual appraisal. Once seated, she looked quickly to either side. The card at the left, penned neatly like the others, First Sergeant E. Kramer, calmed, relieved and elicited a slight smile. In contrast, on her right she read a curiously scrawled Mr. J. Jones. She had questions to ask and, of course, couldn't yell them across the table. Feeling terribly alone and thinking unflatteringly of Fleeta, she ordered a mint julep and waited.

It wasn't a long wait. She knew that gait, had it etched in her memory - but it was a man she watched coming from behind one of the grand columns between her table and the stage, not the boy she had known. His suit of wool cassimere, powder blue with contrasting light gray pinstripes, had some of the elegance if not the flamboyance of those worn by mob leaders like Al Capone. Moderately form-fitting, its cut and padding exaggerated already broad shoulders. His walk to the table was slow and self-assured. After exchanging greetings with Archie and Fleeta and meeting his host and hostess, he moved around the table to stand behind the chair to Rose's left. "May I sit here," he asked. Expressionlessly she answered, "Of course, if you're Mr. Jones."

Happily, other guests began arriving - one or two at a time - as soon as he was seated, sparing them any immediate awkwardness. An exquisitely beautiful young woman took the seat two over from Rose's right. Kitty, or Miss Kitty Luce as her place card read, had been recruited by Fleeta as the perfect Maude neutralizer. For this New Year's, at least, Fleeta's intuition proved correct. Ed, struck dumb just looking at Kitty, gained confidence by being next to Rose, a woman with whom he was completely comfortable. The link was reciprocal, and soon the three of them, Kitty, Rose and Ed were chatting and laughing like old school chums. Mr. Jones, to the contrary, worked hard to become conversant with the strangers on his left.

Dinner was almost over before Rose, relaxed by another mint julep, yielded to the constant, now irresistible, urge to get some clarity. For the first time she looked to her left, and asked, blank-faced and louder than necessary, "Okay if I call you by your first name? What's the 'J' stand for?" Startled, he turned quickly in her direction, and looking directly into her eyes responded quietly, "Jake, just a good old American name, Jake." She looked down, away from his stare, blushed and whispered, "Can I call you Irving? That's an American name, too. A good American name." In truth, the only other Irvings she'd ever heard of were Washington Irving and Irving Berlin.

Irv stood and held out his hand to her. They were the first from the Perkins' table to dance. Fleeta watched, reached into her purse for the pack of Marlboros. A frown from Archie stopped her. She put them back. The brand had just been reintroduced that year as a woman's cigarette - its slogan, 'Mild as May.' Not mild enough, she gathered, for the wife of a Traveler's agent.

As they danced, Irving held Rose at arm's length, right hand at her left waist, watching her brown hair spill out and onto her shoulders from under the beaded fringe of her cap. The words he spoke, "I've always been crazy about you, Rose," completed Fleeta's long, arduous effort to reconcile the two. She had done it. As she would report later to all who would listen, she had re-united the perfect pair. "Missed you, Irv," was all that Rose could mumble.

> *And I beheld, and I heard the voice of many angels*
> *round about the throne and the beasts and the elders:*
> *and the number of them was*
> *ten thousand times ten thousand, ...*
> Rev. 5:11

The months rolled by with no talk of age, ethnicity, or Jack. All clicked for Rose and Irv. They danced, motor tripped, spent time on the beach, went to church, saw films, and enjoyed mama's cooking and approval. On September 29th, the day some believe to be Christ's birthday, Rose took off from work to help Pastor Damschroeder with a special Michaelmas celebration. Irv woke that Tuesday morning noting another cloudless day. September, always one of San Diego's warmest months, outdid itself this year. To Irv, it meant the beach. He knew of Rose's plans, he'd call in sick, meet her at the church and talk her into going with him.

From his apartment, Irv's drive straight down Park Boulevard to Grace Church took only a few minutes. Parking quickly, he ran inside. The choir was singing,

> That angel hosts Thou didst create
> Around Thy glorious throne to wait.
> They shine with light and heav'nly grace
> And constantly behold Thy face; ... .

He slid onto the hard wooden pew next to Caroline. Rose, wedged in between her mother and a young couple Irv did not know, nodded and smiled up at him. After the scripture readings, Revelations 12:1-7, Reverend Damschroeder's sermon, largely plagiarized from German Pastor C.F.W. Walther, first president of the Missouri Synod, tumbled down from the pulpit with little enthusiasm: " ... so in our scripture it's not speaking of a war in an invisible heaven of angels and saints, no war or strife exists there, only eternal peace and blessed rest. No evil spirit can invade that heaven. Rather Satan has been cast out, and his authority taken from him."

After taking Caroline home to the Tenth Avenue House, Irv had no trouble convincing Rose they should go on an outing. Sunny or not, the beach didn't resonate. She had dressed in Sunday clothes and preferred to stay that way. Irv, too, looked special in his new grey suit. "Why don't we just go out someplace for dinner," she suggested. "Dinner? It's barely afternoon, Rose. Are you hungry?" "Not really," she kind of sighed, "Just thought it would be nice to be in a quiet place with you." Irv made his usually welcome response to any 'what-do-we-do-now' impasse. "Would you like to take a drive - then think about dinner?" "What a great idea. I've been wanting to see Lemon Grove. People tell me it's like Upland, where I was born." She would never account for the denial of her true birthplace, Port Townsend, Washington.

Lemon Grove delighted Rose, bringing many childhood memories, most happy, some not. It also provided an opportunity to share a bit of cherished farming knowledge gained from her father. She spoke to Irv non-stop. All thought of dress clothes gone, she dragged him through thickly mulched soil between the trees - pointing to good practice and to bad, explaining like a foreman how a ranch should be laid out, planted, pruned, and picked.

Rose bubbled with pleasure all the way back to Irv's place. She knew they were too dirty to go straight to any of the cozy restaurants she had thought of earlier. She craved a bath. Irv's bathroom was unique. Before he had become a tenant there, a shower had been installed above its claw-foot bathtub by his owner-landlord, a man ahead of his time. A pipe, curved like a shepherd's cane, fastened to the spigots in the tub itself. The shower-head attached at the crook of the cane six feet above, and just below it an oval tube ran the circumference of the tub providing support for a cotton curtain.

Rose took her leave immediately and went to the tub. There she stood, undecided. She had always bathed in a tub, never under a shower. They were rare in the city. She knew of only one other. She undressed and stood. She looked down into the tub and up at the shower, and she thought of Irv. She stood, she thought. She looked down at herself then back at the tub. She opened the door wide enough to reach out, and through that gap held out her arm, held it out to the elbow. "Irv," she called, "Come here please, come to the bathroom and, ... help me ... help me with the shower."

... an invisible heaven of angels and saints ... no war or strife exists there, only eternal peace and blessed rest. No evil spirit can invade that heaven. Rather Satan has been cast out, and his authority taken from him. ...

Chapter 7

The Virgin Birth

Therefore the Lord himself shall give you a sign;
Behold, a virgin shall conceive, and bear a son, and
shall call his name ... .
Is. 7:14

Loretta took little Jimmy from her breast and put him in his crib. It didn't take psychic powers to note Rose's agitation. "Have you been running, dear?" came her quiet non-threatening inquiry. "No," Rose began, then extraordinary for one normally so undemonstrative, ran over and clutched her friend in a tight hug, tears forming and flooding her face.

After getting her calmed and seated, Loretta listened to everything Rose had to say. She heard of her tiredness, of having to get up to 'toto' at night and of feeling nauseous before breakfast this very morning. She put a hand on her friend's shoulder, looked gently and directly into her eyes and asked, "What do you want me to say, Rose, dear?" Now the tears rolled again. "Mama told me to get checked out at the hospital, and ... what should I do? ... What do I want you to say? Say what I ... " Loretta took Rose's hand. "Can I ask a few direct questions?" Rose nodded and she began. "Have you missed your period?" "I had a period just before our ... ," she stopped quickly, then went on, "I'm not due for another couple of weeks." "And you and Irving, did you two ... , have you two ... ," Loretta hesitated. Holy Mother, how could she ask her friend if she had committed a grave, maybe even a mortal sin? Before the question could be fully articulated, she was thankfully, if unpleasantly spared by

Rose's loud and indignant, "Of course not!"

Neither Loretta nor Rose were among the less than 15% of Americans then enjoying home telephone service. So shortly after Rose left, Loretta tucked Jimmy into his spindly wicker-built carriage and pushed him to the new six-story facility at Fifth and Washington. St. Joseph's had moved a year earlier - not long after her stay there for Jimmy's birth. She stopped, first, at the Records Department to once again show former co-workers her fourteen-month-old future priest. After enjoying their oohs and aahs she searched for the new obstetrics unit. There, following another display of the 'little guy' to more clucks of approval, she arranged for Rose to be seen the following day. She circled back on Tenth to tell her friend, remembering to remind her that the new hospital had moved three blocks west and one north of old St. Joseph's. It would add about a third of a mile to her walk.

Rose arrived at the hospital's maternity unit a short time before her 2:00 p.m. appointment. She had successfully followed Loretta's directions through the building, but once inside 'Obstetrics and Maternity' felt disoriented. Standing in a rather large and, in her estimation, space-wasting foyer, she could see directly ahead to the ward windows and a number of the beds intended for women both pre- and post-delivery. The room, perpendicular to her line of sight, didn't allow for any guess as to its size. On either side of her were a number of doors, three on the left, two to the right. She had been standing undecided for what seemed eons when the one on the far right opened abruptly and a nurse, pushing a bassinet made of bent tubular steel and containing a screaming infant, bolted out and headed for the ward. Apparently used to multi-tasking, the woman in white noticed Rose, yelled, "Be right with you," and disappeared.

She kept her word. Returning shortly, she solicited the required information, escorted Rose through the first door on her left into the examining room, seated her on one of its three chairs, asked that her regards be given to Loretta, and left. It was a quick encounter.

Rose assessed the room positively. It had a folksy, homey appeal - calm watercolor paintings of local landscapes, an oriental rug over oak flooring, and a place to change behind drapes. The examination table, not stiff and steel, was actually attractive. Its inlaid mahogany body raised on short turned legs reminded her of a blanket chest. It had three drawers in the center of its side, another three built into its foot-end, and a single door hiding a motor at the other or head-end. The tan leather exam surface looked comfortable. Only the cast iron stirrups, extending from just above the foot-end drawers, evoked a mild discomfort. Functionally, the table operated the same as those used today thirteen years into the following century.

In a few minutes, she was joined by Sister May and Sister Agnes. On seeing Agnes, Rose's facial muscles tightened, those around her mouth creating a noticeable pucker, her mind struggling with, 'Why do they dress like that?' - as her father's had a dozen years earlier. Agnes wore a habit identical to the one triggering Peter's reaction: a somber black tunic, a wimple of white linen encircling her face and extending over her shoulders, and a crowning, waist-length black veil. The only visible flesh outside of her hands, her large, rosy and prominently-cheeked, wimple-framed face, ordinary and pleasant to most, appeared sinister, evil even, to its current observer. With no gap between skin and surrounding white cloth, Rose saw that face as an oversized, puffed-out, pink oval - inlaid with wide-set dark penetrating eye cut-outs, and high golf-ball checks above a long, thin slit of a mouth. The eye cut-out gaze dominated.

Exaggerating those impressions by contrast, Sister May, wearing a long white gown Rose found refreshing, carried herself with elfin lightness, a pixie smile never leaving her pretty young face. Also, the long time milliner couldn't help but be distracted by May's cute white hat. Its wide band, standing upright and curving from ear to ear just back of her hairline, and behind it a tiny peak popping up like a dunce's cap, fascinated Rose. She wondered how it was made, then suddenly remembered the cap as identical to the nurse's who had shown her to the examination room. That nurse had left so quickly, before time to ask about anything. With hats in mind, she looked toward Sister May, then stopped herself abruptly as a barrage of questions, in no way related to hats, rained down from Sister Agnes.

Curtly, and with unconcealed indignation, she answered each question as truthfully as discretion allowed. Between questions, Sister Agnes explained, in elaborate detail, how a pelvic examination could detect pregnancy. Sister May, ever smiling and first looking back and forth between the two, settled - with eyebrows raised - on a stare at her nursing partner. Until the abrupt ending of her exam, and with hats now forgotten, Rose lost all awareness of May, the Sister in white.

The source of Sister Agnes's narrative is unknown. It would, in truth, be two years before a pregnancy could be confirmed by better means than observation of a large belly. Not until 1927, following discovery of the human chorionic gonadotropin hormone, did German Doctors Zondek and Aschheim devise a test based on looking for oversized ovaries in immature animals subcutaneously injected with the urine of a woman suspected of being pregnant. The animals of choice were mice, rabbits and frogs. Colloquially, the test became know as the rabbit test. If the animal's ovaries did increase, the woman's chance of pregnancy was ninety-eight percent.

Rose changed into an examination gown, another hospital staple unchanged over the ensuing decades, and took her place on the table. The exam began with a probe of her breasts, a search for tenderness. "Oh my, dearie, your nipples are quite large," Agnes proclaimed. "Do they feel sore?" Blood surged up, reddening Rose's entire face as she screamed out, "I have big nipples - yes, yes, they're sore, be careful, you're hurting them." Agnes flicked the index finger of her right hand summoning Sister May to her side where she whispered, "Positive!" her lips pressed against the younger nurse's left ear. She reached into the top drawer of the table and retrieved a speculum, the third piece of medical equipment little changed, this time over the past century and a half. Much earlier versions, found in excavations at Pompeii and dating from not long after the death of Christ, attest to the sustained popularity of the instrument.

Sister Agnes explained how her search for tissue changes within the vagina might cause mild discomfort. She had May perform the time-honored task of running hot water over the speculum, rendering its cold, hard surface more acceptable to the organ it would soon offend. The good Sister could not have predicted her own reaction to that first clear view of Rose's vagina. There, barely inside and covering it like a sentry protecting against all interior access, stood a membrane, thick and perforated, like the lid of a salt shaker. Agnes thought she had seen them all: half moon, annular, white, pale pink, translucent, protruding. This was different, her first look at the rather rare cribriform hymen, a stretch of tissue intact and holey.

In one continuous motion Sister Agnes reached her left hand back into the drawer, grabbed a scalpel, drove it down across the membrane, her right hand ramming in the speculum and squeezing it full open. Rose's scream, heard three rooms down on the ward, met with smiles as the sign of a successful birth. A simultaneous attempt to leap from the table had been thwarted by the hands of Sister May pressing gently but firmly down against her shoulders.

Agnes tossed the instruments into the basin on an adjacent table and, her pink forehead knit in a scowl, passed by May on her way out the door. "Pregnant and a virgin," she mumbled, "Blasphemy!" Sister May, as startled, if less shaken than Rose, did everything possible to care for her sobbing charge, getting her calmed, cleaned, dressed and on her way. "Say hello to Loretta for me," were her final words.

Irving showed up at The Tenth Avenue House around seven as scheduled, singing in his flat, raspy, half-in-tune way, "How ya gonna keep 'em down on the farm, after they've seen Paree?" They had plans for the Spreckels that night. Rudolph Valentino would be playing a Russian Cossack officer in a new movie, *The Eagle*. Irv wasn't much of a Rudy fan, but Rose went nuts over him. Rose was his girl now and he was happy. Happy until she met him at the door, said hello, and he saw the tears begin cascading down her cheeks. "Let's go to your place," she whispered. "We have to talk."

The real issue, her pregnancy, took a back seat to the rage surging through Irv over Rose's treatment at the hospital. He transitioned quickly from livid to a state of sustained fuming fury. It took considerable time and talk before he could finally acknowledge that acts of violence against the hospital or members of its staff would be of little use. His alternative provided the last shock to Rose's shocking day. He had her sit on his lap, stroked her hair, and while they cried together made his announcement. It was neither an offer or a command, simply an announcement: "We'll need to get married as soon as possible. Can you get a few more days off?"

Both Rose and Irving regretted leaving Mama out of their plans. Caroline's step-son, August, had eloped, and now her daughter planned to do much the same. The agreed-upon scheme, the inspiration of Fleeta Marly, called for them to wed on an undisclosed date, a date guaranteeing legitimacy if a child was truly on the way.

"It won't work for you to get married at Grace Church, even a City Hall ceremony is risky - too easy to be seen. You might end up a news item, and you'd have to get a public license." Fleeta went on to explain a law unique to the state, the California Confidential Marriage Contract. Enacted in the late eighteen-seventies, section #4213 of the California Civil Code was the state's answer to religious organizations denying marriage to couples who had been living together. "California couldn't stand having so many bastards," Fleeta went on. "You don't even have to go to the County Clerk. A minister can act like what they call an 'officiant,' and Archie and I know just the guy."

Rose stared frowning and wide-eyed, scholarship had never been a trait she attributed to her old friend. "How do you know all that, Fleeta?" she blurted. Fleeta looked down at her shoes, a big grin wrinkling her nose. "People ask," was all she volunteered.

Rose J. and Irving NMI were joined in holy matrimony the following Saturday, October 17th, the Rev. D. E. Oakman of Central Christian Church officiating and officiant. The one proviso, required of all participants using a confidential marriage contract: a signed statement certifying they had been living together.

That evening Archie, in his late model 5-passenger Buick Sedan with Fleeta at his side, stopped first to pick up Irving before driving to Tenth Avenue where Rose and her mother were waiting to be taken to dinner. Caroline, keenly aware of her daughter's edginess as they sat together on the oak sofa, said nothing. She had watched Rose's vacillating moods over the past few days. She had seen red-eyed distress. She had seen quiet bliss. She had said nothing. She was told nothing. Once in awhile she looked up and heard herself say without sound, 'Let her be happy.'

Irv ran to the door, brought his wife and mother-in-law of half-a-day to the car, then got into the front seat next to Archie, while Fleeta and Rose flanked mama in back. Caroline expected to hear some discussion of where they were going, but there was none. She thought then, but knew for sure later, as she was led through the lobby of the U.S. Grant Hotel and down to the Plata Real, that something momentous would soon be revealed. Her daughter's character did not include extravagance. At the same time, she felt honored and a sense of excitement to be taken to such a fancy place.

Rose began in German, her nervousness now replaced by giddiness. "This is where Irv and I got back ... I mean got together, got together on New Year's Eve, Mama. We're happy together." Then, without intending to say more about herself and her man before first offering some explanatory preamble, it just shot out of her mouth like an unintended sneeze, "We got married a while back, Irv and me." Caroline looked in turn at each of her co-hosts, then expressionlessly, and with no intonation requiring response, quietly said, "eine Weile zurück" - *a while back.*

Rose stayed with Caroline in The Tenth Avenue House that night. She was picked up by Irving early the next morning and left with him on their first out-of-town adventure. The record of their honeymoon can be found in a 9 x 11-inch, bound notebook - the words Scrap Book printed in white letters across its black cover. She bought it along the way. Like her papa's photo album, the book's pages, thirty of them, were of heavy black paper. Only twenty sides, the front and back of the first ten, were ever used. Pasted in later, and scattered amid souvenirs of the trip - like a postcard photo of the New Hotel Rosslyn - are congratulatory cards or written descriptions of gifts sent from friends and acquaintances after they had learned of the marriage. There are more annotations here than in the album, but like it, all are cursive and in white ink.

Rose and Irving's script, scattered between the glued-in room receipts, programs, bills and menus, provides a peek into the attitude of the celebrants during their first few days of marriage. Their handwriting is remarkably similar, although Irv's appears a bit smaller. After, *"We journey to-gether,"* un-der the only picture in the book - a snap of the couple side-by-side, a suitcase in Irv's right hand, his left around Rose's waist - the narrative begins with: *We spent our Honeymoon at Los Angeles* (here each ensuing city is written down a line) *Upland Ontario Colton San Bdno.* Then: *Our First night* (next line) or (next line) *What hap-pened in Room 463?* Next page, first entry: *Ans: We saw cockroaches in bathroom at 3 A.M.* Further down the page, beneath a six-day bill for $19.10 from the New Hotel Rosslyn at Main and Fifth in Los Angeles, is the word: *Final.* The bill had been fastened upside down and showed a daily rate of $2.50 plus $4.00 for dinner and 10¢ for a local telephone call. The last entry on that page reads: *2nd day: Rose used my shaving cream for toothpaste.*

The Scrap Book accounts for each gift received. There are many. A gift sent with a congratulatory card is described under that card. There is also a page devoted to *"Gifts without cards."* Except for the many electric appliances: iron, toaster, percolator, ... - possibly because of Irv's job at Consolidated Gas and Electric - most are typical of the time: linens, china, and kitchenware. One line on the no-card page lists *mon-ey ... Both mothers.* Envelopes accompany many of the cards, and it is disturbing to note that about half the time the newlyweds' last name is misspelled - a letter had been altered. The change renders an audible reading less Jewish sounding.

Fleeta Marly was becoming increasingly disappointed. As a member of the select few who knew of Rose's condition, it bothered her that 'the woman' just didn't look pregnant. "My God," she spewed, sharing her frustration with Archie. "It's almost Easter, that's almost six months, ... six months, and she's still skinny as a rail."

Rose had, in fact, asked the same question of Stephanie, a midwife currently advising her. "Could be a number of rea-sons. I've seen women almost as thin as you barely showing at seven months. Most probably your uterus is way up here - and in back quite a ways." She placed one hand on Rose's back at her waist, the other just below her ribs. "I've told you your baby's heartbeats are strong. Sorry there's no way for you to hear them." Stephanie had been listening for a couple of months using her fetoscope, a modified stethoscope introduced by Dr. David Hillis eight years earlier. The device looked like a straight, trumpet-type hearing-aid, and it required its user to hold the large flared-out end against a patient's abdomen, while keeping the other pressed into one ear. Not even a contortionist could have used it to hear the sounds of her own child-to-be.

> *Unto the woman he said, I will greatly multiply thy*
> *sorrow and thy conception; in sorrow thou shalt bring*
> *forth children; and thy desire shall be to thy husband,*
> *and he shall rule over thee.*
> Gen. 3:16

Entreaties from both Loretta and Irving did nothing but annoy Rose. She couldn't believe anyone would suggest a hospital birth after what she'd gone through. Sure, Irv had suggested a different hospital, a Jewish or protestant one, but a hospital is a hospital - a white, sterile delivery room with tiled floors and big metal tanks, and hoses and funny-looking stuff all over the place. In her experience children were born at home, attended by friends and family. That's how she knew it. That's how her niece was born. That's how it's done.

Rose's position was not unique. Until the 1920s midwives attended almost all deliveries. After that, upper- and middle-class women typically chose doctors. The change began in 1913 with the introduction of another German medical innovation, 'twilight sleep' - a combination of morphine for pain relief and scopolamine for memory loss - the first promise of painless childbirth. Championed by women's rights advocates hoping to nullify Genesis 3:16, it was strongly criticized by many obstetricians, especially in America. Ironically, hospital deliveries necessitated by 'twilight sleep' gave doctors the wedge to treat childbirth like a disease; to take the practice away from midwives and to bring in more money for the hospitals and themselves.

The new clinical methodology, sedation, cervical dilation, episiotomy and forceps, can all be studied in "Progress Towards Ideal Obstetrics" (*Transactions of the American Association for the Study and Prevention of Infant Mortality* 6: 1915) by Dr. Joseph DeLee, the father of modern obstetrics. Until the use of antibiotics in the mid 1930s, one of the arguments DeLee cites for hospital care - high maternal mortality - actually increased before leveling off.

It's unlikely Irving had any knowledge of these watershed obstetrical developments. He did, however, have a keen awareness that comfortable people, wealthy people, people he aspired to emulate, went to doctors and had their babies in hospitals. If they paid for this service because they felt it best protected their family's health, how could he not do the same? How could he stand tall and tell those around him that his wife bore their child, his child, in a flat assisted by a midwife?

Happily, the issue simply faded away the first month after their marriage without Irving feeling he had been an inadequate provider or Rose appearing shrewish for not accepting that all **"desire shall be to thy husband, and he shall rule over thee."** It came about because Archie had access to rooms at a farm near Warner's Ranch, a natural hot springs resort about two-and-a-half hours, by 1925 Buick, northeast of San Diego. He wanted Fleeta to convince Rose that it would be nice for her and Irv to go there with them on the weekend before Thanksgiving. They could stay on the farm and play at the resort.

Fleeta made her pitch. "Archie and I've had a lot of fun there, Rose. The resort has natural sulfur springs - springs that smell like rotten eggs but are piping hot and supply water to two giant pools. There's also trails and horses, and ... ." "Why not just go to the resort instead of a farm?" Rose interrupted. "Well," Fleeta went on, "a couple a reasons. First, the rooms on the farm are a lot cheaper than the resort cabins. Second, Betty Ann, Jeff's wife, is a great cook and the farm rooms come with room and board. So again cheaper, plus good food." Again Rose interrupted. "You know I don't know who the heck the people are you're talking about, Fleeta."

"Oh, sure ... sorry. Arch sold a policy to a guy on the police force, Lyle Guthrie's his name. Anyway they, Archie and

Lyle, got to be pretty buddy-buddy. Lyle's uncle, Jeff Wagstaff, owns the farm. Kind of a low-income operation - a few fruit trees, some sheep, they take in foster kids now and then, maybe do other stuff too, and then there's the rooms." Rose ended up saying yes, she'd talk to Irv about it.

Archie and Fleeta picked up Irv and his, then less than two months pregnant, wife early in the morning on Saturday, November 21, 1925. Fleeta got out of the car to let Irv in front and took her place in back with Rose. San Diego's November rains fall, on average, less than one day in seven. Today would become one of those days. They hadn't gotten farther than Poway when it started to pour. Arch turned on the wipers and smiled, "Love driving in the rain, Irv. Looks so fresh out and the old tank really purrs." Through pursed lips Rose ventured to her rear seat companion, "Not so nice for horses or sitting in a pool."

There had been little traffic on the black-topped, mostly two-lane roads, and never a need to use the occasional third, or center, lane for passing. Irv called it the suicide lane. By the time they reached the north turn junction at Santa Ysabel, rain pummeled against the windshield making it difficult to see. It wasn't yet noon, but outside conditions and the rumblings of hunger from the back seat led to a unanimous decision to head straight for the farm and some Betty Ann cooking.

The Buick sunk deeply into the mud as it slid its way along the farm road to the front steps of the main house. Alerted by his three dogs, Jeff got to his porch at the same time. He stepped down holding an open umbrella for the ladies. Rose liked the way he looked, a big man, mid-fiftyish, with a round, pleasant face and scraggly beard, kind of a young, messy Santa Claus. Once he'd gotten them inside, and comfortably seated around a hot pot-bellied stove, Fleeta began the questions.

"Where's Betty Ann? I'm starving." Jeff was as frank as he looked, he didn't take Fleeta's inquiry as rude, just honest. He responded in similar fashion. "Afraid Betty Ann's not here right now; she's delivering a baby." Jeff pondered over the length of time his guests remained silent. Shock didn't occur to him. Irv spoke first in a voice louder than necessary. "Why aren't you with her?" Then, injecting himself into the expectant father role and not waiting for a response, added, "Do you have other children?" Now Jeff, completely puzzled, wavered between asking Irv what he meant, repeating himself, or just answering the questions. Where possible he chose the latter.

"I don't usually go with Betty Ann when she delivers a baby. Only if it's for someone she doesn't know. Like an emergency. And yes, we have three children. They all live in the east. What did you mean by other?" "Oh God," Fleeta yelled, Jeff's words getting through to her. "Betty Ann told me she did some part time stuff."

Betty Ann Wagstaff was the perfect complement to her husband, physically and in character, a bigger than life Mrs. Claus. She returned in time to cook an impressive enough meal for everyone to forget the sandwiches they had made themselves for lunch. Her simplicity also matched her husband's. During dinner she kept reminding her guests, "This is good," or "Isn't this good." It was.

Rose found herself drawn to Betty Ann. The questions this veteran country midwife asked were the right ones, questions that dulled the fear of pregnancy, freeing her to share concerns. Irving, too, listened, and surprisingly, liked and trusted what he heard. Before the rain-drenched weekend ended, a plan had emerged. Rose would come stay with the Wagstaffs whenever she wished. She could even watch or help with some deliveries, if she wanted, before it was her turn. Betty Ann knew Stephanie in San Diego who would help out until then, and Jeff would make up a room for her in the barn, something he'd been wanting to do for future foster kids.

Less than a month had passed since her outburst over Rose looking too skinny to be pregnant. Now her friend began to show a bit. A slightly fuller waistline was all, but enough for Fleeta Marly to be delighted. She gushed, "Oh Rosie, you look so good, like a little mommy-to-be." Rose said nothing. Pursed lips and a furrowed brow should have broadcast her displeasure at the comment; with Fleeta, it wasn't clear. Easter had passed a couple of weeks ago. They had gotten together to talk of Rose's plans; when she would quit her job and when she would be moving to the country. Stephanie had told her she should be delivering in a little over two months.

"What should I tell people at work, Fleeta? A few friends in the department know, but not any of the bosses. I don't want to jeopardize my job." Fleeta's whole demeanor changed; she started to laugh, and the laughing went on and on. Now Rose's brow really wrinkled up. She crossed her arms over her chest, and short of stomping a foot, stared down at her smaller friend. "What job?" Fleeta started between snorts. "You're going to have a baby. Are you going to go back to work after that? Is that what you want to do? I know Irving wouldn't want you to." Rose was stunned. She hadn't given any thought to the consequences of children, or how her life would change.

Rose resigned the following week after thirteen years at Marston's, eleven in millinery. Of the even dozen milliners in the department, only one, Stacie, had been there longer. The girls, as she would always refer to her co-workers, formed a group they called the Sapphire Club. In later years they began meeting once a month, rotating through the home of each member. The meetings continued until only one member remained alive, fifty-six years past Sapphire's founding.

Irving drove Rose to the farm three weeks after her resignation. The day in late May was spectacular. New blooms and late April survivors - goldfields, indian paintbrush, ceanothus, and bush poppy - grew on the lands near the hot springs. As they motored up the dirt road toward the farmhouse, grazing sheep - herded by two young Cahuilla Indian men from nearby Los Coyotes reservation - could be seen on the unplanted hills to the rear of the property. A hodgepodge of fruit-producing trees - lemon, orange, peach, plum, almond, apricot, golden delicious, granny and fuji apple - as well as vines - cabernet sauvignon and thompson seedless - covered the fields in the foreground surrounding the house.

It all looked disorderly to orange rancher Rose, interesting but messy. Her entire stay at Wagstaff farm would seem that way. A room in the barn for starters. She'd been told about it before, but it hadn't registered. There, besides things for her - bed, dresser and wardrobe - a thin rectangular box-like structure had been pushed up against the outside wall beneath the single window. "That looks like something our cow used to eat out of," Rose confided to Irving. Betty Ann overheard, "Yes, Jeff built that for a horse we had, but the horse was sold and we never used it. Looks nice doesn't it? I made the feather mattress inside. Take a look."

And she brought forth her firstborn son, and wrapped him in swaddling clothes, and laid him in a manger; because there was no room for them in the inn. And they came with haste, and found Mary, and Joseph, and the babe lying in a manger.
Luke 2:7-16

Rose had her baby one day following the summer solstice and two days before the June full moon. The child, a 7-pound, 7-ounce 19-inch boy, came with thick, curly, blonde hair. When told of it by Jeff, the lad's hair aroused wonder in the Indian shepherds. They had planned to soon perform parts of the Sundance ceremony, borrowed from their Plains People allies to the east. The sun, the elder fire above, the divine Light - perhaps symbolized here by a ball of glowing blonde locks - could perhaps be reached, could ignite the light within.

And all they that heard it wondered at those things which were told them by the shepherds. But Mary kept all these things, and pondered them in her heart.
Luke 2:18-19

Part II

The Early Years

Chapter 8

String, The Early Years

*Then will I sprinkle clean water upon you, and ye
shall be clean: from all your filthiness, and from all
your idols, will I cleanse you.*
Ezek. 36:25

When it came time to pack up little 'Snoozer,' as the
plump golden-haired putti was now called by his father,
and to leave the Wagstaff farm, Rose would be moving into
an unknown world. She did have prior knowledge of the new
house and the new neighborhood. Had, in fact, helped her
mother pick out the wood for the dining room cabinetry. She'd
enjoyed the snobbery of calling it southern gum, not eucalyptus like those familiar trees buffering from the wind the orange
groves of her youth. Motherhood, not location, would be the
stranger, the foreigner she was to meet.

Caroline choreographed the physical changes. Having absorbed her daughter's a while back marriage, she realized the
need to deal with her own circumstances - first as landlady in a
house too big to live in alone, and now as a *Großmutter*. In the
past half-year, she had twice rented the extra room and bath
- both times to tenants who had come and gone. Too wise
to give any thought to house sharing with the newly coupled
parents, she offered them an alternative, a gift that upwardly
mobile Irving couldn't refuse, a house of their own.

San Diego's population just short of doubled in the 1920s,
increasing that decade from 74,361 to 147,995. Many would
settle to the east. In that direction, about a mile from Hill-

crest and The Tenth Avenue House - and with Grace Lutheran Church halfway in between - Caroline found the community she sought. Its developers called the new area North Park, and were slicing it up into around seven residential lots per acre.

The rectangular plot on their map catching Caroline's attention fronted Pershing Avenue for more than 50 feet on its short side, and ran perpendicularly for half a block down Landis Street to the alley, a distance of about 120 feet. The Avenue, named for General "Black Jack" Pershing, Commander of American Expeditionary Forces during World War I, led to a jog three blocks south, then onto Pershing Drive, a thoroughfare and shortcut to downtown. Two blocks in the opposite direction, the 'Number 7' electric trolley ran along University Avenue, a major east-west artery and a straight shot to Grace Church or past it back to Hillcrest.

Pointing at the small marked out area on the map, she told the realtor, through her interpreter Frieda Rudeloff, "That's it. We'll take that one for the two houses." "You need two lots for two houses," came back a quick reply. The snappily-dressed young man's acumen would prove no match for Caroline's, a woman with literal horse-sense who had sold a farm and bought a property, one which had substantially increased in value over the twelve years she had owned it.

Then there were the coincidences. It may not have been a coincidence to have chosen Frieda as her translator. Frieda, about her daughter's age and height, but rounder and more fluid in the places that caught men's attention, was a natural flirt; not directed and knowledgeable like Fleeta Marly, just graced with an abundance of libido-enhancing hormones. It seemed impossible for her to sit without her skirt hem ending up midway between her knees and thighs.

The real coincidences were (1) that Frieda lived with her mother on Wightman Street, only a block from the Pershing at Landis site under discussion, and (2) that Caroline and Frieda's mother had been exchanging Christmas cards for 34 years. The two women, when just fresh from Germany, had met a few months before the opening of Ellis Island and a year-and-a-half after the closing of Castle Garden at a temporary immigrant processing facility, the old Barge Office, on Whitehall Street near the southern tip of Manhattan.

The contractor's realtor had no chance to haggle. Caroline simply instructed Frieda to tell him what she wanted, and Frieda smiling seductively, rolling her eyes, touching his arm, and shrugging, passed it along. Some things she chose not to translate, "*Wir wollen einfach nur ein Ort, und weitere nicht Farm Leben.* (We just want a place to live 'and' not another farm.)," others she rendered word for word, "*Warum zwei Garagen, wir haven nur ein Auto?* (Why two garages, we only have one car?)" Caroline even got a price reduction by noting the construction of three rental units behind the house across the alley on Landis in an area on the chart marked: "Single Family Housing."

The end result: two very similar houses, each around a thousand square feet, and one 1920s-car-size garage were built on the indicated 6200-square-foot piece of land. The ground along that block of Pershing, as well as some adjoining land, leveled off about three feet above the street, necessitating stairs and a drop-to-road level. Retaining walls were built for some homeowners, but the clay earth didn't require it, and the street side lot edges of the corner house on Pershing and its counterpart on Landis were simply planted with grass and curved down abruptly to the sidewalk below. The drop-off came to be known as 'the slope' and because of it, lawn mowing, watering, and grass integrity at the property's northwest corner would become recurring annoyances in the years to come.

Caroline bequeathed the Pershing Avenue house, the one with china cabinets built of the southern gum selected by her daughter Rosa, to Rosa and Irving. She chose it as the gift more expressive of her love than the one on Landis because of its greater prestige - prestige derived not from its cabinets but from its corner location on a major street. Adhering to then-local building codes, the Pershing house was located only three feet from its larger stucco neighbor to the south, and the garage the same short distance from the alley at the opposite, eastern end of the lot. The houses were perpendicular to one another, with the longer side and front porch of each facing the street of its address: 3691 Pershing Avenue and 2715 Landis.

Until his army years, and later his incarceration and subsequent trial for his life, 3691 Pershing Avenue was the only home Rose and Irving's son would know. String, as he came to be called, absorbed that house and its surroundings over his early years, slowly and totally, as a cat internalizes its environs. His skates knew every sidewalk crack and irregularity around the block - the gradual downhill coast on Pershing, the left turn at Dwight and along it and across the alley to another left on 28th, and the final turn onto Landis and home. He could tell you what car belonged in any garage in the alley between Landis and Dwight, how many cans you'd see by each on trash day, and when Mrs. Zimmerman and Mrs. Fox were likely to motor past in their Packard 740 sedan. The soap box contraptions he built, as did the car he later parked there when its battery ran low, relished the hill on Landis that dropped down quickly to the west across Villa Terrace.

The time between String's baptism and his age at first hand-induced orgasm, or outrage over his mother and sister's alleged disregard for the sanctity of the church, is more of a collage than a sequence of events. No defining moment, no specific happening in time, for example, saddled him, or perhaps enhanced him, with his name. The name emerged during his last two or three years at Jefferson Elementary School when he could often be seen hanging out with his closest pals, Lloyd Estep and Richard Anderson. Lloyd's height, always average for his age, weighed in at well over the normal range, while Richard, with a perfect build, stood a head shorter. Rose's boy, like his Ambuehl forebears and described by her as "skinny as a rail," topped both friends - one head over Lloyd, two above Richard. In the bad-punning and label butchering Ambuehl tradition, Rose referred to the trio as The Three Beans: Lima, Pinto, and String.

The image of an upright refrigerator box with *The Goons* scrawled in blue enamel over its cutout access door, could well be the icon stuck on the collage-backing to represent The Three Beans. Like most youngsters of the time, the Beans were Popeye aficionados. The club they named in honor of the comic strip's long-nosed, fur-garlanded giants stands out as their most remembered enterprise and possible group-image. The actual box had packaged String's parents'

second refrigerator. Their first machine, purchased while daddy still worked for the Gas and Electric Company, used sulfur dioxide, not freon, and had acquired the name "Monitor-Top" because the round compressor above its cabinet looked a bit like the gun turret off the iron ship USS Monitor of Civil War years. String formed a strong dislike of the Monitor-Top once he understood it to be responsible for the man from the Union Ice Company on El Cajon Boulevard not appearing several times a week and presenting him with an icicle broken off from inside his truck.

Pinto, Lima and String wedged the Goon Club edifice between the rear of the garage and the fence separating Grandma Ambuehl's house from the Coleman's backyard. Besides housing Irving's car, the garage became a sanctuary for String. It was there he puttered endlessly at the workbench on its inside wall, the one away from the alley. It was there that disturbances annoyed him, especially calls to dinner. Building things in the garage became his passion. It didn't matter if they worked or didn't work, and increasingly over time they didn't. They became de facto objects of art; perpetual motion machines of magnets and fly-wheels that ran on for days before they proved themselves false; a radio built from plans taken from an *Amateur Radio Relay League Handbook*, but with a critical amplification stage left out; an unfinished car-spring cross-bow and a soup-can submarine.

Initially it was different, two successful toy transports; a skate disassembled and nailed to each end of a two-by-four, then attached at right angles to another, made a great scooter; while the wheels from a discarded Radio Flyer Red Wagon mounted to rotate on two-by-four axles, one nailed to the back of a one-by-six, the other pivoting beneath it and under a wooden box in front - a true soap-box car - allowed him to soar down the Landis Street hill. Loretta's husband, Oscar, once gave him a junked Chevy steering wheel. With a rope attached to each end of the front two-by-four-axle and wound about a broomstick fixed to that steering wheel's hub, he could steer like a race driver - unless he attached the rope to twist around the broomstick in the wrong direction, as he sometimes did - then the car would turn right when he steered left, and vice-versa.

> *In whom also ye are circumcised with the*
> *circumcision made without hands, in putting off the body*
> *of the sins of the flesh by the circumcision of Christ:*
> *Buried with him in baptism, wherein also ye are risen*
> *with him through the faith of the operation of God,*
> *who hath raised him from the dead.*
> Col. 2:11-12

Perhaps before all else, a cross or maybe a cherry bowl should be glued diagonally across this collage, and pasted somewhere near it a rather small Star of David. String was circumcised, not on the 8th day as Hebrew law decrees, but as soon after return from the farm as arrangements with a doctor, not a rabbi, could be made. It was an act of health for Irving, not of faith. String would later regret his circumcision, believing it unnecessary, and clumsily and amateurishly done.

His baptism, on the other hand, became a festive occasion, remembered by its attendees for their first visit to Caroline's place on Landis, for her cooking, and for the cherry bowl sprinkling. Lutherans don't dunk, they sprinkle. The vessel itself would long remain a mystery to String, who would hear from adults over his entire growing years of his coming to Christ in a cherry bowl. The porcelain bowl, decorated with hand-painted cherries and identified on its underside as *F B* (under a crown) *S Germany* was, in fact, one of the few non-essentials Caroline had brought with her from Bavaria.

Among the guests was the master of ceremonies Pastor Damschroeder, his wife and two sons - six-year-old Clarence Jr. and three-year-old Matthew. After a briefing of the sponsors, the pastor attended to necessary preparations. Caroline warmed the sacred water; the pastor's wife laid out white napkins near the bowl and lit the paschal candles, their flames symbolizing the risen Christ. Damshroeder probably hadn't appreciated the subtlety of his choice for a hymn to begin the service. It had been written about 200 years earlier by two Lutheran theologians, a composer from Switzerland, and a lyricist from Germany. He asked everyone to stand and sing: "God's Own Child, I Gladly Say It."

God's own child, I gladly say it: I am baptized into Christ!
He, because I could not pay it, gave my full redemption price.

****

Should a guilty conscience seize me, since my baptism did release me
In a dear forgiving flood, sprinkling me with Jesus' blood?

****

Death, you cannot end my gladness: I am baptized into Christ!
When I die, I leave all sadness to inherit paradise!

****

Though my flesh awaits its raising, still my soul continues praising:
I am baptized into Christ; I'm a child of paradise!

The baptism began in earnest when the Reverend intoned in his rich baritone, "Dearly beloved, Christ our Lord says in the last chapter of Matthew." Here scriptural quotes, starting with Matthew, Mark and Peter, interspersed with litany and expressions of belief deriving from Luther's Catechism, droned on. With the minister's pronouncement that "The Word of God also teaches that we are all conceived and born sinful and are under the power of the devil until Christ claims us as His own," Irving winced and the curly-haired baby he held spit up a bit of partially digested milk. Undeterred, Damshroeder added, "Therefore depart, you unclean spirit, and make room for the Holy Spirit in the name of the Father and of the Son and of the Holy Spirit," and beckoning Irving to his side made the sign of the cross on the forehead and on the heart of the little guy, saying, "Receive the sign of the holy cross both upon your forehead and upon your heart to mark you as one redeemed by Christ the crucified." Then even more solemnly he prayed: "Almighty and eternal God, according to Your strict judgment You condemned the unbelieving world through the flood ..... preserved believing Noah and his family .... drowned hard-hearted Pharaoh .... so that, with all believers in Your promise, he would be declared worthy of eternal life; through Jesus Christ our Lord. Amen."

With his hands on String's head, the Reverend Damschroeder asked all to join him in the Lord's Prayer. "Our Father who art in heaven ... ... and the power and the glory forever and ever. Amen." He then announced, "The Lord preserve your coming in and your going out from this time forth and even forevermore. Amen," and asked the group to sit. The selection of sponsors had been left to her mother, as no one Rose suggested was Lutheran. Caroline chose Karl and Greta Nachtbauer. They answered for String the seven questions asked him: "Do you renounce the devil?" "Yes, we renounce him." "Do you renounce all his works?" "Yes, we renounce them." "Do you renounce ... ?" "Yes, we renounce ... " "Do you believe ... ?" "Do you believe ... ?" "Do you believe ... ?" "Yes, we believe." "Yes, we believe." "Yes, we believe." "Do you desire to be baptized?" "Yes, we do." At this point String was sprinkled three times, each time being told, "I baptize you in the name of the Father and of the Son and of the Holy Spirit." Hands were once again placed on the tiny head and he was assured that "The almighty God and Father of our Lord Jesus Christ, who has given you the new birth of water and of the Spirit and has forgiven you all your sins, strengthen you with His grace to life everlasting." The newly-cleansed Lutheran looked up, first at the man of the cloth, then at his father. He appeared to be giggling as the dampness shifted from his curly head to his hindquarters.

String began going to Sunday School the same year he started kindergarten. Lutheran churches awarded their young members for regular attendance, presenting them with a gold pin if they made it through a year without missing a Sunday. It was an attractive little item, five-eighths of an inch in diameter, with a cross at its center contained within a shield-like heart, in turn surrounded by five other hearts, their tips tucked under the shield. It read "Lutheran" around its top, and below, "Sunday" and "School" to either side of its unique feature, a small changeable number. It came with a '1'. The plan called for the insertion of some type of jewel, along with a gift of the Holy Bible, when the count got to ten. String's pin got to six. Much later he showed it to a Jewish friend, who viewing it upside down and thinking it read nine, joked, "You're a lousy Jew. Any good Jew would have stayed the extra year and gotten the Bible." What most impressed String when he first received the pin was its pinstem-top-opening safety catch. He had never seen one before.

During his formative years, Jesus played a big role in String's life. Letting the San Diego sun beat down on him as he sat on one of the two stairs leading from the small, gray backporch off the utility room behind the kitchen to the side yard between his place and Grandma Ambuehl's, he would think of Jesus. The thoughts, warm, toasty, secure, encompassed him. The church, itself, didn't have much to do with it. Except for the terrible, itchy discomfort of wool trousers, not much improved by either cotton linings or pants over pajama bottoms, he neither looked forward to nor disliked Sunday School. Whether at his house or at God's place, Grace Lutheran Church, he made an internal connection with Jesus. It amused his dad. Rose heard him tell Archie, "The kid'll end up a preacher."

Kindergarten provided Rose with a greater challenge. She would walk String the two blocks to Jefferson Elementary and leave him there with Miss Meeks, only to find him sitting on the back steps shortly after she returned home. The struggle continued for several weeks until his first captivation by a contemporary. Freckly, red-haired and vivacious Mitzi Shiller turned it all around. He wanted to go to school. Even after his fight in the kindergarten sandbox where he tried to verbally bully a classmate who preferred to hit, he wanted to go to school.

Mitzi lived just past Mussies corner grocery on Utah Street, where the two would sometimes go together to buy penny candy. Mitzi's mother liked String. She welcomed him to come to their house and play whenever he wanted. Rose didn't say much negative, but she clearly had reservations that couldn't be ignored. Reservation like she had for the Colemans next door. They were Jewish.

> *And said unto them, It is written,*
> *My house shall be called the house of prayer;*
> *but ye have made it a den of thieves.*
> Matt. 21:13

By the time a '6' had been inserted into String's pin, he found Sunday School less of a draw than church. Sitting on the hard wooden pew in a nave illuminated by a dozen or so triple-cylindrical hanging lamps, and looking at the stained glass windows at his sides, at the radiant, seven-tipped glass image of Mary above the altar, and up at the triangular beams an unbelievable distance above his head, he would experience a kind of fullness - not the warmth of the kitchen steps, but of awe.

On one occasion, in a congregation settling before the service to the sounds of heady organ chords, Rose took a small paper bag from her purse. He heard his mother explain to his sister, seated at her side opposite him, "No Honey, nonpareils were too 'melty' to bring; these are Licorice Snaps and Sugar Babies." Activated by a shift from awe to rage, String's too-quick-to-measure motor response resulted in a bag of candy stuffed into his Sunday coat pocket, and a sustained scowl directed toward his mother and sister.

String might well have chosen the image of an apron and a rolling-pin to represent his Grandma Ambuehl. The apron as a weapon of destruction, a rolling-pin as one of pleasure. Until her death, Caroline would be his cherished teacher, best friend and protector. She taught him about the big and little hands of the clock and how to figure out what they meant, and she saved his pride by showing him an easy way to tie his shoes. He needn't struggle trying to push one string over and under a loop in the other; instead he could form two loops, one between the thumb and first finger of each hand, and simply roll them around one another.

His earliest happy memories included being bounced on her knees and squealing with delight as she finished reciting what probably started as *Reiten, Reiten, das Pferd* ... and sounded to him like:

> Rida rida der fet
> Der gulder is nix vet
> Rida rida eva grava
> Fulter nigh so much is hava
> Botch licked the drek

He guessed it must have something to do with riding a horse and falling into the dirt. He would never learn what caused that fall. She also read him 'funnies' from the German paper, and they laughed together at the antics of the German-speaking figures, one of whom looked to him like Krazy Kat, but like the reason for falling from the horse, he never knew what the characters really said.

Sometimes, when he'd be with her for the day, Grandma would start in the morning to fix him his favorite dinner, noodles and applesauce. Caroline's kitchen table was beneath the window facing her daughter's house. She'd move her cutting board there from its slot beneath the counter next to the sink, gather her eggs and flour, and pile a mountain of the flour onto the clean board. After mixing it into a dough ball with water and eggs, and leaving it covered for about half an hour, she would push it down, spreading it out on the board, then roll it flat with her rolling pin. String never tired of watching this part of the procedure, it was magic. Her rolling pin didn't have fancy little rotating handles like Mama's, it was just a round stick of wood about two and a half inches in diameter and a foot and a half long. When the dough had dried enough, she sliced it, with the help of a yardstick, into varying width noodles, most less than five-sixteenths of an inch. The finished treat, served piping hot and bathed in butter, was cooled to the proper slurp up temperature by plopping on a just right amount of applesauce.

Caroline didn't live alone for long. String was too young to remember when Sophia Ambuehl - everyone would call her Sophie - arrived, but Rose made fun of her, like she did later of dust bowl refugees during the second half of the 1930s. "They think a toilet's a place to wash their feet in," she once told him. Her embarrassment of 'hillbilly' Sophie, fresh from Uncle Samuel's Illinois farm, stemmed from the time she saw 'that first-cousin of hers' brush her teeth outdoors between the two houses. What if Dr. Bell's wife, Lilly, had also seen it from her corner house across Landis? Sophie would become a pillar at Grace Church, first as general gopher, then secretary, and finally, assistant to the Reverend Damschroeder - working for him until his retirement more than thirty years later.

If asked, String would have said Grandma always had an apron tied round her waist. That's where it started, at her waist. It hung down from there to just above the knees. He didn't know why she wore it, had never seen it stained, or any other use for it until one sunny day in late May when he heard his mother scream. She was next to the red brick chimney, pruning a dingleberry bush - fuchsia its non-Ambuehl name - in the small plot of dirt between the house and the cement path that led from the stairs at the top of the slope, when Grandma heard the cry. She dropped down her backdoor stairs arriving across the yard and next to her daughter almost before the bloodthirsty emission ceased. Rose pointed to a black creature swinging against the bricks, its underside showing a bright red hourglass. String heard only "Himmel" from Grandma as her hands flew under the apron and met one against the other, the condemned black widow squashed between. String never definitively decided whether his Grandma's look of disgust or verbal exclamation had been directed at the bug or at his mother.

During the Christmas recess, the one after String had begun second grade, the unimaginable happened. The family - Rose, Irving, String, and his sister Carolyn - drove to Colton to spend the holiday with Uncle August and his extended family. Carolyn, two years and four months younger than String, rode behind her father in their now five-year-old sedan. String, always behind his mother on the passenger side, loved being lulled and joggled along in what his dad called "the old '28 Essex." He'd watch the scenes pan by, especially on the roads to Colton or Upland where they passed acre after acre of lovely green orange groves, then rest his head against the upholstery behind the rear window and drift into a peaceful sleep.

String hated leaving home that Christmas, the time of the traditional surprise. Before the day itself, the 25th of December, his home would show no sign of festivities to come. Then, on the eve of that day, the French doors between the living and dining rooms, open every other day of the year, would be shut and curtained. On Christmas Day when he and his sister were allowed to penetrate that barrier, they would enter a magic realm. The burgundy mohair sofa against the outside windows would have been pulled toward the front door, making room for a six- to seven-foot tree between it and the matching upholstered chair in front of the built in wall-desk just left of the fireplace. The tree, wrapped around in tinsel garlands, hung with family-treasured ornaments, sparkling from long pointed bulbs of many colors and draped meticulously, branch by branch, with silver tinsel, held String and Carolyn's attention for longer than expected for their new treasures would be at its foot. There, a familiar white sheet hid the tree's stick-cross support, and the presents would partially cover the oval three-rail track encircling it. String didn't remember when he first got the Lionel diesel-engine train set, or even if it was his. He did know both he and his father would later have fun with it, play with the dial and switch atop its transformer - its speed and direction controls - maybe even get it to jump the tracks.

String's peevishness at being away from home over Christmas abated significantly when he saw Grandma come out of Margaret's house to greet them. She had come by train two weeks earlier to become acquainted with her third grandchild, Joanne, Margaret's four month old daughter. Margaret had married a World War I flying ace, Milton Van Voorhis, the owner of a full service gas station less than two miles away, and the two had bought the house next door to her parents. The Ambuehls weren't a hugging bunch, but String felt hugged when Grandma stepped down from Margaret's front porch and smiled at him.

Christmas in Colton seemed pretty ho-hum to both him and sister Carolyn. Sure, everyone treated them well, and the Christmas trees in both houses looked okay, not as special as theirs would have, but nice enough. He did like seeing his uncle, no longer jumped when August hid around the corner of the house and barked at him, and enjoyed what everyone else wished would go away, the almost omnipresent whistling, rumbling and shaking from the trains.

August's place stood at the end of the block with no structure intervening between it and the passing railcars. Only the Schell house, kitty-corner across the street, was closer to the tracks. Widow Schell, founder of the Schellite religious study group, held weekly services on its spacious, screened-in front porch. With help from her small, dedicated congregation she had produced a number of teaching aids, including a large glossy poster depicting heaven as a multicolored double pyramid. A copy, hanging just to the left of the front door in Aunt Bessie's living room, always drew String's attention. Perhaps less elegant and more attainable to a seven-year-old than Dante, it none-the-less puzzled. Bessie eyed him with rare favor, offering innocent explanations when she caught him staring at it.

Christmas came and Christmas went. It was three days later on a Thursday - they were to have left for home the following Saturday - when String's world temporarily ended. The boy, awakened by a stone-faced mother, was told the person on earth most precious to him was no more. Grandma Ambuehl was dead. Irving came by shortly after, crying audibly. The boy had never seen or heard his father cry, and thinking he was being mocked, lashed out at him. A stunned Irv responded slowly, "No, ... I loved your Grandma, too." Another first, 'love', a word he had never heard a family member say. He would later learn she had died of angina, and how angry it made his father that she wouldn't be bothered taking nitroglycerin pills.

Margaret's house became the place of convergence, the pot-luck site to wish Caroline her final Goodbyes. It swarmed with guests: Schellites, family, friends, neighbors and acquaintances, most of them strangers to String. The culinary offerings brought to uplift the spirits of the bereaved could have fed a multitude. Irving took String and his sister home the following day. Rose accompanied her mother to Ontario where they laid her beneath the swastika stone next to Peter August.

At the dawn of the Great Depression, String saw his father for the first time in a snappy police officer's uniform, cap and all. Family legend has it that the three-year-old sobbed, "I don't have a daddy anymore," and needed assurance the policeman present was still his father. At the time he quit, Irving had been with the Gas and Electric Company just two weeks short of receiving a ten-year pin. It wasn't because of the market crash, and the impending hard times. He had worked hard there, and but for being stuck at the same job, felt liked and secure. Why had he never been promoted? He had trained two new hires who later became his bosses, one now well up in the company hierarchy. It was hard to accept, though Archie and even a couple of friends at the company agreed; Irving's name was more Yekl than Jake. A Jew, even a good one like Irv, wasn't likely destined to become a member of the club.

Badge number 359, **Patrolman, San Diego Police**, together with a small bronze medal symbolize Irving on the collage. The badge, a typical gold shield topped by a spread-winged eagle, black letter embossed and bearing the city crest at its center, adds brightness to the thus far assembled icons, and anticipates character-altering circumstances ahead. The medal, hexagon in shape and an inch across its opposing points, reveals both the competitive and thoughtful aspects of the man. It may also help soften harsh police realities.

Pride, ambition, the itch to achieve, to compensate for being left behind, drove Irving during his initial years on the force. He'd do whatever it took, and he'd do it as well - better - than the next guy. And much he did do: early motorcycle cop in the years when you owned your own bike, fingerprint expert with the 'I bureau,' patrol car and ambulance driver, beat walker, vice squad member, and 'expert with the pistol.' That was the raised inscription on the medal he gave his son, Goon Club member, String. "**EXPERT WITH THE PISTOL**" it read over the letters **SDPRC** and under the relief of a tiny revolver pointing to a target at its left.

Irv had, by then, over a hundred medals, this one the only ever given away. The gift came shortly after returning from a road trip with San Diego's nationally recognized police pistol team to Camp Perry, Ohio, a trip combined with a side junket he took on his own to visit his mother and siblings in New York City. He wrote six letters while away a day over three weeks, the longest he'd been apart from Rose and the kids. The first two suggest he didn't care for the drive, but history would show he traveled to New York a number of times between then and World War II - visiting family, stopping to buy cars in Detroit, then driving them to California to keep or to resell. What the shooting expedition and family get together meant to Irv can best be seen in words of his own. Below are copies of his fourth and fifth letters, one written before, the other after, his sojourn from Camp Perry to New York.

9/2/36
Camp Perry, Ohio

Dear Maw, Toots & Snoozer : -.

Rec'd your welcome letter to-day & was glad to hear from you all. The shooting is going pretty good only mine is rotten, but I'm saving my best for the 45 matches.

Rodney took 1st place in the 22 match & our 4 man team took 4th place & our 5 man team took 3rd place. We were 7 points behind 1st in the 1st one & 8 points behind 1st place in the second one.

I found out there wasn't any shooting from Sat. noon until Tuesday morning so I went to the Depot & asked about a trip to New York. I found out it cost $13.55 each way on the coach & I can leave Toledo on the 3 o'clock train on Sat & be in N.Y. 7-30 am Sunday morning, be there all day Sunday and Monday till 3-30 pm & get back in Toledo @ 4-55 AM Tuesday morning, which gives me plenty of time to get to camp for the match so I sent Ray a telegram right away & told him to meet me at the Grand Central Station Sunday morning. Its a little expensive but I dont know when I would get to see them & also it gives me a chance to see everybody.

How are all you folks at home? O.K. I hope -

I want String and Carolyn to be good & not tire mama out -

I had to get a new pr of kakhi pants - I was all naked on one knee & I didn't want to disgrace the team.

The car runs fine & the radio has a swell tone. When I go to N.Y. I am going to drive to Toledo & put it in a garage until I come back.

The weather out here is very changeable - Two nights I had 4 blankets on my bed & it wasn't any two warm then. Be glad when I can snuggle up to mugzie again.

The bunch are up watching an open air picture show in camp -& Bob & I are going to Port Clinton.

No more to say for this time so will close with oodles of Love to all.

Daddy

Sept. 7th 1936
New York, N.Y.

Dear Rose & Kids.

Arrived here yesterday after riding all night. Had a swell time & certainly was treated royally - Yesterday I went around & visited all my relatives who were just as tickled to see me as I was to see them. Jean cooked a swell breakfast & dinner. I ate about a two pound porterhouse steak.

Then at night Jean fixed a light supper & Ray dolled me up in one of his suits which fit perfectly & we all went night clubing in Greenwich village. O_We went to two night clubs. Had a couple of Tom Collins in the first place & saw the floor show - Quite a bit different than ours - By the way I'm finishing this up on the train where you see the circle & dash up above.

Then we went to another night club & 4 of us had a steak dinner & two of us chicken dinners & more drinks- The treat was on Jack- He spent about $20. By the way you would be crazy about Jean and Jack. Both families were very fine - nice children -

About noon we went to Jack's store & he picked out 2 nice dresses for you & for Carolyn - then nothing would suit mama until she could buy me a suit- Then se bought me a hat= and Jack pulled me into a shoe store & bought me a dandy pair of dress shoes- then on the way to the station mom happened to think that poor little String didn;t have any thing & she went in & bought

him a sweater, so I'm riding on the train now between
N.Y. and Yonkers & instead of the small grip I bor-
rowed from Beckett I'm loaded down with pkgs-
  Ray also gave me a pen & pencil set & Reduciners
pocket watch & he bought me a carton of cigarettes to
take back- They all came down to the train to see me off
& Birdie was bawling on the way down because I had
to go so soon - no more for this time -Will write again
when I get to camp -Love to all -
    Daddy

When Irv pinned the blue ribbon supporting the "**EXPERT WITH THE PISTOL**" medal to his son's shirt, he admonished him not to tell other officers about it. "A lot of guys I work with try really hard to shoot well, Squirt. They never get good enough to get a medal. I don't want you to tell them I gave you one."

To suggest he was touched by his father's gesture would be a great understatement. String sensed how special he'd been as a baby, that fat little blonde haired infant. He'd heard talk and seen pictures of himself laughing while sitting on an upturned palm, held at arm's length high over his also laughing father's head. He didn't know what had changed - didn't think of his skinny limbs, his fear of the ocean and his repulsion of the YMCA's steam room - physical pleasures Irv had tried to share with him. And his dad, not the gentlest of teachers, would toss him shivering and scared into an oncoming breaker, then leave him on shore while swimming almost beyond sight into the sea before body surfing blissfully back from the crest of a distant wave.

String's retreat would be to the safety of the beach umbrella and ground-covering blanket that shielded his mother from the hot sand and sun. He would not have recognized that woman of earlier years, cavorting on the same sand and splashing hand-in-hand at the edge of the surf with this same man, his father. Now she sat stoically, watched, and kept her charges, Carolyn and String, fed from the picnic stocked larder toted to every outing in her large rectangular wicker basket - the one secured by inserting little hanging pegs into straw loops.

Promotion didn't come any easier for Irv on the police force than it had at the gas company. After seven years and three successful scores on the sergeant's exam he remained a patrolman. One shooting buddy had actually made captain, two others sergeant, but his closest friends stayed on, like he, as simple cops. This time it appears that factors apart from ethnicity - financial interests outside of work, alleged philandering, policy conflicts with top management - may all have played their part.

Irving had always wanted to make it financially. It wasn't pretense. He couldn't be called a social climber. His thinking didn't include class - upper or lower. He wished only for wealth, not riches but wealth, secure, comfortable wealth. Those dreams scared Rose. The family had plenty of food and a warm, nice enough place to live. Sure, it took most of his salary, but isn't that what a salary was for? Why must he be so discontent? When he spoke of mortgaging the house for a little capital, or to invest in a bigger place, she felt punched in the stomach. How could anyone risk a home?

Taking his wife and the kids for rides around town, another of Irv's savored off duty recreations, often only added to Rose's anxiety. He'd drive by places that were part of his beat, Logan Heights or even grimmer places, seedy places, places where prostitutes hung out. Then, by contrast, he'd stop to have them look at newly-built houses in an upbeat place like Point Loma, a few blocks from the yacht club, and to the thrill of the children, speak of buying.

The business he did support, with a few dollars skimmed here and there from his salary, had to do with shooting. String disliked sharing the garage with his father's cars, but it delighted him when daddy would drag out from its back door a plumber's gasoline-fired, lead-melting stove, and fill its cast iron pot with squashed up slugs dug out of the mounds behind the targets at the police pistol range. Once the burner was fired up and the lead had melted, Irv would fill a long handled dipper with steaming, 621.5° F, liquid lead from the pot and pour it into a bullet mold, also supported by long wooden handles. The mold formed six 38-caliber bullets, which, after cooling to a solid state, he would dump into a water filled basin.

For most bullet makers of the time, creating a finished cartridge once the projectile had been molded, required a number of tedious steps. The casing - its shell - would have to be resized, its primer or firing-cap knocked out and replaced, just the right amount of powder inserted, and the slug greased and fitted into the shell. Harry Newcomb changed all that. He had designed and built a machine that would perform all those steps with just one pull of a handle. Each pull created one ready to fire round of ammunition. Irving was hooked by both the device and the man. He liked Harry, he liked the machine, and he liked its commercial prospects.

As for String, what a great time it was to grow up in, to be a part of all this! His favorite magazine, *Popular Mechanics*, prophesied tomorrow: nuclear cars for one, even those that flew. He and his family already had much of it: a telephone since dad joined the force, a radio, his crystal sets, and the appliances - even a grilled-cheese-sandwich maker that Reddy Kilowatt, the Gas and Electric Company's little lightning-bodied advertising imp, urged them to buy to take advantage of all the cheap electricity the company offered. String didn't think of his daddy as a handyman, knowing much about machinery or fixing things, but here he was pouring lead and making one ready-to-shoot bullet every few seconds.

Harry got the machine patented, # 2061977, and he and Irv sold quite a few, not enough for the business to survive, but to some impressive customers like a whole string of police departments from Victoria, B.C., Canada to Tijuana, Mexico with Los Angeles in between. Even San Diego's Sheriff's Office bought one; the San Diego Police Department a notable, if not surprising, exception. Scuttlebutt had it that Irv had earlier expressed a few opinions not well received by then-chief George Sears.

Before becoming chief, Sears had served as lieutenant in charge of the vice squad at the time Irv worked in that unit. Ending prostitution and enforcing prohibition liquor laws ranked tops on the Sears agenda. Irv had been heard laughing about his own minimally successful attempt at making beer in the family bathtub, as well as voicing opinions that eliminating prostitution would only increase the risk of rape. "We've got a lot of transient laborers passing though town. You want those horny guys roamin around looking in your windows? Haul in the girls once a month, have em post bail and let em go. Just an extra tax the city could use." Not words Sears and his cronies hoped to hear from a subordinate, especially from one seen displaying considerable friendliness when booking certain of the hookers.

Irv unintentionally found escape from the disappointing career by being hurt. A drunk had positioned his feet against the patrol car's door frame and pushed back forcefully as Irv attempted to lift him into the back seat. After initial spasms, the wrenching motion left him with lingering back pain, a condition exacerbated by repeatedly kicking down against the lever that started his motorcycle.

Before taking medical retirement, an action welcomed by the Chief, Irv spent a number of weeks lying in a room in Mercy Hospital's recovery ward with weights hanging on lines running through pulleys and attached to both of his legs. The cheerful young man sharing the two-bed room had lost his right arm during a construction accident in the federally-funded Central Valley Project, an early depression era attempt to move water through canals to the dry lands farmed by California's inland growers.

Until his brief return to the police force to help reduce a war time manpower shortage in the fall of 1943, four and a half years after the firing of Chief Sears, Irving wrestled over defining himself. Living only on his retirement income was intolerable. He worked as bouncer in a local ballroom for a short period, always fearful it would jeopardize a back injury based pension. He took a number of car-buying trips east, each time visiting New York and adding to the speculation that staying with his sister-in-law, Jean, on the long nights when her husband, String's Uncle Ray, worked his shift at the post office, might have been for reasons other than free lodging.

Irv usually brought someone along when he drove home from Detroit; a person to talk to, keep him awake, even help drive. He'd look first in *The Detroit Times* to see if anyone had posted an ad for a ride west. A passenger could bring in a few extra bucks, enough for gas maybe. If that didn't pan out, he'd pick up a male hitch-hiker, given they would agree to being patted down to make sure they weren't carrying any kind of weapon.

On one trip, *The Times* yielded an ad for a young minister on his way to a convocation in Los Angeles. Paul was his name. He turned out to be a good, careful driver and an interesting storyteller. Irv enjoyed his company. Paul decided to stay on for the entire trip to San Diego, then later take a train to Los Angeles. Irving let him off at the downtown YMCA with an invitation to dinner in the evening. All went pleasantly. Paul decided to stay in town an extra day for a visit to the famous San Diego Zoo. String agreed to be his guide.

String lacked the maturity to anticipate future trouble as he watched Paul, who in turn and with a fixed intensity, watched the spider monkeys. "Aren't they cunning," were the words String remembers. Two of the males, young males, sat on branches near the front of the cage stroking their penises. They were motionless except for one moving arm, its hand's long, delicate fingers curled around, squeezing and pulling the captured organ to its uncircumcised length - each movement ending in a kind of foreskin enlargement.

Paul would have stayed on longer had he not been sensitive to the fidgeting of his small companion. They moved on, viewed more animals, took the trolley downtown, and ended up in Paul's room at the Y. There he suggested taking a shower together. The idea did seem very strange to String, but not threatening. Paul had been nice and he expected no harm from a man of God. After the shower, the strange became weird. Paul put the tip of his penis against the wall mirror, let it drop, then reached out, grasped String's little organ, and held it against his own - tip to tip. Now, at last, the alarm bell sounded. String announced his departure, and against pleas to say nothing and to be taken for an ice-cream soda, dressed quickly and left.

String said nothing to his mother about what had happened. He waited - not altogether patiently - until his dad arrived. Livid is a weak adjective to describe his rigid, crimson-faced father. "Was he pumping?" Irv managed to ask. String nodded, not clear what that meant or had to do with anything. Irv returned a couple of hours later, soaked his puffed up right hand in hot water, and announced to his family, "I put him on a train for L.A.; let him know he'd better never ever be seen in San Diego again. Couldn't run him in - tell them at the station I'd come across the country with him."

Rose had made friends with the wives of a number of Irv's fellow officers, his confidants, traveling and shooting buddies. Several times String overheard his mother tell one of them her husband had been a really nice person until he became a cop. He couldn't see it that way. His dad's uniform, his medals, his status in the neighborhood, all made String proud. Every Fourth of July daddy would pick up bags full of fireworks - ground spinners, bottle rockets, fountains, the works - from one of the Chinese shops on his beat, and put on a show right there in the middle of Pershing Avenue. He'd give String a few packages of firecrackers and pass out sparklers to Carolyn and other kids on the block.

And the dogs he brought home; first Petey, who turned out to be Peggy, and Peggy's pups - Wimpy, Salt, and Pepper; to name the few that were around for awhile. Pepper, the survivor, became the longtime family member. What a gambler he was, always chasing something. Once he jumped out the rear window to chase a little white ball as the car passed the golf links on Pershing Drive, and another time they had to stop everyone on the police pistol range from firing after he chased the puffs of dirt blown up by bullets striking the mounds behind the targets.

Even so, had String been forced to choose a parent, it would have been mom. She was always there for him; there when he needed support at school, there around the clock when strep throat almost took his life; there when he faced, a death sentence for treason against the United States. Sure, molding him to behave as a 'good boy' around all her friends, as well as the neighborhood old ladies, sapped him. Standing behind her at the front door as she spent forever, first saying good-bye to Loretta, or some other friend, then starting on a new topic, brought him close to screaming: "Stop, stop it, I'm so tired of standing here," but he never did. She had taught him well. He was a 'good boy.'

All his life he would retain the pain he saw on her face as she looked down at him. He was standing in front of the laundry tubs on the service porch and had just called her a bitch. He couldn't recall why, only that he was in first grade at the time. But there it was, he would never forget it.

Mom should merit an important symbol on the collage, a tribute to her uniqueness in String's life. All that comes to mind is the bun of hair at the back of her head. Rose's hair fell to her waist. Every morning she combed it out, rolled it into the bun, and fixed it in place with hairpins. String remembers seeing it once, only once, unpinned and hanging free.

His bed had always been on the inside wall of the bedroom across the yard from Grandma's house, while mom and dad shared the big brass bed in the master bedroom on the Pershing side. Now, after String's first wet dream, the brass bed gave way to another set of twin beds, and Carolyn swapped rooms with her father, pairing Irving with String in the back room, and Carolyn with Rose in front

As he remembers it, the bedroom shades must not have been drawn, and the moon large enough to provide him light to see and be in wonder over the apparition flowing between the beds, bending, and slipping noiselessly beside his father. To him, it had to be very late at night or early in the morning, but it could have been anytime after sundown. Only with effort did he grasp that the long-haired vision, draped in a sheer, almost translucent gown, light green and flowing, was his mother.

He would later have magnificent wet dreams, but that first, the only one he told his mother of - the one precipitating the separation from his kid sister - came in deep sleep and without joy. He simply awoke to find himself wet. Embarrassed and ashamed, believing his bladder responsible, he sought his mother's help first thing in the morning. She looked at him poker-faced, told him not to worry and returned to her morning chores. Why? How could she not have explained to him about growing up, about his body, told him something? Was this the same Rose who had suffered her own 'menstrual surprise?'

While she shared much of the Ambuehl character, wit and speech in particular, the adult Rose differed considerably. She approached events and others more quietly, controlled, subdued, with an outward coolness extending even to her own mother. String would never get to know the laughing, dancing, fashion model of her youth. Ambuehl family words, however, understood only as everyday speech and not as anything cute or clever, persisted. One should pick up and discard little *fuzzelies* (dust balls), and make satisfactory *poo* each day - not just a couple of little *pebbleies* (round turds). If you can't *poo*, *drick* (push hard). *Fersimmel, snitta, franzel, smuttsy, schnitzel, smeary, knarful, flappys,* ... , the words were countless.

String saw his mother unique in ways other than her bun. She was older than the mothers of his school chums. Kids, noisy kids, kids who rode their bikes or walked across and killed the grass at the corner of the slope at Pershing and Landis, upset her. Sophie upset her. Lilly Bell and her sister, String's Aunt Tanny, in the house at the other end of Landis got dignitary-like treatment. And mom didn't like change. It didn't matter what anyone said about electric washers and dryers; no one was going to replace the double iron laundry tubs on her service porch. She scrubbed the family's clothes against a washboard in the one on the left, rinsed in the other, and hung them out to dry on the lines between grandma's house and the Coleman's geranium-covered fence. That's the way clothes should be washed and dried.

Things he didn't notice: she ran her house meticulously - ashtrays wiped clean after each dropped ash. She prepared each, taken-for-granted, evening meal using every group in the food pyramid - meals that Irv might criticize, not for overcooked vegetables, but for a steak or roast not pink enough. Pies and cakes, on the other hand, never got a thumbs-down, her baking skills maybe learned from Caroline, who each Christmas presented them with a few loaves of bread that, sliced and served, melted on the tongue. Bread she called *Birnenbrot* (pear bread), and made from prunes.

String and his sister also relied on mom when they were sick, not an unfamiliar occurrence. They had fevers, earaches, sinusitis, all the drippy, snotty stuff kids get. Carolyn even had a double mastoidectomy, a tough operation for a tot. She reportedly bit the elbow of her attending physician. String's strep throat, though, taxed Rose in an unexpected way; she had to opt for something new.

It was late summer 1937. For three days, String felt himself ebbing and flowing in and out of blackness, growing to room size, his hot head and body throbbing, pounding, filling the space around him - then he'd shrivel and shrink back into dark, hollow sleep. Rose never left him. "He might not make it," was the harshest of Dr. Belford's unforgivable pronouncements. On that third day, he called her into the little hall leading to the bath between the bedrooms. "There's been a new discovery," he pontificated haltingly. "Gerhard Domagk, a doctor at Bayer Labs in Germany - you know, the aspirin makers - almost lost his young daughter to a streptococcal infection just like your boy's. Domagk treated her with a drug he concocted - even before it had been tried on people. It worked, she pulled through. I can try it with String if you agree." He added, not knowing why, maybe to make it sound more impressive, "It's a derivative of sulphanilamide." She agreed.

Aside from the operation behind her ears, and the two broken arms she got rolling down the slope between her house and grandma's (she used the casts to wallop her big brother whenever she had a chance), Rose had little trouble with her daughter, Carolyn. Daddy's happy princess managed physical activities with great care, the slope-rolling a rare exception. When asked to try walking, "No, I 'fraid I fall," became a pat response until she did try, at well past her second birthday. Talking and making her preferences known began for her at the infant age of six months.

It was no different at school; Carolyn content, String pushing for this or that. He seemed to be perennially on the cusp between actuality and aspiration - not a part of the 'in-crowd' but kind of accepted by them, always in the top academic group but at its bottom, seldom winning but often placing in playground events not requiring much skill. Early in the semester new arrivals from Oklahoma overflowed Miss Van Orshoven's fifth grade class, splitting it into two groups; the 'ins' joining young Miss Wright, the 'not-so-ins' remaining. Rose fought to keep him alongside the expected achievers, including String's favorite, a lovely dust bowl refugee. He'd never told anyone, but leaving Miss Van Orshoven was a relief in itself. It made him uncomfortable when she'd lean over Roy

Munn's desk and suck on a strand of his hair.

Lima and Pinto were left behind, but String's social maturity never matched that of his fellow Miss Wright students. Kissing games confounded him completely. Once, at a popular classmate's backyard party where several young lasses were practicing that sport, he asked to be kissed only on his glasses - a prop newly acquired that year, allowing him to read the blackboard from a front row desk.

Both String and his sister liked traveling with their mother. Rose lightened up, became more alive, especially in Upland where Emma and Katherine treated her like royalty. With Papa Rudolph dead and her five siblings all married and living in homes of their own, Katherine and her mother were the only regular occupants of the big old house on Euclid. String's first recollections of the place date from when he was four, although it became impossible for him to sort out which visit went with which memory.

That fourth year, 1930, Mama Emma threw a party to celebrate Rose's 38th birthday. She invited all her own children - Alice, Katherine, Rudy, Helen, Mickey and Ann. Rudy and Mickey didn't come. String doesn't know if he ever met Rudy. He kind of recalls mama being angry over getting no card from daddy, then laughing it off a few days later after receiving his five-page letter. She showed String the envelope. It had a red, two-cent stamp with a picture of George Washington pasted neatly in its upper right hand corner. He heard mama read some of it aloud to Katherine. "*I've been bumming around town going to all the shows. ... I went up to Nashold old fashon dance & chewed the fat with Sgt. Adams who works up there nites as spel officer. He said he would give me a chance at it sometime when he wanted to take off if I wanted to. Friday to the fights ... .*"

String would retain the memory of two, several times repeated, happenings unique to Euclid house. Both of them associated with a tightness in his loins, a tension falling between thrill and fear. He'd be sent to nap in one of the bedrooms, a gracious room, far more spacious than any he'd known - a room with chests and mirrors and drawers, a room inviting investigation. And investigate he did. He'd look both ways, sidle to a dresser, then alert, fearful the room door would open, pull out a drawer and, item by item, examine its contents.

The second memory recorded a custom of his hostess. An overnight visitor seldom left Emma's without being served a fresh, full-course, chicken dinner. Preparing seemed almost a personal ritual, undertaken alone if need be, or with the invited children of her guests. "Come along," she'd beckon them in her broken English, and head out onto her mini-farm backyard of vegetable plants, fruit trees, hens and roosters. The latter were in wire cages along the fence, as were a few of the hens. The other hens roamed free; some ran clucking to her feet as she stepped off the porch. Like picking the ripest peach from the tree, she'd choose the proper hen, then bend her over-75-year-old body down carefully, grab its legs with her left hand, and carry it squawking and flapping to the large, knee-high tree stump just left of the porch stairs. There she would curl the fingers of her right hand around the handle of the heavy, well-honed hatchet, lay the bird's head across the stump, raise her arm and ... . At this point, and before the blade came down, Carolyn would scream "mama" and run through the back screen door. After watching the animal hop headlessly about the yard, String would stay with 'Auntie' Emma for the kitchen plucking.

Trips to Colton also stored memories, those treasured and those less welcome. That bit of awkwardness, present in most families, existed with playful, yet uneasy, teasing between brother and sister, and maybe less playful between skinny Rose and her plump sister-in-law. For String it was mostly fun. He got special treatment from Cousin Margaret; Uncle August would take him to work once in awhile, show him how to pull the switches and share a lunch Aunt Bessie had made. Then there was the little girl his mother called his shirt-tail cousin, Margaret's daughter Joanne. He liked her in ways he didn't understand. When eleven and pushing her in the back-yard swing, he wanted to touch her, pull the swing up close to him, up against his own body. But he didn't. Afterwards came the thought that Aunt Bessie would sense what he had wanted. It scared him. He didn't know why, but it did.

At home, neighborhood playmate inventory and evalua-tion constituted a final maternal duty not left to chance. The blocks around Pershing and Landis were blessed with children of all ages. Each belonged to one of Rose's five categories: desirable, acceptable, permissible, tentative, and strange. Only Lilly Bell's sometimes visiting nieces, possibly Joan Walsh across the street in the brick house, and Duane Ecchols the chiropractor's son on 28th Street made it to the top echelon. The great bulk drifted back and forth between acceptable and permissible, depending upon their behavior during the activities of the day - from toy car road-building and driving in the yards of Cappy Swift's parent's rental properties across the alley, to creating fairytale hide-outs with chalk on the brick columns of Grandma's front porch. Mitchell Kapitas, catty-corner across Pershing and Roy Munn, by the alley opposite Aunt Tanny, always fell into the strange class. They were possibly joined there by the two kids halfway down the hill beyond the brick house on Landis Street, after their father committed suicide in the days following Wall Street's collapse.

> *For all that is in the world, the lust of the flesh,*
> *and the lust of the eyes, and the pride of life,*
> *is not of the Father, but is of the world.*
> 1 John 2:16

Pretty, caramel-brown-haired Joan Walsh had become a favorite neighborhood game sharer of String's during his last half-year at Jefferson. He couldn't, and didn't want, to shift his thoughts away from her that Saturday. Rose had taken Carolyn to rehearse for a piano recital scheduled for the following day. Dad was at work. String had slumped into the big golden-yellow overstuffed chair in front of the built-in bookcase on the side opposite the fireplace from its smaller burgundy counterpart. He stretched his feet onto a matching ottoman, opened his belt, unbuttoned his fly, slid his hand through the slit at the front of his boxers and started stroking a penis that had previously begun its growth. It was a first, it was good, it was a surprise, it was not in his power to describe. The skin-covered tissue, cupped between the fingers and palm of a coaxing hand, filled the room and howled, a glow ran up and dissolved his brain, and a sticky, thin, white paste filled his hand. When it passed and full consciousness returned, he found himself wet, startled, sure he would do more of that, and looking about with that same sense of being watched as when going through the dresser drawers in Upland.

String confided in his mother when he thought he had wet his bed. He told his father when he'd been treated in a creepy way. He shared with no one when he had snooped through drawers, wanted to touch his cousin, or masturbated. Where had he acquired this knowledge? How did he know who to tell what?

Chapter 9

First Aside - End Game

O death, where is thy sting?
O grave, where is thy victory?
1 Cor. 15:55

Regretfully, because of the possibility of death, my death, String's narrative will be interrupted. Why, you ask, should this writer's death matter? It matters because my story was to have been placed in the pages following his. When learning I might not be around for that, I refused to honor an advance payment made to me by my publisher, HeronDrivePress, unless they showed me published components of the work in progress. Their compromise agreement calls for a first, serial publication of the book - they will release each chapter as soon as I complete it. They further agreed to allow me to include details of my medical condition, now an integral part of the tale.

Cowards die many times before their deaths,
The valiant never taste of death but once.
Julius Caesar II, ii, 32-37

	total population: 67.59 years
World	**male:** 65.59 years
	female: 69.73 years (2012 est.)

	total population: 78.49 years
United States	**male:** 76.05 years
	female: 81.05 years (2012 est.)

The two entries pasted above were copied early in 2013 from "Field Listing: Life Expectancy at Birth" in *The CIA World Factbook*. I'm a U.S. male, apparently quite a bit past due on the world clock, and by a number of years even here at home in the States. If you plug your gender and birth date into the Social Security website's 'Online Life Expectancy Calculator,' it will show you the average number of additional years you can expect to live. They don't give me a lot. I'm fine with that, or at least I was until a little over four years ago. Then a biopsy, taken on January 27, 2009, showed I had prostate cancer.

People, even old geezers like me, aren't typically aware of aging. Sure, we slow down, lose this or that, initiate an icky, messy mannerism or two - the kind you might see Craig Ferguson mimic on *The Late Late Show*, but we look out of our eyes, out only, and can't see ourselves - even in the mirror. We can and do see others, old acquaintances, friends, colleagues. They get old. We don't.

Since the biopsy, my subsequent treatment, its failure, and the search to decide what's next, all that has changed. There are things I want to finish - like this writing - and I can't get death out of my mind. "Hang down your head, Tom Dooley" is the refrain that keeps repeating itself. Calpurnia may have been encouraged by her husband's words, but I'm afraid I can't be counted among the valiant. What I'm most aware of is the passing of time, the ever-present tick, tick, tick of the clock. Don't get me wrong. I'm not writing this part to bitch about dying. Woody Allen excepted, it's something we all do. The message has to do with the way my illness got juggled around in the medical community, upsetting the old "Que Sera Sera."

I'm an engineer by training, PhD, Engineering Science,

U.C. Berkeley. I've always been a merit badge collector, and a PhD was a badge I yearned to have. At an age twice some of my classmates, an undergraduate education more in the biological than the physical sciences and questionable intellectual capability, I can't claim to have been a typical Berkeley grad student. I snuck into the elite electrical engineering department, then ranked second in the world, only because of early experience with computers and the pull of an influential boss at the Lawrence National Laboratory in Livermore, California where I worked.

I bring this up because I believe an engineer looks at biological events differently than physicians. Engineering is logical thinking about practical problems, not airy-fairy poetry science like some 'origin of the universe' theories, or the let's all agree, then try it and see, crap shoot of medicine, a discipline that should maybe be studied not practiced. Again, not to be misunderstood, there's a place for all of it: poetry, medicine, music, a big bang theory, you name it. Just don't mix it up.

What I'm about to write isn't meant to deny them their often innate, vigorous intellectual capability, but M.D.s are taught to move in lock step, think alike, work like the Borg in *Star Trek's Next Generation*. In one sense that puts them ahead of the rest of us, only now catching up on mass brain sharing, mind melding through blogs and social media: Facebook, Twitter, et al. And physicians are privy to great information, much of it from compatriots and their statistician allies, hunched up over benches in the laboratories of pharmaceutical houses, universities and other, often government-backed, enterprises across the nation. Many specialists need also be given credit for being superb technicians, employing consummate skill in their handling of the dangerous tools - robots, scalpels, laser beams, radiation - they use to penetrate the human body.

The knowledge doctors acquire from their laboratory associates provides a body of disseminated information, an unbound bible of sorts - albeit an ever-changing one - suitable for pontificating on what to do next: what food to eat, what test to take, what drug to use. Bear with me, or skip ahead a page or so, as I digress with an example, the often cited "atrophy of the vagina associated with post-menopausal women" problem. This was, and still is by some, considered an under-recognized and under-treated 'disorder,' with symptoms including dryness, itching, burning and not enough smeary stuff to have sex without pain. All that changed in the 1950s when menopausal women were directed by their gynecologists to take an estrogen pill made from the purified urine of lady horses. The women followed doctor's orders in record numbers. Premarin had, by the 1990s, become the most frequently dispensed drug in the United States.

In 1975, two articles published in *The New England Journal of Medicine* indicated women on the drug were experiencing a significantly increased risk of endometrial (uterine) cancer. Back to the laboratories. A study from Kaiser Permanente showed the culprit to be the absence of progesterone, so progestins were added to the therapy and prescribed by doctors. A while later, the same *New England Journal* reported a link between the drug and breast cancer, and in 1989 a Swedish study showed that risk doubled when taking a progestin (Prempro) and not estrogen alone. Back to the laboratories.

After half a century of record-setting prescription writing, a comprehensive study, conducted and reported in 2002 by the Women's Health Initiative of the National Institutes of Health - finally stopped because of health risks to its participants - determined that older women on estrogen therapy had a higher number of heart attacks, strokes, blood clots and dementia, in addition to their greater risk for uterine and breast cancers. So, do doctors prescribe hormone replacement today? Some do, some don't. The pharmaceutical companies are still out marketing, science and statistical workers remain in the laboratories, and the holy book of 'what shall I tell my patient' produces advice of the nature: let each woman be advised to consider, individually, the risks and benefits associated with hormone replacing medications.

One can buy from the health services company Athenahealth, Inc., a package of software routines, Epocrates Essentials, that includes Integrated Drugs, Diseases, Diagnostics, and a Medical Dictionary. The programs can run on smartphones or other mobile devices, doing just what their titles suggest: diagnosing and recommending appropriate pharmaceuticals. Over 50% of all US physicians have copies.

If estrogen decisions had been left to engineers, would history have been different? Probably not. The path to ageless women, great sex until death do us part, is unlikely to have been scrutinized by even the most anal of engineers, especially not by those with a penis. Circumstances calling for a more invasive intervention, a vasectomy instead of birth control pills - another instance of women's bodies undergoing hormone alteration - might prompt a look at outcome statistics: the number of failures, how many men bruise, swell, get infections or lumps from sperm leaking into surrounding tissue. Engineers tend to probe more deeply as the nature of the proposed medical fix becomes increasingly harsh - a heart lung transplant likely leading to a few weeks at a local medical school library.

In my case, the quest to decide what to do with a rogue prostate began over nine years ago in my primary service provider's examining room. 'Primary service provider' is what my HMO calls him. Here I'll call him Duno. There are a number of adjectives I'd use to characterize the physicians I'm about to speak of, but I know far too little law to feel comfortable doing so. A Google search turned up a paper by Eric Eden informing me that:

> Anybody can sue you for libel or defamation if they think you damaged their reputation, but if you can prove what you say is true, chances are that you won't end up in court.
>
> "Make it clear when you are stating your opinion," says Donaldson (editor of Legal Bytes) "Always state the facts that your opinions are based on just to be safe. You probably won't lose a libel or defamation lawsuit if you can back up what you write with solid facts."

While it is assuredly my opinion that one of the physicians I saw deserves the appellation 'arrogant little prick,' it would be quite difficult to prove in a court of law. Hence, the hesitancy to couple that opinion with his actual name. I will thus refer to each MD by providing a 'D' for doctor, followed by an abbreviation of the descriptive, invective, or, for one at least, praiseful name that comes to me when I think of him. Dalp, for example, will identify the **a**rrogant **l**ittle **p**rick.

Duno's a nice enough guy, keeps up with all the latest medical injunctions, and carries his Epocrates-loaded smartphone with him at all times. He'd been bugging me to have pieces of my prostate cut out and examined - biopsied - since 2005, when my PSA measured 5.22. The rules that year called for testing everyone over 50 annually until the PSA number exceeded 4.0 ng/ml, then recommending the biopsy. I'd skipped 2004. In 2003 it had come in at 3.38. PSA - prostate-specific antigen - is a protein produced by cells of the prostate gland. A simple blood test measures the level of that protein in the blood, and is typically reported in nanograms per milliliter. Laboratory statisticians, using the correlation between the amount of the antigen and prostate cancer, come up with the height of the hurdle, the number alerting doctors to yell, "Let's you and me worry about cancer."

It may not be cancer at all, just a big gland. Prostates do grow as you age. Being old-school as well as old, the DRE test, and WAW, appealed more to me than a biopsy. Read DRE as medical nomenclature for bend over and D-digital (finger), R-rectal (no identification needed), E-examination, and WAW as watch and wait or watchful waiting. Unlike a number of other cancers, many in the prostate grow very slowly and without symptoms. So if you're an older guy, forget about it; you'll probably die of something else before it gives you any trouble. I told Duno, "Let me know when you can feel something hard up there; then we'll do the biopsy." I think he would rather have had a urologist worry about me than do the DRE, but he accommodated me; that's the way he is.

It's difficult to grasp any account of my medical dilemmas without some knowledge of the prostate. So again a digression is in order, and, as before, if you know - this time about the workings of male parts - skip the next paragraph.

The prostate is a little organ, about the size of a walnut (the more scholarly works call it chestnut-sized), that goes bang when men have orgasms. It's part muscle and part gland, sits just below the urine-storing bladder and in front of the rectum, through which it may be clearly felt, and concocts much of the juicy, milky part of the sperm-bearing semen. During an orgasm the gland contracts repeatedly, pumping the gooey stuff first into the urethra, then through it and out the penis into a waiting hand, vagina, mouth, whatever. Unfortunately for getting rid of it, the prostate wraps itself tightly around the urethra, the tube essential for getting pee from the bladder to the outside world.

Late in 2008 it was a done deal. Duno said my walnut-sized gland felt hard to him and my PSA was over 12. Time to honor my agreement and visit a urologist. For both known and unknown reasons, PSA wobbles around a bit. Sex and DREs are thought to push it up. Mine hit 15.56 a couple of months past Duno's exam. It may have been shortly after getting another DRE from the urologist. I can't remember. My notes show it dropped to 11.13·two months after the biopsy. Since predictions are based on this number, we with prostate cancer, or suspected prostate cancer, hang onto its fluxuations like a new mother watching the rise and fall of the thermometer during her baby's first fever.

Duno referred me to a likable urologist, senior and experienced, who promptly scheduled the biopsy. His name here, Darf, reflects the bad and the good: about to retire, but fine. Biopsies are not unhurty. The prostate is most commonly accessed for the procedure through the same channel as the DRE, this time with an ultrasound probe and a needle gun - not a digit. After a couple of days on an antibiotic and a morning fleet-enema emptying, an embarrassingly cute medical technician positions you on your left side, crunched up in a rear-end-exposed fetal pose, and leaves you for the eternity it takes until the arrival of your 'provider.' Darf didn't give me the expected upbeat greeting. No, "How are you?" or even, "I'm here." Just some quiet words to the tech. I loved him for that.

I'm not sure, but I think I must have received local anesthesia, probably lidocaine, as I felt very little when the ultrasound probe - used to see where to shoot - was poked into place, or during the first half-dozen or so pops of the gun as it shot needles - each a half-inch long by a sixteenth-of-an-inch in diameter - through my rear-end wall and into the offended organ. Then the pops started making themselves known, each more intensely than its predecessor. Once the twelve tiny cylindrical samples were placed, one by one, into small glass containers, Darf excused me to attend to a scary, because bloody, urination and be on my way.

On Monday evening, six days later, Darf called me confirming Duno's concern and awakening my obsessive indwelling engineer. I obtained a copy of the surgical pathology report, plotted its findings on an 8½ x 11 sheet of white paper, and initiated the search for the perfect method to eliminate prostate cancer. The outline for my diagram, taken from a drawing found on page 1360 of Henry Gray's *The Anatomy of The Human Body*, 1959 - given me that year by my now long-dead wife, Joan - showed the prostate as two pulled-apart ear-shaped lobes - kind of a stretched sideways Valentine's heart. The report provided details of each tissue sample, and identified its place of extraction from my prostate. It's that information I laid out in a corresponding array on the chart: twelve regions - base, mid and apex from top to bottom, and from left to right: left, left transitional zone, right transitional zone, and right. (No, that's not incorrect. Henry Gray called the part on top next to the bladder, the base, and the underside of the prostate, the apex - you figure.)

While the report's data would prove helpful, I don't know why I needed it to be so artfully displayed, or worse, why I want to bore you here with its description. Perhaps to reemphasize the engineer's modus operandi, exemplified in a middle school joke - not clever enough to warrant being repeated - here or anywhere else: "What did the constipated engineer do? He (it's always a he) worked it out with a pencil."

An inspector from the U.S. Department of Agriculture determines one of the eight grades of beef: prime, choice, select, standard, ..., ..., partly by examining fat marbling patterns in the carcass's ribeye muscles. Similarly, the pathologist seeks out patterns in magnified tissue slices, matching them against the way prostate cancer looks in one of five stages, numbered, uncharacteristically for the medical community, 1 through 5. The greater the number the more aggressive the cancer, the one more likely to spread. He chooses the most commonly matched pattern, then the one next most common, and adds their numbers together for a total called the Gleason score. The meat inspector figures age, as well as appearance, into his final grouping.

Prostate cancer staging calls for more than a single additional factor: tumor size (T score), lymph node involvement (N score), distant spread or metastases (M score) and the familiar old PSA taken near the time of the biopsy are all figured in, but it's the Gleason number that gets kicked around by the cancer novitiate in his interactions with pals who've been through it.

As long as the cancer is confined to the prostate, methods used to get rid of it are surprisingly simple. It's excised with a knife or robot, zapped with radioactive beams or seeds, frozen stiff, or in less restrictive countries, Canada for example, roasted with ultrasound. I studied them all ad nauseam, talked with an old friend, Ernie, who'd had his chopped out in the mid-nineties, and exchanged emails with an acquaintance living near Princeton, Jack, who'd been recently embellished with the glowing seeds. They honored my unnecessary plea for discretion, hush hush being another trait of the newly diagnosed, shared their stories in much detail, and helped me on my way.

Jack pointed out that I had a favorable Gleason of 6 (3+3). His was 7 (3+4), luckily not 7 (4+3). He seemed quite pleased with his treatment. It had been started with beam radiation, then switched to the implantation of permanent seeds when a previous artificial hip replacement made reaching parts of his prostate difficult. But radiation, the treatment typically touted to geezers, and the only one Darf had spoken of, appalled me. Fresh thoughts of pictures I'd once seen post-Hiroshima and Nagasaki, thoughts of days at Lawrence Livermore Lab wearing a little radiation detection badge, thoughts of Edward Teller, chilled me, prickled my flesh.

I kind of liked what Ernie had to say, although it happened to him so long ago, and with such a different procedure. Ernie underwent classic surgery. Today a robot can work through a few tiny holes in the abdomen, and pop the gland out through a one-inch incision. The big ah-shucks comes about because in order to whack out the prostate, the urethra, the pee-draining tube, must be sliced in half, and has to be reattached - another possible middle school story - this one about the plumber and the leaky pipe.

I enjoyed this medical excuse to spend time with Ernie, even though his hearing loss from the big guns off Iwo Jima made communicating a challenge. I'd always admired him, thought of him as one of my best friends when his wife was alive and his kids at home. Now that he lived without them, sharing his big house in the Berkeley hills with grad students from all over the world, I didn't know. I felt more of an oddity from the past than someone he wanted to be with outside an occasional lunch at the Durant or the Faculty Club. Lunch, even lunch, had to be at lunch time. Ernie was orderly in all things: chores, contacts, pleasures, it didn't matter - there was a time for it - and lunch time was twelve noon.

We were at Lawrence Livermore together until he left to teach. Ernie collected and nurtured an odd group of fellow workers, an unusually bright assortment from the Physics and Computer Divisions. He may have mistakenly included me among them, this gang we'd today call super nerds. Not only techy nerds, but one at least who'd questioned an Einstein equation or two. We'd sit around his living room with our wives - looking far down at San Francisco Bay and the Golden Gate Bridge - after some great meal Sal, his wife, had prepared. That's when Ernie would see if he could start something going between us, some kind of a discussion - I hesitate calling them arguments. Our wives would drift off into other rooms, those not filled with his houseful of boys or kids of their own, while we squirmed around Ernie's dialectic of the day.

He's sore at me now, and we're out of touch. I think it's because he misunderstood my intention when I bad-mouthed Google about going so commercial and betraying its initial calling, right after he'd praised them, but it could be for different reasons altogether - maybe just my turn to call. It happened once before. That time he stopped all contact for over twenty years. I thought my unfaithfulness to Joan caused the rift, but he told me later it was because I'd yelled at him. Anyway, at the time of the prostate visits he was a real help, a friend who'd survived being cut the old-school way, been cured, and had only an occasional dribble plus the need for a few post-op sex aids.

I finally made my choice, or thought I had. I'd first see how hard it would be to get my prostate baked with ultra sound, the least frightening of the procedures. If that didn't work, I'd go for the robot surgery. I tend to heal quickly after any cut or injury, painlessly, and only once with a scar. The surgery seemed a natural. It's called a prostatectomy, a radical prostatectomy if they take out the whole gland. Cooking it goes by the name 'high intensity focused ultrasound,' or just HIFU. Besides Canada, many places around the world, France, Japan, Mexico, ... all the way down to South Africa, do HIFU. It's not cheap for a foreigner, and scary to head offshore and have strangers fiddle with your reproductive system. I'd see if it could be done here at home.

When the FDA says a medical procedure is disallowed, think clinical trial. I learned that after my Livermore Lab days, when I'd worked on, or built, a few medical devices: blood typing instruments and gadgets that measured bodily activity no one's ever heard of. There'll always be some group trying for grant money to test out and evaluate what can't be done legally. I typed http://www.clinicaltrials.gov/ into the address bar on my old Dell Inspiron's home page, clicked on the blue arrow and *voilà*, better than I had hoped, a HIFU trial at the University of Colorado, Denver, close to where my daughter lived. Wow, a cancer cure and a visit, life couldn't get much better.

The trial coordinator I got on the phone, can't remember his name anymore, couldn't have been more accommodating. At my request, Sergio, Darf's front office man, sent him copies of my biopsy report. He called back positively, asking for more information: volume in cubic centimeters, and size, the prostate diameter, front to back, in millimeters. I felt quite cavalier about all this, anxious to answer his questions, get through the paperwork, and call United for my tickets. His response to my laughingly asking why he needed so much trivia, provided a wakeup shock, and my first clinical trial learning experience. It was a quiet, unembellished, "Got to follow the protocol."

I told him I'd call Darf's office and have them send him what he'd asked for, hung up the phone, ran upstairs to my laptop and returned to clinicaltrials.gov. This HIFU fix, this trip to Denver, this chance to visit my daughter was now a must. Could they really keep me from it just because my sick organ measured, in one direction or another, a millimeter more than they thought it should? My god, look at the period between these brackets [.]. Put two of them side by side and that's their millimeter! I called Sergio back, got his assurance that my walnut fell within required limits, then re-read - carefully this time - the section in the trial description headed 'Inclusion Criteria.' Now panic, total anxiety, descended. Inclusion criteria 5 of 34 read, 'PSA equal to or less than 10 ng/ml.'

The hunt was on. There had to be something, some medication, that would lower my reading. Google led me to it quicker than expected. Several drugs did just that - cholesterol-lowering statins, even aspirin - but the ones that caught my attention, the ones with the greatest effect, were those prescribed to grow hair for folks suffering male pattern baldness. The package insert on the one I chose states under '**WARNINGS AND PRECAUTIONS**': "Finasteride (brand names Proscar or Propecia) reduces serum prostate specific antigen (PSA) levels by approximately 50%." Perfect! Now all I needed was a prescription, or did I? Back to Google.

All pharmacies appear to ask for prescriptions, but several around the globe require questionable verification. I don't remember just how, but ' EASYMD' accepted whatever proof I sent, and for USD $59.50, 30 5mg tablets were on their way. And come they did, from one of the lovely South Pacific islands in the Republic of Vanuatu. I'd flip a "So there" to my local pharmacy if it hadn't all been in vain. After less than a month of diligent pill popping, I received a "Thank you, but" message from the University of Colorado. Forget the privacy forms you have to sign every visit to a doctor's office, and congratulations to improvements in medical records keeping, my PSA history was just that, recorded history. On to plan B, the prostatectomy.

Darf didn't do robotic surgeries. He left them to a young associate in the adjoining office, but instead of sending me to him, referred me to the radiation oncologist, Deat, **e**verybody **a**grees he's **t**ops. Deat, one of those rare medical sweethearts, greeted me with "Hi, Doctor my-last-name, I'm his-first-name." It was a first, first for me. We talked. He told me all about radiation and the treatment I'd receive. All to no avail; with HIFU off the table, it had to be surgery. I shared my preference without mentioning death rays or any of my other negative thoughts about what this good man did for a living. I wanted him to know I was in pretty good shape for an old fart, so mentioned that I'd done the local AIDS ride the previous year. It's a seven day, 545-mile bicycle ride from San Francisco to Los Angeles to raise money toward helping treat and stamp out that disease. I was the oldest rider. Joyce had gotten me into it, and ridden with me, eight years earlier.

A word about Joyce. She agreed, foolishly maybe, to edit this, so if you can read it, she probably did. Joyce retired as a librarian after managing a couple of libraries down in San Ramon about thirty miles east of San Francisco. She reads vociferously, averaging about a book a week, well over a thousand since we met. We live together, have for nineteen years, same as the difference in our ages. She's the younger. Joyce is a great partner, with all that implies, and to keep it that way I'll say no more of our relationship - except for comments like: 'Joyce went with me, I asked Joyce about this or that, or ... .'

I don't remember getting a referral to see Dycl, young chicken little. I think I just asked Sergio, whom Dycl shared with Darf, to put me on his schedule. I asked Joyce to join me. Dycl came into our assigned examining room carrying my chart, introduced himself, sat on his little round stool, and staring at the chart without looking up asked, "How old are you?" Now almost everyone knows the two pieces of information scrawled boldly on the front binder of a chart are: the patient's - I hate to call myself that - name, and date of birth. I am sometimes snotty with Duno, a failing I regret, but its hard to sound off to one you're about to ask to cut into your sensitive zone and extract a rotten walnut. The words, "Can't you subtract the dates, asshole!" choked in my throat; I did not say them. I later felt I should have asked, "Physical or chronological age?" Instead, I simply answered his question, honestly and feebly. It went back and forth from there, Joyce taking notes - my assertions of health, his over and over characterization of urinary incontinence. Finally, either out of exhaustion or a realization his next patient would have to wait even longer than requisite, he caved; he would do the surgery.

Sergio gave me a number for the person who did the urology group's surgical scheduling. I called, conveyed my information, and the pleasant, helpful voice responded, "I'll set it up and get back to you." I waited a week, a long while at my anxiety level, before calling back. The voice, the same pleasant one as before, appeared as nonplussed as I. Dycl's office had not responded to her repeated query. Back to prostatectomy square one, calls, confusion, and the scheduling of a second appointment with Dycl.

"I just got back from a national urology meeting in Chicago," he told Joyce and me. "I spoke with several of my colleagues about your case. They all said I'd be crazy to do it." Many of the 'scholarly papers' I'd been reading on the subject agreed with Dycl. Others, at a few notable institutions, the Mayo Clinic for one, saw things more as I did. A man's general health would be a better indicator of success than a number on his chart cover. "Who would you recommend to do it then?" I asked. We went all over the place with that one. From whom would my insurance cover - to finally, who in this group had the capability. Why, of course, one of them, Dalp, had done more of these robotic procedures than anyone else - ever. Round and round it went till at last, Dycl acknowledged he'd be pleased to assist Dalp, or even do it himself with Dalp looking on.

Joyce drove me to Dalp's office high in the Oakland hills. The young woman behind the polished counter stared at the few papers in front of her, then shuffled them around a bit before looking up. Quite of number of doctor's office workers - Duno's were a bit like that, while Sergio and the people at Deat's John Muir Radiation Center were exceptions - appear trained to make office visitors feel small and insignificant. Maybe so they'll deserve the long waits and first name indignities inflicted on them. When Professor Einstein walked into his physician's office, the receptionist probably handed him an array of papers to fill out, privacy form, list of current meds, ... , asked for his insurance card, and told him: "Take a seat Albert, the doctor will see you soon."

In due time Joyce and I were seated in the stark little examining room, Joyce in the only chair, me on the table, feet dangling, butt against crumpled protective paper. Dalp, a short man in his early sixties, strode in crisply, and with a little nod from the waist, gave us his name. To his credit he did intend to assess my health. Deat had given me a thorough exam, while date of birth had been sufficient for Dycl. After the usual questions - meds, family health, past problems, ... , Dalp told me to drop my pants, then extended his right arm, palm up, and with three little flicks of his curled fingers, summoned me to his throne, the small, swiveling doctors-only stool he was perched upon. There he probed my privates, told me I had a hernia, asked if I had a left testicle, and after hearing I had, acknowledged he'd found it. Why he hadn't walked to the table for his feel, I do not know. It was a first for me.

Exam completed, he left after telling me to dress and for us to join him in his office across the hall. His corner office exuded everything the exam room had not, from large shiny, dark brown, cherrywood desk to full bay view. There Dalp shifted immediately from examiner to teacher, and started leading us through prostate narrative 101. He was at, "It's about the size of a walnut," when he slowed a little, just enough for me to push my own narrative. "It would be so great for Dycl to have an opportunity to work with you," I began, then embellished on that theme ad nauseum, or at least until he had the time to stop me with his question. "What kind of treatments do you know about for prostate cancer?" My answer threw him. His face showing obvious surprise when cryotherapy popped out of my possibilities list. He did not expect me to have heard of cryo, the procedure he was about to propose. Dalp, a master of the we know, you don't system, created during priesthood days and enforced by the title 'doctor,' brought the session to a close. He'd get back to us. In parting I suggested, "You can fix my hernia while you take out the prostate." Joyce took notes.

My recollection and above description of our meeting may be overly heavy-handed. There must be many a good doctor, as well as priest, but I know of only one doctor, Deat, who wipes away the goo after performing a DRE. In any case, Dalp did call the following week letting me know he had not the time to do surgery. He would do the cryo if I so chose. I asked if I could have the name of one of his former cryotherapy patients, and he told me to call his secretary for a number. I asked how many he'd done and he said six, this man who had done hundreds of robotic prostatectomies.

Resignation settled - to be or not to be - to be zapped by a man I trusted and admired, or frozen by a jerk. It was no choice at all. I met again with Deat, Joyce took notes, and on June 7, 2009 sent friends the following email: "Sorry it's been so long. I've decided to go for the radiation treatment. Not because I think it's the best option for me, but because the guy that does it is the only one of the MDs I seem to be able to get along with. So much for objective, logical reasoning, and five months of study. Anyway, I'll begin getting zapped sometime in early July - 39 times, 5 days a week for eight weeks (minus a day)."

The treatments began on August 3, not in July as planned. On June 23 Darf screwed four gold "seeds" into my prostate as targets for the radiation machine. Deat allowed two weeks for any swelling to abate, and did CT scans for measurement to set the control algorithms. The scans showed some odd-looking tissue outside the prostate, so Deat ordered additional scans, contrast scans from a local radiologist, left instructions with a colleague, and went on vacation. Not to worry, the weird stuff turned out to be just an unusually large, funny-shaped bladder. With my concurrence, the colleague punted and we waited for Deat to return before starting anything.

I bought a little Honda Rebel 250cc motorcycle for traveling the 14.2 miles to and from the clinic. A rebel to match mine. I believed carrying my helmet into the dressing room would be uplifting. For whom? I'm still out on that one. I rode the bike for only a week before almost hitting the center divide when returning on Kirker Pass Road, and deciding that dying of prostate cancer was the better option.

My sessions were scheduled for 10:30 each weekday morning (11:00 on nine of the days). We, all the patients, had bar coded IDs. We'd scan ourselves in at the reception desk - across from a table of cookies, graham crackers, juice, fruit and coffee, then pass through white gates, looking bizarrely like the entrance to a bar in a western shootout, grab appropriate garb - for me it was pajama bottoms, suit up in one of five dressing rooms, and wait together in a cozy, five-chair room until called to our assigned machine. It was in this waiting room I realized how lucky I'd been in this life. My wait-mates, both men and women, ranged from early middle to late old age. They came in wheelchairs or with canes, some with little hair, some so disfigured they were difficult to look at. Many were upbeat and clowning. Not once did I hear a complaint.

After some positioning by one of the two therapists, John or Reynaldo, my time on the machine would be less than half an hour. They would align me by the three dots tattooed by my hips, snap verification x-rays, and leave me to drift and dream.

The machine would shake me into place - then whir, rotate and click around for roughly twenty-five minutes while I lay motionless on its steel slab.

The staff and I parted company the last Friday in September, accompanied, on my part, by a strange sadness. We exchanged gifts, small boxes of chocolates from me, a certificate of completion, signed by all, from them. I liked this gang, they did their job with passion. This isn't the place to bitch about this or that ache, but I'd be remiss if I didn't share my belief that the notion of a free-lunch medical procedure is a fallacy. Urinating became increasingly difficult as my walnut grew in protest to its abuse - on and off lethargy became my companion for the next few months, and gastrointestinal issues which I am loath to share, and which destroy valuable morning time, linger on.

As crude an indicator of prostate cancer as it is, PSA monitoring is ongoing after an attempted cure. It's a delight, dancing time, when it hits its nadir, its lowest point. Mine did just that, falling down to 0.89 on December 2, 2010, fourteen months and a week after that last session on the machine. By then I'd read of General Petraeus's very similar treatment at Walter Reed Army Medical Center. That became my health explanation to any new query: "Yea, I had the same thing done as General Petraeus. Uh-hah, only six months after him."

It's déjà vu all over again.
Lawrence Peter Berra, aka Yogi

Then less than a year later, arbitrarily, without warning, and in completely bad taste, it started up again - my PSA, that pleasure sapping, little-meaning measure of unwanted protein in the blood, began its rise - hasn't stopped - and has increased, not once but seven times, to this year's 2013 reading of 5.73. After three consecutive upswings following radiation therapy, the medicos called it biochemical recurrence, relapse, failure - 'biochemical', when PSA is the only sign of disease - no pain, no biopsy, nothing but a growing PSA. This PSA-princess's kiss of possible disaster awakened my dormant engineer to the obvious, the need to find, once again, tools squeezed out in the laboratories - the best guides to salvaging and predicting the future of a failed cure.

Salvage is the word the men in white use for cure after failure. *Merriam-Webster Online* gives as its second definition of salvage: "(a) property saved from destruction in a calamity (as a wreck or fire), or (b) something extracted (as from rubbish) as valuable or useful." Its first definition has to do with nautical stuff. For me, predicting came first, how long would I be around? Extracting life from rubbish would have to wait. On my first go around, I'd harkened sloppily, far too wishfully, to the popular, upbeat literature, the hype that read: "Most men will be cancer free after undergoing therapy, radiation or surgery." 70% shouldn't have read 'most' to an engineer.

I quickly learned how to calculate the approximate date of my relapse, July 29, 2011, a year and ten months after treatment. That time span would be a survival clue. Another, more frequently cited indicator of cancer progression, the speed at which PSA increases post failure, is known as the PSA doubling time, or PSADT. Mine appeared to be around eight months - kind of *meso meso* - more than twelve is good, less than three, scary. Mind you this is all statistical, an engineer's delight. There was, as one might expect, a complication. Dicy, is conservative for a youngster, my new urologist - Darf had made good his threat to retire - had me on finasteride - this time legally - to shrink my prostate and make it easier for me to pee. If you'll recall, that's the drug that lowers PSA.

A fourth-generation urologist, Dicy had been a commercial real estate broker before returning to his heritage and taking up the scalpel. I felt a kinship with him for that temporary rebellion. For a while he even laughed at my disparaging asides about Dalp. Then, over time, he settled in, becoming another in the group to take date-of-birth seriously. Colleagues may have gotten to him. He acknowledged my PSAs read considerably lower than they would have if I was not on finasteride, but failed to provide me with any way to extrapolate truer values. In particular, I wanted to know how long it would be before I got accurate information once I'd stopped taking the drug. It wasn't doing any good anyway. I couldn't get an answer. It was back to Google.

This search proved the hardest of all - uncovering only one source - a paper written back in 대한비뇨기과학회지

제 48 권 제 12 호 2007. I guess that's sometime in 2007. Its title Finasteride를 투여하는 전립선비대증 환자에서 전립선용적이 혈청 전립선특이항원과 유리형 전립선특이항원 백분율에 미치는 영향 wasn't much help either, but I was grateful someone had done their homework, even if they were off in Korea. Thankfully, it came with the subtitle, "The Influence of Prostate Volume on the Serum Prostate-specific Antigen Levels ... during Finasteride Medication," and 'Purpose,' in English, as well as a set of tables. Numbers are universal. I now had enough information to estimate my fate with a nomogram worked out by folks at New York's Memorial Sloan-Kettering Cancer Center. It used my T-stage and Gleason score at time of original diagnosis, and my current PSA and PSADT, to predict that I had a median progression-free survival of 14 months - that's the time before metastatic cancer would show up in a bone scan. The odds were about one in four I'd be bone scan free for two years. Dicy had ordered such a scan soon after my PSA started ballooning. I was fine for now. His only recommendation to me was Androgen Deprivation, men's hormone therapy in reverse.

Without testosterone, prostate cancer growth slows down to a crawl. An anti-hormone regimen works like castration. The American Cancer Society lists the 'possible side effects of hormone therapy' - their parenthetical explanations, not mine - as: "reduced or absent libido (sexual desire), impotence (erectile dysfunction), hot flashes which may get better or even go away over time, breast tenderness and growth of breast tissue, osteoporosis (bone thinning) which can lead to broken bones, anemia (low red blood cell counts), decreased mental sharpness, loss of muscle mass, weight gain, fatigue, increased cholesterol, and depression." Not something to jump at.

Salvage procedures for prostate cancer are, not too surprisingly, the same as the originals: hack, zap, freeze or bake. Only now the gland may be more obstinate, trickier to work with, depending upon its initial handling. For example, during a prostatectomy it's harder to sew up a severed urethra made crispy by radiation. Pondering these options was less fun than the first time around. I knew no one who'd been through it twice. Ernie remained out of touch, and even if he'd been around it felt odd, kind of pauvre moi, to bring it up with anyone, except maybe Joyce - and then how do you ask a woman what she'd do if her prostate was fucked-up? I was on my own. With a prostatectomy requiring great skill, HIFU still banned in the U.S., and radiation like adding insult to gastrointestinal injury, only cryoablation prevailed. These obsessive conjectures blissfully ended on reading an article in U.C. Berkeley's quarterly alumni rag, *California*.

I usually flip ahead to "In Memoriam," part of the magazine's last few pages, see if anyone I know isn't anymore, leave it by my bedside to read later, and forget about it. This time, Spring 2012, I didn't make it to the obits, but got stopped by W. Ravven's short piece, subtitled "A scientist trains the immune system to recognize and attack cancer." It told of James Allison's attempt to get T-cells to attack cancer, an autoimmune story in reverse. Yes! I thought of Joan - how after they'd cut off her breast they wouldn't listen to her, gave her meds she couldn't handle, and how she gave up on them, the whole doctor lot. What if there'd been an effort like this back then? I mentioned the article to Dicy on my next visit. Told him the idea of immunotherapy really appealed to me. "Oh yea, Provenge," he said, and later, "I think UCSF might be doing a clinical trial."

> *"There you go again."*
> Joe Lieberman, Ronald Reagan,
> Kenny Rogers, Sarah Palin, and others

There it was - way too easy, http://cancer.ucsf.edu/clinical-trials brought me right to Protocol No. 115510, "Randomized Phase II Trial of a DNA Vaccine Encoding Prostatic Acid Phosphatase (pTVG-HP) versus GM-CSF Adjuvant in Patients with Non-Metastatic Prostate Cancer." Perfect, I'd call them - but first I wanted to find out more about how immunotherapy worked. I crossed my fingers about some of Wikipedia's reporting and looked to see what they had to say. It took a few extra clicks since they identified Provenge by its generic name, sipuleucel-T. I first learned it cost $93,000 for a one-month three-infusion treatment. And second, that it "extended survival by median 4.1 months." That pronouncement baffled my engineering soul. Even more so, when later I saw in a *Forbes* magazine report: "Provenge boosted survival by 4.1 months." No mention of median, distribution or sample size - the number was meaningless. I amused myself by imagining a group of eleven men, each paying the ninety-three big ones - the first six lived exactly 4.1 months after treatment, while the last five lived on for another 20 years. Their median survival would then be 4.1 months, while the average would make it for 11¼ years. Not that bad a gamble. Those reporters weren't doing much to promote immunotherapy, or to help Dendreon, Provenge's manufacturer, sell stock.

I found Wiki's section on the process's mechanism pretty obscure. Think vaccine. The body's white cells don't normally recognize enough of the invading cancer cells as baddies. A vaccine nudges the immune system into taking a better look. In this procedure a type of T-cell is taken from the donor patient and exposed to a prostate cancer protein along with a kicker molecule that will stimulate cell reproduction. These loaded blood cells are re-infused into their host where they and their buddies will now know - by eyeing the protein - who's an offender, and then go after it.

Was Provenge for me? Immunotherapy certainly, but at Provenge cost I'd want to keep the same - geezer active - state of health I was in, and have 11¼ years guaranteed. I soon learned Medicare pays for it - yep, the whole 93 Gs - but only if it's used "according to approved criteria." Namely, "for the treatment of asymptomatic or minimally symptomatic metastatic castrate resistant (hormone refractory) prostate cancer." Thankfully, I didn't qualify; I had no proven metastasis and hadn't been castrated, chemically or otherwise. A close scrutiny of UCs protocol showed they had no such restrictions. One only needed a good healthy case of biochemical relapse.

I sent an email to the contact address on the clinical trial listing and got a phone reply within the week. Everything I would like to have heard, I heard. I needed to provide only a few salient records of my history with the disease. With typical courtesy and alacrity, Sergio transferred all they required. Two months and one week later, a miraculously short time period for medical decision-making and scheduling, I was on my way to San Francisco's Western Addition for a meeting with Ducu, **U**niversity of **C**alifornia **u**rologist, at the UCSF medical Center, Mt. Zion.

The experience I had at the Center, a tribute to every staff member I encountered - from front desk clerk to medical top gun, popped up my spirits, elevated me like a blissful pull of happy grass. After a thorough physical exam by an associate, a resident-in-training, Ducu, focused and intense, reviewed key elements of the trial. Joyce had driven to Washington state for a visit with her daughter and two-year-old grand-twins. She couldn't take notes. Ducu pointed out double blind study meant half of us would get no vaccine, not sipuleucel-T in this case, but the pTVG-HP they were testing. Not bad odds, 50-50, and in my estimation even if you didn't get the vaccine, there were no losers. Everyone got GM-CSF, a growth factor used to stimulate production of a variety of white blood cells. Ducu went on to assure me I was in fine shape physically, had a PSADT within their range of interest, and an encouraging Gleason score. A tad dramatically, he tore off the last page of a fat, clinical trial consent form and sketched out his summary of my options and what might be going on in my body.

The drawings showed three possibilities, a circle, a circle within a rectangle, and a stick figure man in a box. My cancer could be local - the circle, local-regional - the circle in a rect-angle, or it could have spread and be systemic - the little guy in the box. He asked why I hadn't had a biopsy after the radiation therapy, and we bantered on awhile about age issues and dis-crimination. He urged me to have one done now, pointed out that the trial was not a cure and that if I was the circle, with or without the rectangle, I might still be curable. Ducu said he would write Dicy, left the room to ask a colleague about him, and returned saying, "D??? knows him, says he's fine." Then he changed his mind about writing and added, "I'll call him tomorrow." Both of us signed the consent form. He left, and a young woman, Beth, appeared, told me the coordinator of the study I'd just signed onto would be on vacation until the following week, and would call when she returned. She gave me a handful of her own cards and left.

I didn't hear from the coordinator as expected, called the number on the cards - Beth's number, got a name - Allison, and contact number. I rang it a bunch over the next sever-al days before getting a live voice. Meanwhile, I spoke with

Dicy and set a date for the biopsy, a simple in-office procedure I judged he'd seemed reluctant to do before speaking
with Ducu. I came on like a bear on that first direct one-on-
one with Allison, blustering into my old, not very smart, Mo-
torola Razr, "I expected to hear from you before now. I'm
told you've been back from vacation for a couple of weeks."
Her voice, constrained, a bit testy and slow to begin, seeped
out, "I've been waiting for all your information to come in. I
need to see if you're qualified." "Qualified," came back my response in a greater number of decibels than intended. "I'm in
the study, Ducu signed me, I need scheduling dates from you,
and ..." "You need to have some tests done, two more PSAs,
a bone scan, and ... " "What date will my blood be drawn for
the vaccine?" And so it went, until Allison stated slowly and
firmly, "I'm the person responsible for seeing that all the criteria required by the study are met. Ducu has nothing to do with
it." Would I ever learn?

The whole cancer crap was getting to me. I remembered
Joan's talk of leading a life - not being a patient. "You can't let
the disease identify you," she'd said. Strangely enough, cancer
itself had never bothered me, given me one iota of trouble.
Treatment, office calls, tests, decisions, just being in the system
- when you're in the system, you're in the system - mentally at
least - that's what was painful. I'd say the worst was agonizing
over what to do next - who to listen to - nobody fucking knew
anything, and everybody thought they did. I tried to adhere to
Joan's advice, dined out with Joyce, took small trips, walked
and worked out on my rowing machine, but it seems I only got
out of my jeans to see some doctor, not to be out on the town.

After the biopsy, I got back to Allison and made my peace.
She told me what tests I still needed, put me in contact with
an insurance helper, and set up a tentative start date. You'd
think, I did anyway, that all clinical trial costs would be gratis,
paid for by the outfit doing the research. Not so. They take
care of whatever's being tested, in this case the infusions; all
else - exams, tests and consultations - are up to the applicant.
I'd already been through a hassle with Health Net for my first
visit with Ducu. Now, I learned, I'd need another visit with
him plus the tests. The system does what it can to keep up the
anxiety level.

Dicy gave me a call as soon as he had my biopsy results. Happily, I thought at the time, they had found cancer in five of the twelve cores he'd sent to the lab, down from the pre-treatment ten of twelve. Happily because I might not be a stick figure in a box, only a local circle - the cancer may not have spread. It was impossible to know for sure. No scan definitively rules out cancer. A bone scan will show the obvious, anomalies in skeletal growth that may indicate cancer has reached the bone; a finding that's likely taken time. In the interim, any micrometatastes, small numbers of cancer cells spread beyond the original site, won't be seen. Other techniques, CTs, MRIs, ... , also look for clues, some found in the pelvis, some in lymph nodes. If nothing is uncovered, great but ... .

Ducu, next to call, offered his congratulations - I guess I can call them that - and prompted me to contact his colleague Duco, **U**niversity of **C**alifornia **o**ncologist, the investigator running UCSF's clinical salvage brachytherapy - radioactive seed zapping - trial. Yes, l have to admit to being a slow learner. It took two weeks for me to fully understand I'd been key party in a "Catch 22." When Allison stopped me from going on about results of the PSA I had just received and the good news that Health Net had finally authorized my upcoming visit with Ducu by asserting, "You're no longer in the trial, ... " - shock and complete disbelief don't fully cover my reaction. She had to be wrong. "We can't have anyone in the trial with confirmed disease," she repeated.

A visit with Deat followed each twist in my search for the cure. Once every three months I would sit in one of his examining rooms reviewing, dumping, listening. I always came away feeling better. I had pressed him by phone to call Ducu, to find out what really went down. Typical compassion accompanied his explanation. "The study only covered biochemical, not real evidence. You knew you were out if you had metastases, you didn't know you were also out if you had confirmed local disease." "But he didn't tell me I had to have a biopsy," I protested, "I thought it was just a suggestion." Before parting, we agreed cryoablation, freezing the gland to death, might be my best option. Many weeks passed before I looked again at Ducu's sketch. There in the bottom left corner he had drawn two small rectangles, one beneath the other. To the right of the top box he'd written 'DNA vaccine trial,' the box below read 'Biopsy.' Neither box had been checked.

Fast forward. Ducu, without further input from me, got insurance authorization and left directions for me to make an appointment with Duco. Like Ducu, Duco proved an engaging researcher with able assistants, a nurse to take sexual and waste elimination data, and a resident to look me over. As a competent salesman, he made a good case for his high-dose-rate seeds, a technique basically offensive to me. Joyce took notes. Before we parted he asked if he could give me a physical then, or wait and have another consultation if I decided positively. "Sure go ahead," I answered. His exam was a DRE.

Dicy punted when I called about cryoablation, said he didn't do them anymore, and referred me to fellow urologist Dwot, way out there. At our first encounter, after fencing around some initial doc-speak, we seemed to connect. He laughed at date-of-birth, and at my not liking the man in the adjoining office, Dalp. More to the point, he talked almost like an engineer, ordered a more meaningful scan, ProstaScint, designed to look directly for a specific prostate antigen, and asked me to come back for a flow test. Joyce took notes. Unfortunately, only two places in the Bay Area could do the scan, Stanford and UCSF. Health Net didn't authorize it.

The flow test is kind of like writing your name in the snow when you were a kid, only you aim at a bucket with meters, not at the white stuff. I've done them before and always fail, trickling not squirting. The results bothered Dwot. He took a closer look through a cystoscope, peeking inside from penis tip through bladder. "If we do the cryo you might not be able to urinate," he warned afterwards. I guess I looked pretty downcast, because he added quickly, "I could do a transurethral resection of the prostate first, before cryoablation. That would open up the space in your urethra below your bladder." "Is that anything like a TURP?" I asked. His answer, a dry, "It is a TURP," somehow surprisingly amused me; I don't typically like being caught stupid.

Tomorrow is TURP day for me. Dwot will go up my urethra with some instruments and cut out a piece of the old prostate. He'll finish the job with a laser, a fairly new technique, that often reduces healing time. I got off the phone with the pre-op nurse about an hour ago. It was mostly questions from her, with answers from me. She'll pass my medical history on to an anesthesiologist, and said whoever it is would call me tonight.

Since seeing Dwot I've been exercising my urine-flow-cut-off-muscle - don't know what it's called - by doing kegels. Four years ago contemplating having my urethra snipped in two during a prostatectomy seemed a piece of cake; today, thinking of a simple puncture through it, scares me.

I decided to glance back over this chapter before calling it a day, and while rereading what I wrote early on - "There are things I want to finish and I can't get death out of my mind," I couldn't help but think of what Gene Hackman (Little Bill Daggett) said to Clint Eastwood (William Munny) in *Unforgiven*: "I don't deserve this ... to die like this. I was building a house." And Eastwood's wispy reply, "Deserve's got nothin' to do with it."

Part III

The Unknown Years

Chapter 10

The Unknown Years - Junior High

*Enter ye in at the strait gate: for wide is the gate,
and broad is the way, that leadeth to destruction,
and many there be which go in thereat:*
Matt. 7:13

That short period of time, those days between early fall 1938 and the summer of 1941 when the world to the east and the one to the west exploded - most of America, the good old U. S. of A. including even Navy town, San Diego, didn't seem to give it a thought. In September '38, two-and-a-half weeks after String began classes at his new junior high, Germany received permission from its neighbors to the south and west to annex a part of the sovereign state of Czechoslovakia. It was a heady time for both String and British Prime Minister Neville Chamberlain. The Prime Minister claimed to have achieved "peace in our time." String felt alive, liberated.

Why he had begun feeling stifled by the familiar blocks he loved so much, the ones surrounding the two homes he thought of as his own, he couldn't say. He'd backed away, it seemed long ago, from his Goon Club pals, and "corny" was the word he used to describe those idyllic days when Rose packed him a lunch and the three of them, Pinto, Lima and he, took streetcars to the Coronado ferry, where for a nickel they'd spend an entire day riding back and forth across the bay. He knew only that where he now found himself was exactly where he wanted to be - right there - attending a school butted up tight against the zoo and the park he cherished. South, beyond the fence at the back of the school, he could squint through the chain link fence and catch sight of a camel or a fast-moving ostrich, the sounds of monkeys and peafowl were omnipresent. A fifteen-minute walk farther on would take him to the Museum of Man and the art gallery, the very hub of Balboa Park.

Auntie Bell and Aunt Tanny had, a year earlier, given him a junior membership in the San Diego Museum of Art. It came with membership card, a print of Goya's *Boy in Red*, and several hands-on activities, including making a papier-mâché diorama of the park itself in a tower room of the imposing old Museum of Man - just a block west of the gallery. The painting reproduction pleased and puzzled him. Was it all in the artist's imagination, or did the model really hold a bird on a leash, and with cats watching? He hung it on his bedroom wall next to the three-foot cardboard cutout of archangel Gabriel, a protector above his bed for longer than he could remember.

The skinny kid, String, never felt shy, self-aware, when wandering about either museum. Artifact or fine art, he looked on without discrimination. One object, El Greco's *Penitent Saint Peter*, always caught him, stopped him, held his attention. He no more knew why than he did of his physical growth, or his current contentment with school. He'd sit on the wooden bench in the center of the hall and stare at it, overcome with the same eerie lift he'd gotten while seated in Grace Lutheran's nave gazing at the beams above. Later, he would notice how Saint Peter's thin, Ambuehl-like face clashed with a much muscled, Irving-like body - but that had nothing to do with the way the image spoke to him.

His family had picnicked at the Pepper Grove off Park Boulevard at the edge of Balboa Park since his infancy - Rose providing gastronomical comfort from her wicker basket. It was there Carolyn first walked. String liked to suck sweetness from the drupes, the little pink fruits plucked off the park's namesake trees, and made a distance contest out of spitting their woody seeds. Rose didn't object, as she often would, to the sampling of unpackaged treats, her farmgirl freedom reigned in by Carolyn's bout with trench mouth - a misfortune attributed by Dr. Belford to dandelion chewing. These outings and an occasional concert at the Organ Pavilion were String's introduction, but the big fair, the California Pacific International Exposition of 1935 and 1936, made the park his personal play place. He had traipsed about the exhibits endlessly, watched Queen Elizabeth throw a lamb shank over her shoulder at the Royal Globe Theater countless times, and continued to prize the five-inch-long model of a 1935 Ford Sedan he'd watched being molded out of rubber inside the Ford Building. That blue beauty had made many a trip over Cappy Swift's toy car roads.

At a few minutes before 8:00 a.m. on Halloween morning, Monday, October 31, 1938, String sidled onto the seat of his scuffed oak chair behind its built-in desk shelf. This first month at Roosevelt Junior High had opened new doors, but he would revert tonight, cross-dress in a Red Riding Hood costume, and escort his sister trick-or-treating around the old North Park neighborhood. Teen tricking was still a possibility that year; many a family would wake the next morning to soaped windows or toilet-papered trees.

The bell rang, school had begun, and his homeroom teacher, Winifred Perry, hadn't yet arrived. It was a first. The plainly dressed, tall, stern-faced woman in her late forties had always before nodded unsmilingly at each of her charges as they made their way to their assigned places. Today, carrying a stack of newspapers - the local *San Diego Union*, *The New York Times*, and *The Christian Science Monitor* - she arrived at sixteen past the hour and into bedlam, a class of screaming, paper-throwing, out-of-control vandals. With one look around the room, one glance from left to right, a single scowl, she restored a demanded imperative - thirty-three angelic pre-teens, hands folded and resting motionlessly on thirty-three wooden desk tops.

String did not know what to make of Miss Perry. She was a teacher unlike any he'd had before. As Rose once grouped his playmates, he placed teachers, present and past, into one of five categories: nice, gross, OK, pretty or weird - there were no overlaps. He had no time to consider where this enigmatic presence standing at the blackboard, up front, belonged. She began speaking in a deep, blunt, though carefully modulated voice, and with no mention of the chaos just past. "How many of you heard the story on the radio last night about the United States being invaded by Martians?" There were a few quickly squelched giggles, but no one raised a hand. "How many read about it in this morning's paper?" Still no hands. "OK, let me see hands from everyone who believes there are people living on Mars." A general sense of unease filled the room; many stared down at their laps, others looked toward a friend for the answer to "What does she want from us?"

If she felt any sympathy for her students' silence, nothing in her manner showed it. She wrote Martians on the board, then glancing at the seating chart on her desk, repeated her query, this time directly to the unfortunate girl whose name caught her eye on the chart. "Do you believe creatures live on Mars, Doreen?" The tiny brunette, second row center, put a hand to her mouth, moved her head side to side, and, in almost a whisper, ventured, "I hadn't thought about it." "Think about it now, please," Miss Perry implored, as gently as her nature permitted. Doreen felt almost released. "It ... it doesn't ... creatures ... it doesn't sound right," she managed. "Good!, Good!" the corners of the teacher's lips turned up ever so slightly. "I hope by the time you get to high school, you'll all be able to sort out what is true and what is not. That's our job here."

Miss Perry went on to explain. "Last night, a young actor, Orson Welles, read a story on the radio - his version of an old H. G. Wells science fiction story." She stopped as if she hadn't thought of it before, and threw in the aside, "No, the two men aren't related, they even spell their names differently." Then quickly went on. "Mr. Welles with another actor, Mr. Houseman, told it like it was a news broadcast. A lot of people thought it actually was. You see, here's the tragedy. Many hid, armed themselves with guns, even tried to leave the cities where their homes are." Her voice dropped. "They were unable to think clearly, think 'it doesn't sound right,' like Doreen just did."

Near the end of the period, after further explanation and some actual class interaction, Miss Perry could no longer avoid the large inappropriate grin seemingly frozen on String's face. "Do you have something to add?" she asked him. "Just wondering why anybody would have wanted to dial the radio to a story yesterday. Sunday's Jack Benny night." Luckily, the second period bell rang coincidently with the pronouncement of his final word "night."

For String, these were the years of unremembered friends, a time when quite unconsciously he would begin tapping into humor, his most likely path toward recognition. Success hinged largely on whether his nouveau-Ambuehl wit would make any sense, let alone be funny, away from home. His teachers of the absurd - first relatives, now radio - fashioned his vocabulary, his speech, his notion of timing. And radio came to mean much more to him - a shared family experience, a bit of still-remaining group glue. Jack Benny, for one, literally stuck them together.

To accommodate Fred Allen's 6:00 p.m. *Town Hall Tonight*, Rose served dinner late on Wednesday nights. It left only a half-hour to eat before *The Lone Ranger* aired, a weekly time-crunch concern for String. Allen listening, too edgy for both String and Carolyn and even a strain for Rose, came as a concession to daddy, who implausibly laughed more during that show than during Benny's. Many other programs held them near the large, shiny walnut console, their model 37-630X Philco, pushed tight against the living room wall between the burgundy sofa and the narrow vent door to the right of the front entrance.

FDR's fireside chats had always been among the never-missed. The President's mellow resonant voice soothed String more even than Pastor D's, and in both cases - the words meaningful to him or not - he sat attentively, enrapt. Roosevelt had become kind of a magic overlord, much like Prince Valiant, one of String's favorite comic characters since first appearing in the papers a few months before he'd turned eleven. The voice that brought him so much comfort, visibly agitated his dad. Irving's body moved restlessly. He scowled. He shook his head. He presented a complete contrast to that of his composed young son. The somber stated declaration, "I voted for him the first time he ran - the only time I ever voted for a democrat - and I've always regretted it," was one String often heard him repeat. As the years passed and world events unfolded, he noted his dad listened to the chats with ever-increasing, knit-brow attention.

As good as that first year at Roosevelt had been - it never occurred to him that the school had been named for Rough Rider Teddy, not his idol, President Franklin D. - String welcomed vacation. For starters, ten cents would get him into Saturday matinees at the North Park Theater where he could sit through two features, a cartoon, a newsreel and the weekly serial. This summer, after completing *Flash Gordon*, they'd be starting the first *Lone Ranger* serial, released just the previous year by Republic Pictures. Now, he'd be able to actually see his masked hero, as well as continue to hear him yell at Silver during the Monday, Wednesday, and Friday night radio adventures. String wouldn't know it until becoming a teen a couple of weeks later, but listening would become even better. The birthday present he would receive from his parents that year - a Philco, model 39-71T battery-powered, portable radio, that looked like a vintage tweed suitcase about the size of a large lunchbox - filled many of his previously unbelievable dreams. Wireless portable communication had been an in-the-sky ideal, a vision, since his first crystal set. Now, half that wish would come true. It would be many years before the other, the transmission half, would become a reality - even Dick Tracy's 2-Way Wrist Radio was eight years off.

String both looked forward to, and dreaded, an announced upcoming visit from his Uncle August. An arrival date had yet to be determined. When he did come, he came with a bang - literally. Unbeknown to their nephew, August and Bessie had parked on Landis Street late Monday night, the third of July, and made themselves welcome at Grandma's - now Sophia's - house. At a little past seven the following morning, String woke with a start - deafened, heart-thumpingly scared, and sitting abruptly upright - to the sound of an incredible bang coming from somewhere between his bedroom window and the Coleman house. He didn't hear the familiar guffaw, but saw his uncle's face pressed up against the outside screen.

The "Happy Independence Day, Neph" also did not make it past String's ringing ears. The initial greeting came by way of a now-illegal, big red, 1½ inch-long by 9/16 inch inside-diameter firecracker, a 'salute,' originally called the M-80, and made to simulate artillery fire for the military.

He genuinely liked his Uncle August, but gosh, must he be with him when he has everyone looking for the dog that's barking near the butcher counter in Whitman's grocery or from the back of the streetcar. One time the conductor even stopped the train and walked to the rear looking. String thought of other things, too. He had considered himself a runner after his uncle, seeing him galloping down the beach about six years ago, had asked, "Are you running or flying?" Now he wondered, did August mean it, or was he making fun of my big ears? And the stomach pounding. After Irving had told him how strong he could get by tightening his abdominal muscles and beating on them with his fists, August seemed to do it at random, privately or in public. It came across as an odd kind of way to demonstrate admiration for his brother-in-law.

August would not see Irv on this visit, nor would the neighborhood viewers of his many previous fireworks displays. String told his uncle, "Guess he's gone across the country again. He'll probably be bringing back another car." The boy hadn't given it much thought. Dad would either be away somewhere - all the way to the east coast, to one of the hot springs, Warner's or Murrieta, just around town - or be found sleeping on the living room couch. Little irked Rose as much as Irv's, "Places to go, people to see, things to do," answer to her "Where are you going?" question.

The M-80 explosion wasn't the only silence shatterer that summer. Irving returned from his ballroom bouncing gig early one morning, emptied the cartridges from his 38-caliber revolver, snapped off a few empty chamber rounds at the little black bull's-eye he had pasted over the calendar against the kitchen cooler, then reloaded and went to the fridge for a snack. His hunger appeased, and not quite ready for bed, he'd take a last few pistol snaps when - bang-kaboom - the pistol kicked, its exiting slug making ugly noises as it crunched its way through relish, jams, and home-brewed beer before finding its way into the adjoining dry foods cupboard and coming to rest past the little girl with an umbrella printed on the cylindrical box of Morton salt. "When It Rains It Pours®." String heard none of it this time, having fallen asleep beneath archangel Gabriel, cradling his precious portable, and listening to station KFSD coming live from the top of the U.S. Grant Hotel.

SEPTEMBER 1, 1939

"I sit in one of the dives/On Fifty-second Street/
Uncertain and afraid
As the clever hopes expire/Of a low dishonest decade:
Waves of anger and fear/Circulate over the bright/
And darkened lands of the earth,
Obsessing our private lives;
The unmentionable odour of death/Offends the
September night. ..."

W.H. Auden

Miss Perry greeted her returning students more somberly than ever. It seemed natural enough to them. Why would anyone want to stop vacationing? In truth, no place suited Winifred Perry more than her classroom. It might have surprised them even more to know she understood, actually respected, teenagers. She sacrificed her teaching that day to let them have their fun - talk about the good times they'd just had, and orient themselves for their coming classes. Tomorrow would be soon enough to talk of the horror that had begun just three days earlier. She knew it would mean little to them; she also knew she could not ignore it.

And ye shall hear of wars and rumours of wars: see
that ye be not troubled: for all these things must come
to pass, but the end is not yet.

Matt. 24:6

For the past five years the world had been cooking, throwing off a little steam. The restless, the ruthless, the hungry, the ambitious, the oppressed all tossed gasoline on embers smoldering since the end of the "war to end all wars" - Italy into Ethiopia - Spain onto Spaniards - Japan into China - Czechoslovakia ... ... gone. Now, as the fall semester commenced, boots began stomping, first west to east, then east to west across Europe. Stalin's foreign minister Vyacheslav Molotov, whose name became celebrated as an incendiary 'cocktail' thrown during the Russo-Finnish winter war, signed a treaty of non-aggression - in truth, a secret protocol defining 'spheres of influence' - with his strangely contrary counterpart, Hitler's foreign minister Joachim von Ribbentrop. Over a thousand planes and two thousand tanks helped propel the German boots into a desperately outmanned, outgunned country. By month's end, Poland had been ripped apart and claimed by the two politically disparate powers. Two days after the siege began, Great Britain and France, honoring their guarantee of Poland's border, formally declared war against the Germans. That great conflict, World War II, had begun.

Life went on. Irving had purchased a piano a few years back, a gift for princess Carolyn on her eighth birthday. She'd done pretty well. String didn't think much of it when she played "The Rabbit Revels and Romps Away," but her tempo when playing Pieczonka's 'simplified-score' "Tarantella" impressed him. He'd had a number of music makers, tin-flutes and slide-whistles, as well as his mother's old zither and Grandpa's accordion; now, he wanted to try the piano. Carolyn's teacher had a full schedule and recommended a compatriot, Benjamin Locke, whom, she said, worked well with boys.

Locke met String's needs, if not the other way around. Since he preferred his grand piano to the little spinet - pushed up against the inside living room wall to the front of the yellow armchair, he'd pick String up from home every Thursday afternoon after school and drive him to his place in East San Diego. He drove with no hands on the steering wheel whenever not threatened by an imminent collision. When asked about it, he mumbled something about the need to live dangerously, and told the boy he practiced the tenets of Rosicrucianism. The connection between that organization and reckless driving never became clear, and his passenger never shared this, the most interesting part of his lesson, with others.

String's progression didn't compare favorably with that of his sister. No matter what the musical offering, he'd attempt to play it faster and faster. Beat the old man's time seemed to triumph over other practice goals. In this second year at Roosevelt, Locke spoke with Rose and recommended a different instrument be tried. The timing couldn't have been better. The junior high orchestra suffered from no cellists that year, and the director offered instrument loans and free afternoon training to anyone interested. String may not have acquired much additional aptitude for music, but it did improve him physically. He had been walking to school and pocketing the allocated dollar-a-month streetcar pass money. Now he'd do the walk with a cello - no small feat - down Landis, left on Texas, past the park swimming pool, and up Morley Field Drive to school. As a toddler, he'd taken that route to the park with his uncle and learned: "Texas tecks-us to the park."

Music, literature, paintings, none of the arts commanded prominence in the house on Pershing Avenue. When upbeat, Irv continued off-key singing of old war favorites, and Rose encouraged her daughter's piano practice, but no new recordings had been acquired, and the long-forgotten Victor Victrola could be found stored, unused next door in Sophia's front room. Dishes, pitchers, gold-trimmed tea sets, together with ceramic knick-knacks, including a couple of Hummel figurines, constituted the household's complement of art objects.

String grew up on classic *Mother Goose* and *Uncle Wiggily*. He doesn't remember seeing his mother read, except out-loud to Carolyn and him. Irv read *The San Diego Union* daily, long and laboriously, section by section, moving slowly, carefully, sometimes running a finger beneath each printed word. The only books belonging to him alone, *Everyman's Calculus*, *Everyman's Algebra*, and T.G. Cooke's *Finger Prints Secret Service Crime Detection*, could be found side-by-side on a shelf of the built-in bookcase behind the yellow chair to the right of the fireplace. The most prominent and most used volumes, *Funk and Wagnall's New Standard Encyclopedia*, appeared as twenty-five, 6-inch-high, $1\frac{1}{8}$-inch wide, gold-embossed, Dartmouth-green spines, in one long row three shelves up from the floor. The order of the children's books below was disturbed, here and there, by a Halliburton book, String's favorite author - *Seven League Boots*, *The Flying Carpet: Adventures in a Biplane from Timbuktu to Everest and Beyond*, *The Glorious Adventure* - books that pushed him to read and to dream.

It was alleged that one could learn to dance at Roosevelt

Junior High. The activity - for second- and third-year students only - took place in the school gym every Friday immediately following sixth period. Two hours of swing and sway to the recorded music of Tommy Dorsey, Duke Ellington, Glenn Miller, Benny Goodman and others, followed a half-hour of questionable instruction. The girls swung, the boys, with a few notable exceptions, swayed-away. String fought terror to never miss a session. While he desperately wanted to hold, to lead, to spin a beautiful young lady - most looked beautiful to him - around that polished basketball stage, the only contact he made came about tenuously, during the oh so awkward teaching period, when, right hand at his partner's waist, left blissfully clasping hers, he moved with the grace of a penguin, not an average penguin, but a stiff, half-frozen one.

After the lesson, the boys would line up on one side of the court, the girls on the other; a few remaining on the floor to dance with one-another or with the couple of the braver or more sophisticated lads. One dancer stood out above all others, boy or girl. He dipped and glided, pivoted and guided, his entranced charges - choosing a new hopeful for each dance. String knew only that they called this tall, graceful phantom, George.

He was to hear differently of George later that semester - a baffling contrast to the image he'd formed. It came from Miss Perry during a talk to her homeroom about 'thinking.' No one expected anything unusual to be said; 'thinking' seemed an inexhaustible subject for her. She'd spend most of her teaching day in the laboratory, showing how frogs should be dismembered, how to use a microscope, how to grow mold, and the like. This morning the 'thinking' narrative drifted to an experience she'd had in yesterday's general science class.

"I was explaining heat," she'd begun. "I have several thermometers, some measure Fahrenheit temperature, others centigrade. I showed the class how to convert from one to the other, when we began discussing the range of temperatures animals are able to withstand - polar bears to moths. Someone brought up the solar system and we talked a little about absolute temperature and temperatures on the different planets. I mentioned that life couldn't be sustained on the sun because of the temperature. I was saying it was 'just too hot' when one of my best students couldn't contain himself. He yelled out 'Those creatures on the sun are probably looking down at earth and saying no one can live down there - it's just too cold.' That young man was thinking. He's a year ahead of you, but maybe some of you know him. His name's George, ... George Talbott."

" ... Let us therefore brace ourselves to our duties,
and so bear ourselves, that if the British Empire
and its Commonwealth last for a thousand years,
men will still say, This was their finest hour."
Winston Churchill - June 18, 1940

As much as school pleased, lazy vacation beckoned. Saturday after Saturday, String sat in the darkened North Park Theater watching the latest *Movietone News*, films of bombs falling on the British people. It was no more real to him than the new Columbia Pictures' serial, *Mandrake the Magician*, his primary reason for not missing a single Saturday - no more real than the pictures on the bubble gum cards he'd once collected, those showing Italian guns pointed toward Ethiopians with spears.

France fell near the end of June that year. Only one major Western European enemy remained pitted against Germany. The Nazis had a plan, Unternehmen Seelöwe - Operation Sea Lion. They would cripple England from the air, then conquer her with amphibious troops from across the Channel. The plan unfolded in the North Sea where the Luftwaffe, the German air force, destroyed over 2,500 merchant ships before turning to the Isle itself, where sustained assaults began day after day against the airfields and radar stations of the RAF, the Royal Air Force. The Germans could put more than three-and-a-half times the number of planes into the air - on any given day - than their British counterparts. Even more frightening, the British had lost many of her pilots over France. Training new ones took time. They could build three new planes during the time it took to train two pilots,

Then - after Portland is bombed, after Andover is bombed, after Southampton is bombed - the unexpected begins. Forty Luftwaffe's planes are brought down by Spitfires and flak; seventy-four more, launched from Denmark and Norway, go down. The Luftwaffe's commander, Hermann Goering, orders his fighter pilots to challenge the Spitfires in the sky rather than risk his bombers in attempts to pound them on the ground. It doesn't work - airfields are hammered once again. Two hundred RAF fighters are lost, but the Luftwaffe loses more, three hundred and thirty planes.

As the fall semester got underway, Miss Perry tried to provide her disinterested class with news of the conflict. String's thoughts were elsewhere; besides, he'd heard it all before, seen it all on *Movietone News*. This would be his last year at Roosevelt. He wanted to do something special, make a mark, be known. Even so, it proved hard to ignore his teacher's story. She told it straight, unemotionally, but there was sadness in her eyes. Hitler, in an effort to break the resolve, the spirit of the British, had ordered the bombing of London over the bombing of strategic RAF airfields and installations. On the night of September 7th, the skies over London were filled with close to a thousand German planes, 617 fighters and 348 bombers.

String's plan formalized. Why not be top-dog, become the school governor? At Roosevelt, they called the two highest student office holders, governor and lieutenant governor. 7th, 8th, and 9th grade leaders retained the typical designations, class president and vice-president. All officers were selected at a general election held a month after the opening of each fall semester. Candidates for governor and lieutenant governor were voted on by the entire student body, other officers by their respective classes.

String had no doubt he would win, a belief incomprehensible to the first person to learn of his intentions. He needed two faculty sponsors. Miss Perry was now not only his homeroom, but his science teacher. She knew him for pretty much who he was: shy, curious, reasonably - but not exceptionally - bright, and a incorrigible speller. She had just this week written on the blackboard his answer - "gas, lickwood, solid" - to a question in her first science quiz: What are the three states of matter? Today, puzzling as it seemed, she accepted, with her usual sensitive restraint, his form requesting permission to run for governor. "Well yes, of course," she kind of stepped back and forth - foot to foot - almost like one of her teenage pupils, "I'll be glad to sign for you. You know," she added quietly, "there'll be a lot of competition ... ?" but stopped without saying, "Don't be too disappointed, one of the popular kids always wins."

Heart pounding a bit, he approached 22-year-old Ruby Christian for the second signature. He'd only known Ruby - Miss Christian, that is - a little over a week, but he knew he loved her, and their eight-year age difference, wasn't that just a few months more than his parents. Fresh out of U.C.L.A, she'd joined the Roosevelt faculty just this year. She'd be teaching romance languages. That sounded right to String. He'd signed up for her last period Latin class, and found a seat front-row-center in a class of only eighteen students - all but four, girls. Miss Christian, pert, blonde and a bit too heavy by Hollywood standards, taught while sitting cross-legged atop her desk, posed prettily, skirt not far above her knees, and only an arm's length in front of him. Heaven. Unlike Miss Perry, Ruby had no way to judge String's electability. She knew only that he adored her, had carried her books to her car after the Latin Club meeting she'd organized, and seemed to be really into the Latin language. She signed for him willingly, offering any help she could provide. Heaven.

Each student-body-office aspirant received from the principal a four-by-six card showing approval of their candidacy, their name, and the name of the office being sought. String put his in a cheap gold frame bought at the local five and dime, tied a string to its wall-mounting eyelets, and wore it hung round his neck. A week before election day, in the grassy area behind the gym, while chasing a classmate who had grabbed his last Rose-packed lunch cookie, his right toe caught on a low bench he'd almost jumped clear of, causing a hard fall onto his outstretched left hand. Getting back up with his left arm sticking straight out from his elbow, and in the wrong direction, he knew something had broken. Miraculously nothing hurt. He took himself to the nurse's office, all the while holding in place with his right hand the strangely jutting appendage. By her first reaction, he thought the nurse might faint. She didn't.

She summoned Rose and he was taken to Dr Belford's - all the time vowing loudly he would let no one force him into that dark tunnel of dizzying, sickening ether, the anesthesia Belford had used years before during his tonsillectomy. He awoke from far pleasanter nitrous oxide, angry at no one, and wearing a much-admired cast. By noon the next day, $8\frac{1}{2}$ by 11-inch sheets of mimeographed paper bearing the message 'Elect String for Governor - Cast Your Vote for the Boy with the Cast,' could be found pinned to every accessible Roosevelt school wall.

Miss Perry smiled at each of them as they filed into class Monday morning, September 16, 1940. The gesture stunned String and his fellow homeroomers. "Yesterday," she began, without introduction or explanation, "Air Marshal Frederick Bowhill sent every squadron of England's Royal Air Force after the German bombers. They shot down eighty planes. It looks as if the wanton destruction of innocent civilians may stop." Some bombing did continue, but her general prediction proved correct. While that Sunday, now known as "Battle of Britain Day," may well have been the war's pivot point, all, at Roosevelt, was back to normal by Monday afternoon. String, along with fellow members of her general science class, winced as Miss Perry, preparing to demonstrate how bacteria grows, leaned over a Petri dish and spit. It wasn't a gentle feminine spit.

As the curtain went up - sitting on stage with his fellow candidates - he stared out at around seven hundred faces, a crowd greater, maybe twenty-five times greater, than any he'd ever stood before. He expected to feel fear. He didn't. He felt buzzed. His turn to speak, second to last, was the only negative so far. Waiting, he thought, would be tough. It turned out not so. He listened to his opponents. They talked of the school, what a governor, or whatever they were running for did, should do, would do, had done. They bored the crowd. Great. Each candidate, each repetition bored a little more.

When his time did come, String relished it. He introduced himself playfully, he was a natural ham, he knew it. He later heard of someone quipping "a ham can't really be cured." That sounded right. Today he was on fire. Each speaker had been limited to a certain number of minutes, perfect for hit and sit comic punch. He started speaking of his first grade teacher at Jefferson Elementary, Miss Anna Stole. Told how she had expected great things from him and how he hoped his friends out there wouldn't disappoint her. He sensed groans from the stage - the popular kids in Miss Perry's unspoken thoughts - but his audience - he had his audience - he knew it - knew he especially had the under classmates. String won his victory overwhelmingly. He had done it. He was Governor of Roosevelt Junior High.

At the close of the year, each officer gave a talk explaining his duties to a group of parents and teachers, members of the PTA. She may have, but String doesn't remember his mother being there. On his way out, at the conclusion of the talks, he heard one of the mothers tell another, "The higher the office, the worse the talk." It hurt a bit, but he regretted more the school paper quoting him as saying "apples," not "noodles and applesauce" were his favorite food.

Chapter 11

Second Aside – Loose in Livermore

But as it is written, Eye hath not seen, nor ear heard,
neither have entered into the heart of man, the things
which God hath prepared for them ....
1 Cor. 2:9

It's probably not necessary to acknowledge that I survived the TURP. Aside from a night in San Ramon's 'Regional Medical Center' with tubes both in my arm and up my penis, with legs wrapped and mashed every thirty seconds by a compression machine, it wasn't much to complain about. What Dwot said he'd do, he did, painlessly and with dispatch - hospital excepted. I'm capable once again of pissing my name in the snow, but the TURP has to heal completely before I'll know what's next for the cancer. It'll be awhile.

Unlike mine, Joan's cancer did not make itself known by any subtle, man-devised blood test, but by the dense, insidiously frightening lump her hands uncovered in her left breast after showering one morning in the late fall of 1971. We had recently moved from Livermore to Berkeley. It was the third home we'd owned in our thirteen married years. Joan welcomed Berkeley as a coming-out place, a place where a city girl who'd been stuck in a backwoods community could find herself, add other contributions to raising kids and taking care of a house and an ambitious husband.

I'd known I wanted to marry Joan soon after we met. Why? Because of her beauty. Sound callous? Sure - even though it didn't register as genetic engineering at the time. Marriage wasn't anything I gave any thought to. It was a generational thing - just something you did. I never liked the way I looked, and I wanted my kids to be handsome, beautiful. I wanted them to look like the gorgeous redhead I chose to marry. Don't misunderstand, Joan had a brain under that attractive facade. If she suffered any notable defect, only shyness comes to mind. Born thirteen years after the youngest of her five siblings, she took on the probably unlikely burden of the un-wanted child. It took her time to get her voice. I remember our first major date at one of the city's long forgotten Russian res-taurants. Neither of us had been saying anything. After being stared at for awhile, her lips curled into a nervous smile, and to win a couple of flattery points I remarked on the whiteness of her teeth. Her mouth remained open, the smile dissolved, she paused, looked down, and quietly confided, "They've been capped."

Our first house, one-bedroom and owner-built - what re-altors would call a charmer - shared its quarter-acre lot near downtown Los Altos with a couple of dozen apricot trees. We paid fifteen thousand and thought we'd made a killing because we sold it for twenty-two at the time of the Livermore move. Years later, during the Silicon Valley boom, a guy bought the property for $900,000, tore the house down and built an abomination that now covers much of the land.

At the time we bought in Los Altos, I worked for Philco as 'Western Computer Support Manager' - trying to keep the sales gang a little honest about what they told potential buy-ers. The boss there used the word "software" to describe the stuff I'd been writing for the past five years. I thought he was putting me on. The computer we marketed, Philco's Transac, the first commercial one to use transistors, stumped the ex-perts. Once, at a conference, I heard a speaker lament that a "refrigerator manufacturer" had done what the electronic wizards at IBM had been incapable of. The small staff out of our Palo Alto office managed to get a contract with Califor-nia's DMV to build a system capable of registering the State's 8,532,571 - and growing number of - vehicles. Another un-expected kudo for the refrigerator manufacturer. Ironically, I left them to work on an IBM machine, to help out with the operating system on the then-largest, fastest computer in the world, Lawrence Livermore's 7030 Stretch. IBM had made a public release of all the Stretch's specifications, excepting its direct operator interaction device, a slick little unit with printable characters projecting from a golf-ball-like gizmo. We were told to keep quiet about it. They called it a "Selectric."

Commuting to Livermore seemed better than living there, and on most trips my share-the-ride companion, African-American physicist Reggie, kept me entertained with his conservative political observations. In the early sixties, you had to be white to buy property in that archetypical cow-town, then fast filling with Lab employees the natives liked to call "sexual intellectuals." Blacks and Asians, whether included in that designation or not, had to live elsewhere. Reggie or I drove with great care from the town's downtown flagpole out East Avenue to the Lab, wary always of adding to the city's wealth through the efforts of Chief Michael's patrolmen as they practiced traffic watch on the 'they-don't-look-like-one-of-us.'

My driving had become so cautious that when at a little past midnight the time arrived and Joan yelled, "Let's go!" I had difficulty keeping my foot to the pedal to maintain the seventy-plus miles per hour down El Camino Real, the speed necessary to get us to Stanford's obstetrics ward on time. We'd been sitting in classes and practicing natural childbirth - coaching, breathing and all that - for almost half a year, and had picked a doctor, a many diplomaed specialist who advertised that's what he did. All his deliveries took place at beautiful Stanford Hospital. He assured us Joan would have her baby there awake and drug-free. For reasons soon to become obvious, I'll call him Dfkh, the 'h' is for head.

When we left home, Joan's contractions screamed out pretty regularly, right around every five minutes, and they lasted forever, probably over a minute. They'd slowed down a bit by the time we careened into the ambulance entrance, and after we'd been directed, parked, advised, and finally settled into the ward, they became as intermittent as firecrackers at noon on the Fourth. The nurses showed great sympathy, tried several times to contact Dfkh, and failing, had Joan seen and attended by a resident.

Dfkh arrived at precisely 8:15 the following morning, ordered Joan wheeled into delivery immediately, stunned and blocked me from following with questions and directions from a number of nurses and attendants, ordered an epidural block from the anesthesiologist, preformed an angled posterior vulvar incision, a type of episiotomy, and delivered our daughter - no less beautiful for her traumatic passage - with large, 1848-vintage, Simpson forceps. Our life was too filled with her loveliness to obsess over the medical profession. I bought clay and spent weeks staring at her and modeling her head.

I'm going to afford my kids, and later a few others, even more anonymity than I extended Joyce. I'll not divulge their names. My daughter and my son - born at Livermore's Valley-Care Hospital on East Stanley Boulevard by induced labor two years and two months after his sister's Stanford appearance, and at a time and date agreed upon weeks in advance by both mother and obstetrician - were wonderful as children and, in spite of considerable paternal neglect, grew into caring, productive adults. I couldn't be prouder of them. Incidentally, both are good looking.

Tiny house notwithstanding, everything about Los Altos suited Joan. She delighted in turning the big guest closet off our only bedroom into the baby's bedroom. She became part of the town's visual landscape - a striking redhead pushing a stroller with an even redder-haired offspring down colorful sidewalk-less streets. She dried apricots on rented racks in our backyard jungle, and she helped, as a 'friend of the library,' with fundraising and plans for a new building, the one to be built near the civic center. Sadly, we left a few months before construction began, the drive to Livermore had become more than I could handle.

I shared my first office at Lawrence Laboratory, LLL, with mathematician and computer programmer Edna V - a room to the right and just inside the west entrance of the wooden, barracks-like quarters that housed us. The building, like many at the Lab at that time, had been built in 1942, twenty years earlier, soon after the Japanese had bombed Pearl Harbor. Known back then as the Livermore Naval Air Station, this former 629 acres of cowboy-land had as its first mission the training of pilots for the war that had just begun.

Across the hall from my desk by the door - Edna had the one by the window - and farther from the structure's outside entry, stood the always open door to the office of Sid's secretary, Marge. Always-open could not be said for the door between her desk and the office of her boss, Sid F., the Director of Computation. I came to think of her more as watchdog - a diviner of the favored - than a creator and mover of paper. Sid, small in size, big in presence, personified enigma: friendly, stern, flexible, unyielding - all the contradictory attributes - and with notable political skills, Marge among them.

At our first meeting, he made an unexpectedly gracious impression. He wore, or had with him, a bow-tie, two-strap Birkenstocks, and a cigar stuck in the left corner of his mouth - accoutrements which I later found to be as much a part of his daily appearance as his receding hairline. On those rare occasions when he was without the smoke, his lower lip retained a hollow, as if awaiting the missing prop. Taking over after an introduction by my new boss, a supervisor reporting to him, Sid showed me to my office, made sure Edna and I became acquainted frictionlessly enough to share that space, then left us to seek out Ernie, whom he asked to show me around.

Ernie, tall, pleasant and relaxed, swept away any anxiety I might have been feeling. After the expected initial exchange: where are you from? where did you go to school? ... , he smiled and went on with, "Edna just co-authored a book, a book of over 400 pages, all numbers." My only response, "What?" elicited an even bigger smile along with a quickly blocked chuckle. "Edna, your new office partner. She and the astronomer, Joe B. - he used to be in charge of the old IBM Card-Programmed Electronic Calculators - they just published a book called *The Heliocentric Coordinates of Mars, 1800-2000.*" That explanation didn't help me fathom his message about a book full of numbers. I already had an unaccountable awe for the place, an organization created to design things most of us wished didn't exist, life-ending weapons. I opted to let the coordinates of Mars alone, and instead asked questions about where things could be found and how to get around. Ernie took me on a tour, then for lunch at the cafeteria, and finally to meet bright, handsome Bill C. a friend of his who worked in the main weapons division. He would become my friend as well.

Coming from industry, the lab looked to be a sort of hog heaven - both for its computers, its support staff - tech writers, mechanics, machine operators, ... , - and its supplies. The open stockroom, while squeezed into much less space, could be favorably compared to a free Staples or Office Depot - just walk in and help yourself. As for computers, LLL would make even a modern geek drool. I read an editorial, while there, claiming the number of computers Sid had obtained - stacked one atop another - would allow one to climb to the moon. By then, I understood the role of the Mars coordinates, how LLL contributed to the space as well as the weapons race with the Soviet Union, and why, post-Sputnik, getting to the moon figured into that struggle.

I hadn't done much to please the Stretch's system programmers - having spent much of my time getting the machine's Selectric interface to successfully spit out red characters - so they summarily traded me off to one of the math supervisors. My assignment from him - to rewrite in FORTRAN a frequently used numerical routine, then coded only in machine language - left me dazed. I had no trouble with either the machine language or FORTRAN, but the entire purpose of the program eluded me. What did it do? Could I make it work without knowing? Luckily, I had the roommate with both the patience and know-how to get me through it. Edna brought that piece of software to life. "It's based on Dick's PhD thesis," she began. "He keeps working on it, making it run faster or improving its accuracy. Has since he got here in '54 after getting his degree at Northwestern. Guess that's why he wants the FORTRAN version. Be easier for him to change."

I knew Dick V. He'd been one of my interviewers, actually the one who took me to lunch. Edna continued, "If you ask Dick about it, he'll give you mathy talk about Eigenvalues and Eigenvectors, but what it does is pretty straight forward; it finds the curve that best fits a bunch of data points. And we work with observation points all the time, ... " Bang! "Oh," I interrupted, a bell going off. "Like observations of the planet Mars." She laughed. Over time she taught me, helped me to understand every nuance of the code.

Joe B. filled me in on many other parts of the story. I liked talking with him, asking him questions. He had a unique set of life experiences and values. And something else made you want to be around this tall soft-spoken man, the quiet pleasure of being with a gentleman. Apart from his family, he had three passions: astronomy, sailing, and tennis. He wouldn't have separated the last two, "Sailing is tennis, tennis is sailing," he once told me. He had joined the navy soon after Pearl Harbor, and spent his first couple of war years patrolling California's coast on a commandeered sailboat, searching for Japanese submarines. I believe he skippered it, but I don't know for sure, nor do I know if he sailed aboard Zaca, the requisitioned, 118-foot schooner bought by Errol Flynn soon after the war.

First off, though, Joe identified as an astronomer. An astronomer of the Kepler, Isaac Newton ilk, not of the 'where-did-the-universe-all-come-from' blarneyers. I never became privy as to why he wanted to, or how he got the Lab's support - but LLL's interaction with space program people began in 1955 when Joe wanted to predict the next appearance of Halley's Comet - coming sometime in 1986, 31 years in the future. Joe needed the positions of all the planets to compute Halley's orbit and make that prediction. The existing coordinates for the planet Mars were not good enough, so he decided to use the program Edna had been developing for the comet's orbit to do a better one for Mars. The rest is, as said, history.

When the U.S. seemed about ready to put up its first satellite, one of Joe's coworkers, Nevin, wanted to use Edna's code to track it. He was telling me this when I asked, "Wouldn't he also have had to have good Mars coordinates?" That question, one that displayed a complete lack of elementary astronomy knowledge, didn't result in any kind of deprecation. Joe actually prefaced his answer with, "Good question," before explaining, "For a satellite around the Earth, it's not necessary. All that's needed is the effect of the Moon and the Sun, and the oblateness of ... " He stopped briefly then went on, "You know, the degree the Earth is flattened in the direction of its axis of rotation, its deviation from a sphere."

This may be difficult to swallow, but Joe told me more of the story as he rowed me around a small lake aboard an eight-foot dinghy, in pursuit of a duck I had badly injured. With the duck too far in the distance to be immediately helped, I asked what I'd long been wondering, "How did Nevin's satellite tracking attempt cause such a stir, Joe?" "Ah," he responded, adding effort to his oar strokes, "that code was ready in

October of 1957, right at the time Sputnik went up. Sid got a call from the Observatory, the Smithsonian, asking if the Lab would track and predict what was going to happen to it." "And that's what you did?" He didn't have time to answer, we'd caught up with the duck.

Joe's home on the shore of this little lake, completely within an incorporated city, had been plagued by a bunch, I guess properly called a sord, of mallards. Besides keeping the neighborhood awake with endless quacking, they were making a huge mess of his shoreline front yard. Joe had called the police who suggested he hunt them, warning simultaneously that any gunfire was illegal within city limits. After a bit of back and forth he learned that other hunting methods, bow and arrow included, wouldn't conflict with city code. Joe found three of us who had the equipment - Tom H., Edna's friend Bob C., and me.

Suffice it to say duck hunting with bow and arrow is not easy. Out of literally dozens of squawking animals, only one was hit, and by me from a distance of less than ten feet. My deer-killer-tipped arrow found its way, and remained a hideous projection from the brave lady's midsection, prompting her quick swim to the center of the lake where our boat chase ensued. After additional fruitless volleys from me - she dove under the water at every approaching missile - Joe managed to pull alongside, grab her, and administer neck twisting salvation. I am incapable of describing my remorse. Joan and I plucked feathers - me lovingly - from the scrawny, once traumatized bird, and Joan prepared her for our scant chewy dinner. As part of a group from LLL, the day hadn't seemed all that strange.

I can't recall who filled me in on the final details of Joe's Sputnik fame, but after the satellite went up, an agreement reached between the Lab and the Smithsonian called for LLL to do the tracking calculations while the observatory sent observational data by Teletype. A message with the precise instant the satellite passed over a certain Washington, D.C. meridian was received every 96 minutes, about the same amount of time it took one of the Lab's IBM 704's to compute its orbit. They needed to use two of the machines to keep up. Those two 704's cranked away for seventy hours straight, Joe and his crew stopping them only long enough each revolution to dash outside and see their target tumble its way across the Livermore sky. They did not sleep for those seventy hours, arriving finally at Sputnik's often-quoted death date of December 1, 1957.

I came into my own at LLL by way of what I later decided had most likely been a relatively innocuous grammar correction. Before that, wandering about the Lab, seeing so much computing equipment I'd previously known nothing of, delighted and mesmerized me. Not just the monster machines, those responsible for the Lab's reputation, but gadgets designed for some odd, single-purpose function. Bill's office, a couple of buildings away, was crammed to the ceiling with a unique, and ever-changing, array of devices hooked to teletypes, cathode-ray-tubes, or just lying around with wires poking out. In another building, Digital Equipment Corporation's initial entry into the computer world, the Programmed Data Processor-1, the PDP-1 - famous for hosting Spacewar, the first game ever played on a small computer - supported a number of quaint peripherals: speakers, photosensors, a light-pen, and a film-reading device called the 'eyeball.' Ervie F., the engineering tech maintaining it, walked me though its features. I had to give it a try.

The PDP's 'eyeball' and light pen tempted me most. The pen looked like an ordinary pen trailing a thin wire that led back to the machine's central processor. For a nib it had a small photodiode covered by a mechanical shutter that opened when pressed against a flat surface - in this case the machine's cathode-ray-tube, CRT, display. You used it like a mouse, to write or point out objects, on the screen - using programs that output dots for the pen's photodiode to either see or not see. It was fun and at that time, with Doug Engelbart's mouse still a few months off, had no similar functioning competitors.

The 'eyeball,' simple enough in purpose and design but far more of a Rube Goldberg physically than the pen, needed to be housed on precision benches in its own darkroom. It allowed one to digitize photographs, film actually, held against a vacuum holder. Programming the eyeball was much like programming the pen, sending coordinates to a CRT which sent light through both the film and a reference filter to be subsequently sensed by photomultipliers. You wrote your own scan, point by point.

I'd talked a physicist into letting me use some of his project money to show how the 'eyeball' could be used with other equipment to add pictures to printed material - something not yet done - and was preparing a paper about it for a conference in Atlantic City when, luckily for me, the lab planned an open house. The Computation Department decided to program one of the super computers - I don't remember if it was an IBM 7094 or Control Data Corporation's latest - to jolt out *Stars and Stripes Forever*, at ear-cringing volume, to the coordinated movement of a dozen or so tapes - spinning with jerks in shoulder-high drives - while console lights blinked in sync with each cymbal crash and beat of a big bass drum. As impressive as it was, our unfunded demo on the PDP-1, Ervie's and mine, attracted equal visitor praise, and lab management status points for me. Alerted by photosensors of someone's approach, the little machine, in a shaky, husky voice would demand, "Pick up the light pen." A picture of the pen flashed on the screen - "Go ahead, pick it up," it repeated, then led its guest viewer - with light pen input - through some eye-catching screen stuff, including an explanation of how it worked.

That year, John McCarthy - after learning they, too, had one that played chess - challenged some Soviet computer scientists to an intercontinental match against a machine in his laboratory. The games, four in all, were played by telegraph, and lasted close to a year. John's machine lost. McCarthy, the man responsible for the expression 'AI - artificial intelligence,' had moved from MIT to Stanford where, two years later, he had founded SAIL, the Stanford Artificial Intelligence Laboratory. He'd been creating computer chess-playing programs long before that, for more than a decade. They fascinated me, even more so because I was - am - a lousy chess player. I tried to follow the action in whatever computer publication had something to say about it.

Every so often Sid would pop into our office to chat with

Edna or me about nothing in particular. He'd stick his head in the door, smile comfortably, and ask about our progress on whatever he thought we might be working on. This particular day, Edna had left early and I was feeling pretty smug about myself, having just had an article accepted by the Association for Computing Machinery's most prestigious publication, its journal. I'd used the 'eyeball' for scanning and displaying curves, the mathematical kind, to pick initial approximations for Dick V's curve fitting programs. Dick did the heavy computational lifting, but because the innovation, the graphics part, had been my idea - and I'd written the article - they gave me the added honor of first author.

Sid pulled up Edna's chair and made himself comfortable, rolled over next to me and looked over my shoulder. In front of me was a highlighted section of Alan Kotok's paper, "Artificial Intelligence Project - MIT Computation Center: Memo 41 - A Chess Playing Program." Sid looked at me, at the paper, then back at me with a kind of bemused frown. He said nothing for awhile then, "You've been busy." I struggled at how to reply - the relationship I felt with him might best be described as slave to respected master. For no thought-out reason I changed the subject, "You missed the quartet on Sunday, they were wonderful." The lab had a small auditorium, another part of hog heaven, and hosted weekly performances for employees and their guests - foreign films mostly, but occasionally live music. I'd referred to a celebrated chamber music group from Europe. Sid nodded, "Sorry I missed it. I hear Edward played the piano with them." "He was terrible," I blurted. Wherever I'd worked, I'd always had a kind of political death wish. This exemplified it. I had no immediate knowledge of Sid's boss, Edward Teller. I'd seen him around quite often, but had never spoken to him, nor he to me. In the past when I'd referred to him negatively, Sid's response had been, "Don't sell him short." Once again I changed the subject.

I pointed out my open office door at the brown-mat bulletin board across the hall. "I see you're looking for someone to lecture at Berkeley. What are you looking for?" The typical enigmatic Sid response I got, "Someone who wants to teach. Do you want to teach?" left me numb. Me, a guy with only a bachelor's degree from an unknown college, teach at the very zenith of academia, unbelievable. I pressed him. "What department is it, Sid?" "Electrical Engineering. Lotfi wants to get some computer subjects started in the department." I didn't know that name, I heard only 'computer subjects.' "How would I apply?" I asked. "I'll let him know you'll call, you set up the appointment." "Thanks, I've been interested in what's going on in AI." Starting up from Edna's chair, he stared back down at my desk, "I see," he said. This time he did show a slight smile. Encouraged, I pressed for one additional perk, "Can I do some chess programming?" As he moved past the edge of my door he looked directly at me, and shot back, "I don't know, can you?" That subtlety, that tiny confusion between *can* and *may*, turned me into a loose Lab cannon, freeing me - at the anguish of my supervisor - to work at whatever struck my fancy - until one day Sid pulled the plug by promoting me, assigning me a group of twenty-three programmers, all working on strange support jobs, most for the lab's electrical engineers. My carefree life, diddling with chess games and facial recognition program attempts, was over.

For everyone but our seven-year-old son, the move to Berkeley had been a happy one. Leaving our place on Pestana Way, one house east off Jensen, took him away from a number of close neighborhood buddies and put him down on Colusa Avenue a block north of Hopkins and next to a house full of girls, all younger than his sister. His very best friend had lived in that corner house on Jensen. A week or two before we left, when the boy's mother told him she wouldn't let her son play, he'd called her "a fucking-ass-hole" - prompting her quick appearance on our front porch where, with screams, she provided all the particulars. Joan, hearing through the bathroom window, just to the left of the porch, yelled back calmly, "Did you tell him you didn't like it?"

In retrospect - culture differences aside - our years in Livermore were good, family-bonding ones. Joan collected friends easily, both labbies, their spouses, and parents of the many kids who hung out with ours. She helped the founders of the

Valley School, physically and with ideas, bring fresh teaching methods into their pre- and elementary-school classes. She got into creative knitting, yarn sculpture, and watercolor painting. I found her often wild, three-dimensional wool creations motivating. My dad's belief that I had used some kind of photographic imaging gimmick to mold my infant daughter's little clay head led me to believe it should be preserved. I made a plaster mold, cast it in clay slip and bought a small electric kiln to fire it off. Success with the project led, first, to a reading of Benvenuto Cellini's *Autobiography* written in 1558 and telling, among other things, how to cast in bronze - then to the digging of a backyard hole, the burial there of an empty fifty-five gallon oil drum, and the purchase of fire bricks, coke (refined coal), and a clay-graphite bilge crucible with a long iron hand shank to lift it and pour. That foundry-to-be, located behind the garage and fenced off from the rest of the Pestana backyard, left sizeable space for our other additions: a cage for Fuzzy the rabbit, a 5 x 5-foot plywood-sided playhouse, a swing supported asymmetrically between a tree and a two-by-six joist, and a six-by-eight foot, cat tempting sandbox.

By the time we left I'd also built a very heavy potter's wheel, one powered by a foot treadle moving an offset crank - like the one pictured on page 1143 of *Webster's New World Dictionary*, 1962 edition, taken from the Lab's stockroom. The dictionary showed the potter standing - my wheel had a seat. It looked great, but the crank arm and bearing-supported shaft of iron plumbing pipe didn't quite line up, leading to an unseen but keenly felt wheel-head wobble. It failed to encourage dreams of a successful potter's life.

Not in everything, or everyday, did life in Livermore engender joy or creativity. The Lab's presence intensified the omnipresent twinge of a possible Soviet-U.S. nuclear war; it brought protestors and the danger of leaking radiation; it encouraged the digging of front yard bomb-shelters by 'strike-first' advocates - a few maybe in sympathy with Major T J "King" Kong, bomb-straddler in the relevant movie of the time, *Dr. Strangelove* - and it remained for many years egghead unfriendly. We'd lived there only a few months before those thirteen days of terror, the days John F. K. and Nikita S. K. remained squared-off over missiles in Cuba. And then - only thirteen months later - on that glum Friday in late November, we sat in front of the TV in Ernie's Livermore home - he would beat us to Berkeley by three years - watching and listening to Walter Cronkite's somber announcement of the young president's death - our three-month-old daughter clutched tightly in her mother's, Joan's, arms.

In the sixties most computer users didn't have much contact with their machines. It was no different at the Lab. We'd punch up a bunch of cards, $3\frac{1}{4}$ x $7\frac{3}{8}$ Hollerith, some called them IBM, cards and pass them off to machine operators along with any necessary reels of tape. We could punch the cards ourselves or jot our programs down on coding sheets and send them along to a keypuncher to do it for us. The operators at the computers would 'batch process' the card decks - line them up one program after the next and let them run to completion. We'd get our decks back along with the results printed on a pile of folded paper. Sometimes, depending on the program, the pile would seem big enough to deplete a forest. One printer in the basement spewed paper across the room at about the speed of a power walker.

The PDP-1 had me under its spell. Interacting directly, watching the CRT screen, light-penning a next move - none of that much changed the job of a programmer. What it changed was the job of the computer. And the new customers I had acquired as supervisor, the electrical engineers our group served, saw that change. They knew of ongoing work, how computers were being programmed to help design circuits interactively. They knew, particularly, of those efforts at Berkeley. They wanted what I had on the PDP-1, wanted all of it plus a keyboard and some function buttons. But how could one little overused computer serve a bunch of circuit designers? It couldn't. I called Bill.

He picked up with his always pleasant "Hello," and I replied with a precisely articulated and not unexpected, "Fuck J. Edgar Hoover." Bill had long been certain our phones were tapped, were monitored by security, and our shared paranoia had given rise to that often used greeting. He got back with a slight chuckle of acknowledgement. "What would you do if you had to provide about half a dozen guys with interactive terminals?" I asked. He answered without hesitation, "Gotta time-share. You know how McCarthy got em started with 'Multics' back at MIT, and now there's 'Genie' at Berkeley and the 'Octopus' right here."

About fifteen years later in a short paper, "Reminiscences on the History of Time Sharing," Stanford Professor John McCarthy writes of his thinking about such systems, thoughts he had as far back as 1955. This is the way he defines time-sharing: "By time-sharing, I meant an operating system that permits each user of a computer to behave as though he were in sole control of a computer, not necessarily identical with the machine on which the operating system is running."

There were two super-bright guys in the six member team I managed to get together to build a multi-user design system for the Lab's engineers. They created most of the software. My job was, first, administrative - like getting the space and the hardware together - then writing up for some computer conference the way it would work, and, finally, giving it a name. Through no fault of J. Edgar's, the mainframe hardware we bought from Scientific Data Systems caused us a lot of grief with security. Vendor personnel, sales and tech help alike, had 'SDS' tastefully embossed on their business cards. Getting them into the Lab was a nightmare. Earlier that year, a student group had launched a protest they called the 'Ten Days of Resistance.' They rallied, marched, and held sit-ins and teach-ins on campuses across the country. The ten days ended in a one-day strike with around a million students staying away from classes - the largest number of student strikers in United States history. The group responsible called themselves Students for a Democratic Society, 'SDS.'

The conference we decided on, the Association for Computing Machinery's 23rd National Conference, accepted my paper, "Design of a time-sharing system allowing interactive graphics." I listed the two hot programmers first, as senior authors. They would also present our methods at the conference. We still needed a name. It came unexpectedly - or maybe not - it came from the funnies. One of my favorite cartoonists,

Gus Arriola, had a character in his comic strip, Gordo, who used a computer to draw cartoons. I wrote Mr. Arriola asking if we could call our system Gordo. Here is his hand printed response:

July 29 1968

Dear -----------------

If only I had known you men before, I could have authenticated that sequence with the mystifying terminology of your paper. Send me the Greek translation so I can understand it more clearly!

Though, perhaps, it should be named the "Windsor Knott," after that harried cartoonist in the strip, we will be flattered to have it called, "Gordo"! Be my guest! A more wonderfully far fetched anomaly I couldn't come up with.

It's encouraging to note that the conference is taking place in that mecca of science and intellectual pursuits, Las Vegas! The de-humanization program there is far ahead of your Lab!

Click!

Gus Arriola

Chapter 12

The Unknown Years - High School

Whom shall he teach knowledge? and whom shall he make to understand doctrine? them that are weaned from the milk, and drawn from the breasts.
Is. 28:9

A part of America must have been aware of the conflict to come. President Roosevelt had, in fact, by the spring of 1940 convinced Congress to substantially increase the defense budget, to build up the size of the army and to add to our fleet of military planes. But to many Americans - maybe most - the war came like a switch had been thrown – a huge brass switch like the one Frankenstein threw to send life-giving shocks through the bolt in his monster's neck in Universal Studio's 1931 horror flick - a quickly thrown switch that turned a country at peace into a country at war.

String and his dad were on the way back from the cabin in Julian. It was mid-afternoon when they stopped at the tiny local market where Irv wanted to buy snacks for the sixty mile ride home. Early that year he and Rose had bought the place in an area just east of a town called Whispering Pines. Rose had regrets. The wallboards smelled stale, the toilet was an outdoor one-holer, she'd found a nest of baby rattlers under the front steps, and the last time Irv left them alone overnight a mountain lion had scurried across the roof. Today, Jeff Wagstaff had driven the twenty-two miles up the hill from his Warner's farm to see if he could help. Irv felt good about his capable friend's conclusions. "Yea, I can line the place with knotty-pine tongue and groove paneling, build a little water closet against the kitchen, and help you get in a septic tank, but I can't do much about the snakes or other critters." "Thanks, Jeff, that might do it for Rosy. Maybe I can scare off most of the things she talks about liking to see at the zoo. How about letting me and snoozer take you to dinner?" Jeff declined, he wanted to get back home. Betty Ann expected him.

String's day with the two men had been special. Jeff treated him like an adult, and private time with his dad was an always welcomed rarity. He knew, with only the two of them, they'd not stop to eat, but it didn't matter. They'd buy munchies and fruit for the ride and with the speed limit recently upped to 55, it'd still be early when they got home. He opted to accompany his dad into the shop - a kind of out-west pre-7-Eleven convenience store. The look of the people inside startled both father and son. All - patrons and clerks alike – were hunkered in a rear corner staring down at the small brown Montgomery Ward's brand Airline Midget table radio. They were listening to the replay of news aired several hours earlier by CBS announcer John Daly. "The Japanese have attacked Pearl Harbor, Hawaii by air, President Roosevelt has just announced. The attack also was made on all military and naval activities on the principle island of Ohau." The quote has no typo; Mr. Daly twice that day mispronounced Oahu. String saw his father's face contort as he never had before. Then it turned and looked straight into his, frozen and white. After Irv's attempt to explain what the broadcast meant and of his own distaste for war, they talked little on the ride home, but String experienced a change in his dad's voice, an unfamiliar softness.

> *"Yesterday, December 7, 1941*
> **— a date which will live in infamy —**
> *the United States of America was suddenly*
> *and deliberately attacked by naval*
> *and air forces of the Empire of Japan. ... "*
> Franklin Delano Roosevelt

High School Principal, John Aseltine, called a special assembly on the day of the President's address, December 8, 1941; a somber assembly about war. All students were ordered to attend. String didn't expect to learn anything new. He'd heard it all, yesterday, from his dad. He climbed the stairs to the Russ Auditorium balcony, where, front left-center, he recognized the short, olive-skinned teen from English class peering intently at an opened magazine. The boy had just stopped turning pages and had flipped open a sheet to twice its folded width. String, both purposefully and with characteristic shyness, moved quickly to the empty adjoining seat, sat, and stared over his left arm at the glossy print, now turned ninety degrees and resting on his neighbor's lap. The image in the gatefold, a tall sinuous model, standing, red flower adorned head cocked to the right and resting against the back of her right hand, wore a pink dress - painted on her flesh from breast tops to ankles – leaving no part of her a secret. Hers was a figure that titillated without shocking, a figure certain to compel the attention of a good many 15-year-old males. The treasure's owner looked up at String and smiled, "I'm Guido," he offered. They spent the hour staring at Varga's November offering, and thumbing through the *Esquire's* other pages, undistracted by Dr. Aseltine and his faculty staff.

Guido, the first of many buddies String would attach himself to during the last of his school years, knew nothing of his companion's difficult transition from junior high to high school - from top dog, in name if in few other ways - to statusless sophomore. It was now exactly three months since the still-sprouting beanpole began his student days at the Grey Castle on the hill. That's what the locals called San Diego High - and fittingly so. The ivy-covered structure, built of massive granite blocks, stood commandingly on a hill overlooking groomed and inviting Balboa Park. With its round towers, parapets, and great doors of solid oak, its architect had given it whimsy, illusion and majesty. It was the proper sanctuary for the diverse group it housed: Portuguese kids, Negro kids – no one called anyone black or African-American back then, Mexican kids, a smattering of Chinese, and a great mixture of European ethnicities. They came from the waterfront near the fishing fleet, from harsh, struggling Logan Heights, from Chinatown, from Hillcrest and North Park, from all of downtown. The groups didn't mix a lot, but there was solidarity, there was respect.

String's Pershing Avenue home straddled, at that time, the

boundary between the district served by tough, old San Diego High and newer, more suburban, more genteel Hoover High to the east. He made his choice easily, without thought. Sure, he wouldn't be able to walk it. He'd have to take the trolley up University, then bus it down Park Boulevard, but getting to Hoover would be even harder. Who would not want to go to that grand castle across from his beloved park, just a mile-and-a-half south of the old Junior High? Two years later his sister, Carolyn, answered that unspoken rhetorical question. She chose Hoover.

String began his high school stay cautiously. He learned the complete campus layout - classrooms, quads, labs, and toilet locations; how to work the combinations on his lockers, and the way to get through gym class without too much hassle. Rose made him paper sack lunches - two sandwiches, one always peanut butter and jelly, an apple and a cookie - which he most often ate sprawled out on the expansive lawn that swept down the hill in front of the school. He sometimes ate alone, but increasingly had the company of a growing number of boys, first Guido, then Robbie, and now Doug.

He took some pride in being joined by Robbie. A strange kind of pride because it took awhile for String to stop thinking of the tall-like-him, but heftier, young man as an intruder, a nuisance, and come to view him as an upper classman. Upper sophomores didn't typically hang out with newbies. String met, or more properly became chosen by, Robbie during his last summer before high school. String still puttered in the garage, making or taking apart this or that. Because of the summer heat he'd leave the two big garage doors open, the ones for the car. Robbie, while on his way to Mussies grocery for a Pepsi - he was a multiple soda a day drinker - spotted String soldering a couple of cans together for a projected toy submarine and came up the slope to watch; came without being asked, as if it were his God-given right. It became a habit. He'd climb the nine-block hill from his house on the north-east corner of Mississippi, a block east of where Landis Street ends, and make himself at home at the end of String's workbench. It escalated one day when, just before noon, he followed String past Sophie's house to the Pershing Avenue backdoor where Rose saw him and offered him a sandwich.

String had no objection, by then he enjoyed talking with this uninvited guest. He also found it natural for his mom to give snacks to anyone hanging out with one of her kids. That continued until, when in college, he started bringing home a couple of friends who played football for San Diego State. Their bulk drove her wild. She complained, "When they walk around the whole house shakes." Another, subtler, Rose-maddening incident occurred almost weekly. Every day but Sunday, on returning from work at Grace Church, Sophie would poke her head against the window above the kitchen sink and yell, "Hello, I'm home." If leftovers remained from the evening meal, Rose would offer them. Sophie's response, as predictable as sundown, "Well, if you want to get rid of them," would set off in the self-decreed 'gracious giver' an equally predictable fist-clenching, lip-pursing reaction.

The English class String shared with Guido was an X-graded one. X-graded not for pornographic content, but because each member had scored high in the literacy test given to incoming students. Guido had tested tops: fastest reader and greatest in comprehension. String took second in comprehension but, in this English class, no one read as slowly.

Doug, also a member of that X class, could be quickly picked from the group by his attire. San Diego High had no uniforms, or even a dress code that anyone knew of. Most boys wore tan corduroys which increasingly became canvases to decorate with inked-on words or short messages. The girls played follow the leader to a lesser extent, choosing skirts and blouses - often under a sweater or light jacket - or simple, season-appropriate dresses.

Only principal Aseltine and, except at picture taking time, three or four teachers dressed like Doug, in a two-piece suit, usually complete with tie. Doug's build, a little like String's dad without the apparent muscle mass, didn't inspire caution as did Hoss, the football team's large Portuguese tackle, but no one was ever heard asking him why he dressed as he did. Every sophomore seemed to have some vague notion - mostly untrue - about the person seated next to them, the person they hadn't known before. A common guess had Doug a product of wealthy eastern parents. He was in fact local, born in San Diego and a fleet-follower-kid in the Navy's one ocean days.

And though, until his senior year he choose not to share it, his dad, Chief Petty Officer W, had been aboard the USS Arizona when she went down at Pearl.

War crept into the city's consciousness slowly, in unexpected ways. Sometime before spring break String first noticed the anomaly, what he took to be a Navy blimp, tethered on long steel cables above the northeast corner of the park, just east of the golf course and across the street from the house Guido shared with his mother. Both boys had been pleased to learn their homes were fewer than six blocks apart, though they seldom met at Guido's. He behaved there with a reserve akin to hiding something; his mother, while always welcoming, spoke little, perhaps because of her accent, and the upscale maid-tended house itself made String edgy.

On this particular day, Guido met String's hesitant knock with unfeigned cheerfulness. He began his greeting with typical polish, an urbanity uncharacteristic of teens. String interrupted him, pointing excitedly across 28th Street and into the park: "I see you've got your own blimp." It took some time before Guido caught his meaning, then, "Oh, the barrage balloon. I talked with the GIs who put it up. They worked me over a little." He giggled. "When I first walked out there, they yelled, 'Halt! Who goes there?'" He laughed again, "Told me I was in big trouble for trespassing. The sergeant finally let me know they were part of the three hundred and somethingth Coast Artillery - Barrage Balloon Battalion - I think he said. He said they'll be putting up more of those things." "What the heck's it for?" String pushed. "They're supposed to keep away low flying enemy planes." Now String took a turn laughing, "Guess they must be working!" They went on to joke about how, when in February a "Jap" submarine shelled the oil field just west of Santa Barbara, everyone got uptight about the lights.

Lights were among the least subtle reminders of the war. No lights were to show after dark. They must either be off or in some way covered - most often by drapes or tightly drawn curtains. Volunteers made sure. Civilians - teens included - volunteered for a variety of defense duties: aircraft spotters, farm help, blackout wardens, messengers, war-bond promoters, even hostesses for a USO newly re-formed to provide servicemen with respectable recreation. String once spent an exhausting day wearing a double ring on the middle finger of his left hand, climbing a shaky ladder, and attempting to pick and fill as many boxes as possible with Eureka lemons. He and Doug had been bused to Lemon Grove - at a time before that town's land had given way completely to single-family homes - to do their part for the war effort and make a few bucks. They'd been taught how to pick without pulling out the stem, and to pick the proper size. If the fruit didn't fit through the 2¼ inch ring attached to the one on their finger, it was fair game. They didn't make much money, they never picked again, and String failed to grasp the novelty of having been briefly engaged in his Grandfather's calling.

Both String and Robbie received official-looking cards after taking a defense message carrier course, but heard no more of it after training. Rose dutifully poured all her grease - mainly from bacon fried in her heavy iron skillet - into empty coffee tins, and turned them over to Whitman's butcher, who sent them on to be recycled into drugs or dynamite. Then there was rationing. Rationing had to have been the most constant and vexing of all the war's reminders. Oscar and Loretta now owned the garage and full-service Shell station on University at Arnold, four blocks west of Pershing. String had once spent a little of his summer vacation pumping gas at the Texaco, three blocks farther west on Texas Street. Oscar invited him to do the same. Even though the job now entailed getting a gas card and a ration-stamp book - in addition to pumping gas, cleaning windshields, collecting money, and checking batteries, oil and tires - keeping any air at all in those tires proved to be the hard part of the job. With tires and tubes close to impossible to get, String spent much of his station time patching tubes and inserting boots - sometimes several - into almost treadless outer remnants.

From newborns up, everyone had a ration book. It would be easier to list items not rationed than those that were. Among the rationed, sugar and gasoline always come to mind. String had a tiny gas engine, a 1939 Mighty Atom, he'd purchased to power a paper-covered, balsa-framed model airplane he never managed to build. It had a displacement of a little under a tenth of a cubic inch. He used a discarded eyedropper to fill its clear plastic tank. The Office of Price Administration issued him gas stamps for it.

About halfway though his first semester, String joined San Diego High's orchestra. He'd heard earlier no cellists were needed, and quite properly understood his instrumental skills didn't warrant any attempt to bump a current player. Then Robbie, the group's only tubist, told him conductor Marcelli needed a bass player, maybe two. String would never learn much of that gifted director's past: never know of Nino Marcelli the composer, the once cellist with the San Francisco Symphony, the guest conductor there - as well as for the Los Angeles Philharmonic and at the Hollywood Bowl, the reviver and two-year director of the San Diego Symphony, and the educator who'd written books for students of both cello and bass. That latter revelation might have discouraged his joining. As it turned out, playing the bass changed his life, not musically but because of the future friendship it engendered.

By appearances, life at 3691 Pershing hadn't changed that much: little showed of the slowly growing gulf between boy and man to be. Even so, String retained scant recall of early giddy days when, with Rose out of sight, he and Carolyn would lift - ever so carefully - the earpiece off the switch-hook fork on the left of their sturdy, black, upright telephone and listen surreptitiously - giggles suppressed - to the conversation of strangers. They had, at that time, a two-party line - two short rings for them, one long ring for the anonymous others. Now the squat dial-model - occupying the same spot on the spindly foot-square, walnut phone-table pushed into a corner of the dining room just left of Rose's southern gum china cabinets - had become a major String irritant. Its placement guaranteed the unlikelihood of making a call without being heard. He couldn't even share a private joke with Guido. What if he were talking with a girl?

The phone's location became symbolic of the fishbowl he lived in and couldn't yet leap from. Privacy was the only part of that teenage purgatory he understood. He'd need Rose's amorphous succor for quite some time, and he still hoped for the seemingly impossible - to please his father. Once, when he'd inadvertently left the bathroom door unlocked while showering, Irv came in to use the toilet and, on seeing his son's genitals lathered up and ready to rinse, smiled, nodded and said, "Good … ." String didn't catch the second word, but the "Good" made him happy. It would be his single memory of direct paternal praise. On the flip side, Irv's need to explain the proper way, the only correct way, to do what needed doing, may have hit an apex the day he parked his car on the Landis Street side of the house, looked up to see String watering the grass on the slope, and offered authoritatively, "You need to be spraying back and forth, not up and down!"

And Onan knew that the seed should not be his; and it came to pass, when he went in unto his brother's wife, that he spilled it on the ground, lest that he should give seed to his brother.
Gen. 38:9

While it didn't stop him, or even much slow him down, String remained forever ambivalent over the consummate joy, the elation, even the relief, masturbation brought him. Would he be, could he be - was it possible to be - perfect like Jesus, if he hadn't had that warm, fist-seeking fleshy-nozzle of bliss between his legs? Why did they call it self-abuse? He doubted that Jesus masturbated.

The bathroom, that single refuge of privacy in a house of eyes, became not only a place to read - if too long on the toilet, then seated on the tissue cabinet, back against the mirrored wall between the towel drawers - but also a sanctuary, a place for delight, for orgasmic elation. He'd lock himself in each Saturday morning, fill the tub with water as hot as he could stand, and bring about his climax in a number of creative ways. Then he'd watch, making sure the stringy, mucusy, white coagulate, floating in the water around him, spiraled its way down the drain to oblivion. Later in his junior and senior years, when he'd get up at five a.m. to sit at the dining room table and finish the homework put off the previous night, it would just happen, happen almost spontaneously. He'd tense up to concentrate, to finish studying before the others woke up, and then it would happen. He'd reach down, grab hold and … , and it would just … pleasingly, smilingly happen.

String spoke of it to no one. He knew some of his friends talked of sex with one another - with him the topic was taboo.

Once while prying through his father's personal effects, in the top dresser drawer to the right of his own, he found a card with the waist-up picture of a lovely naked brunette, each of her hands gently cupping its neighboring breast. The caption, over what might have been a Cotton Club logo, read, "I've got you in the palm of my hands." It startled him to find anything in the house so overtly sexual.

For the most part String's self-pleasuring remained disassociated from any thoughts of the girls at school. Many of them seemed to enjoy having him around - talked and joked with him - but that's about it. Getting closer, having a 'girlfriend,' he couldn't even conceptualize those possibilities. That, in spite of adoring one young lady, buddying with a second, Mary, and being attracted to a number of others, Alice in particular. Cathy, the girl of his dreams, the beauty sitting behind him and across from Mary in English X, would hold his heart for the entire two-and-a-half years of his Gray Castle stay. Co-incidentally, but irrelevantly, both were physician's kids, Mary being the youngest daughter of his sulphanilamide benefactor, Pediatrician Belford.

Now the names of the twelve apostles are these; ... .
Matt. 10:2

By the end of that first year at San Diego High, String had reached an unexpected comfort level, more pleased with school life and more at ease, even, than he'd been at Roosevelt. The group of guys he hung out with had grown to eleven; one more, Kris, would join them next semester. Besides making the orchestra's two-person string-bass section, he'd signed up to run on the cross-country team, and planned to campaign for junior class president in the fall. Politics and athletics had more to do with popularity, merit badges, the garnering of an attractiveness aura, than with any keen interest. With his behavior easily influenced by urgings from certain of his friends, especially Doug, Guido, and occasionally Robbie, he couldn't rightfully be called a leader - and running, well running might get him a letterman's sweater sporting the school's coveted chenille-felt varsity **S**.

With their first summer vacation coming to an end, Guido and String decided on one last adventure. They'd load up their bikes - String's 1939 Schwinn Lincoln New World Tourist 3-speed, and Guido's older, fat-tire Columbia Twinbar Cruiser - with bag lunches, water bottles, a sling shot and an air rifle, then head down into Mission Valley to shoot at - they weren't sure what. There wasn't much development in the valley back then - a number of dairies, some poultry and a scattering of produce farms. Even less after the previous year's relentless spring rains caused the El Capitan Dam to spill over and turn the usually trickling San Diego River into a destructive torrent. The two were at String's house, picking up his lunch and BB gun when Robbie wandered by on one of his Pepsi trips to Mussies. He wanted to come along. If they'd stop by Mussies with him, he'd pick up something to eat as well as the Pepsi.

Sure, Robbie was welcome. Both bikes had racks over their rear wheels. Robbie would ride behind String on the bigger bike. They decided on the close route; instead of riding the more than a mile west to take Mission Grade in Hillcrest by the hospital, they'd go down Texas Street. Heading south "Texas tecks-us to the park," but to the north it leads straight to the valley. After the mile-and-a-half to where Texas meets Adams, just before the big drop down to Camino Del Rio in the valley below, String asked Robbie to get off and ride behind Guido. A later hash-over yielded no apparent reason; String said he wasn't particularly tired; Robbie hadn't remembered being unduly uncomfortable, yet when asked to switch, he complied immediately. Before starting his own descent down the steep hill, String did remember seeing Robbie amble toward Guido's bike - lunch and Pepsi in one hand, BB Gun in the other. String had dropped about half the distance from top to bottom when the cruiser passed him like an apparition accelerating toward the speed of light - Robbie's arms splayed full length still gripping precious cargo: gun and Pepsi. He had not seen the thin steel strap holding the coaster brake arm to the left chainstay snap, and leave them without brakes. He did not see them cross the luckily un-trafficked valley road, leap off the ridge at its far side shoulder, and drop the seven feet into the bushes below. What he did see was a scratched-up, shaken Robbie motioning him over. "Guido's badly hurt, String, get some help quick." String didn't hesitate. He heard the sobs of his out-of-sight friend as he let his bike fall by the side of the road and started running back up the hill.

Still running, and somewhere between Madison Ave. and El Cajon Blvd., a white-haired lady, trimming a hedge by her front porch steps, called out to him, "You all right, son?" The simple gesture turned a plan-less endurance run into actual, possibly unneeded, help. Some time before String reached Robbie's mother on the kind woman's phone, Robbie had flagged down a passing car and help had been summoned. Declining refreshment offers from his hostess, String left immediately, retracing his way down the hill and arriving in time to witness the rescue operation wrap-up.

Robbie lying on a stretcher just behind the ambulance looked up at him and smiled, then closed his eyes. Two attendants were wrapping something around his mid-section. "Where's Guido?" String managed, still out of breath from the downhill jog. "The other kid's in the cab," one of the men answered without looking up, "not much wrong with him, just a green wrist fracture. This fellow took a real shot. Don't know yet how bad he's hurt. We've given him a pain killer." With that, they slid the stretcher into the back of the vehicle, one aide jumping in after it and slamming the rear doors shut, while the other moved quickly behind the steering wheel. They were off before String could even get a glimpse of Guido, but it was he who, later that day, shared the details. Robbie had never lost his grip on the Pepsi, but as the bike came down, the BB gun, wrested from his other hand as its stock hit the ground, remained vertical as he descended onto its barrel - its muzzle becoming the vanguard of a direct anogenital path - rectum to balls. It would be happily confirmed that all motion stopped in less than two inches, sparing entry into his testicles and saving his manhood by a scant quarter-inch. The bad news, his hospitalization would cost him one school semester. He would no longer be an upper-classman.

In the months preceding String's junior class presidency, American troops had arrived in Great Britain; the U.S. government had forced thousands of American citizens, those of Japanese ancestry, to give up their homes and farms and 'relocate' to camps in remote, uninhabited places; the mass slaughter of Jews with the cyanide-based pesticide Cyclone B had begun at Auschwitz; 72,000 prisoners had been forced on 'The Death March' following their surrender of the Philippines' Bataan peninsula; the U.S. Navy had turned the tide at the Battle of Midway in the Pacific, sinking four Japanese aircraft carriers; and, the German Navy had sunk over six hundred U.S. and allied merchant vessels within sight of the east coast shore - from Maine to Florida. Water frolickers could do nothing but watch with terror, revulsion and disbelief as the U-boats surfaced and shot apart the ships they had torpedoed to a standstill. Upper classmen, seniors - some getting ready to join a fleet still rebuilding in San Diego after its crippling losses at Pearl Harbor - may have known of some of those events. If so, it didn't trickle down to many of their classmates, kids still talking of how the school's sprinters, Willis and Smalley, took first place in the 880 relay at the State's championship track meet, of how much unfair homework they had to do, or of student elections. String had won his spot without much fuss. His only opponent, a pretty young woman not part of the student elite, campaigned on academic excellence and raising school standards, while he stuck to much of his successful old recipe, "Don't disappoint my first grade teacher." He got fewer looks of disapproval from the in-crowd than at Roosevelt - winning seemed easier and less eventful than it should have.

High school guys and gals in the forties formed mock fraternities and sororities, clubs they called them, not gangs. String's group wanted to be big shots, like one of the senior clubs, the Barons. They made up a name from the first letter of each of their last names, but decided, after a while, that it sounded too corny, and called themselves the Kings. Take that Barons!

Two Kings, Carl and Max, stood apart, unique from their fellow members. Carl, large, awkward and coarse-spoken, lived to fight Germans. No other King spoke of the war. Carl idealized it, worked his way up in the Reserve Officers' Training Corps, the ROTC - what fellow Kings called the 'Rotten Old Tomato Cans' - joined up as a private immediately after graduating, and ended his service at war's end as a lieutenant colonel in the U.S. Marine Corps. Max, Carl's counterpart in charm, not handsome but the group's true ladies man, danced with moves second only to George's. Along with Doug, and at times and often deviously Guido, Max provided much of the group's leadership. His father owned a mortuary, a great place for a few members to hang out evenings, play pinochle, or just sit around among the cadavers and talk about girls. Starting out as an announcer four years after he graduated, and known as Don, Max became one of San Diego's leading radio personalities – DJ-ing consecutively for stations KSDO, KCBQ, KOGO, and KPOP.

By the time Nino Marcelli stopped the orchestra, tapped his baton against the lectern, pointed it straight at String, and yelled, "Hey you monkey, you with the glasses, that's a D-flat, not a D - tap, tap, tap," German troops had been completely encircled by the Soviet Red Army at Stalingrad; American forces had joined the British, helping them defeat General Rommel's Afrika Korps; Glenn Miller had joined the U.S. Army; and String had added jazz to an already questionable musical repertoire. The latter happened pretty much at Doug's persuasion. He knew of an upstairs ballroom, east on University Avenue past 42nd, that had been idle for a number of years, and learned of its owner from a real estate dabbling neighbor. Meticulously groomed, brown hair carefully slicked down with even more than usual care, Doug forced his way past the man's secretary to make an offer he couldn't believe would be accepted. It was. He could use the space for non-alcoholic dances every Friday and Saturday night for one year. In exchange, its proprietor would receive twenty-five percent of all net profits - an amount, if not paid monthly, could have been written in red.

Robbie put Doug onto a fledgling band, most from the

school's marching unit, who'd played a few tunes at the school's mostly DJ'd dances. Not used to being around instruments neither blown nor beaten, the marchers welcomed String. Though trying hard to sound like Tommy Dorsey, they still didn't much impress the handful of attendees Doug's telephone-pole-stapled ads brought to the first weekend's events. String faked his way through the scores, ending up Saturday night with the three central fingers of his right hand bloodied from two nights of pulling and plucking - never bowing - a rented bass. His dad mail-ordered a new one for him, one beautifully pictured in Montgomery Ward's latest catalog. It arrived looking fine when viewed from the front, but its dimensions sideways measured less than half those of a normal double bass. Irv sent it back and bought him an early Kay Musical Instrument Company model from a pawn shop on one of his old beats. He'd been called back to Police duty, working once again in the 'I' bureau, filling a spot for one of the many officers who had left to serve in the military.

On the second weekend of 'Music Live at the Loft,' entrepreneur Doug took extra care during ticket sales. He'd been stuck the previous week paying taxes on a couple of hundred optimistically purchased, but unsold, tickets. No one had told him you couldn't just throw them away, that the tax people wouldn't believe you hadn't sold them unless you turned them in - in good shape and untorn. About halfway through Saturday night's session, while counting the tickets for packaging, an older guy, a guy almost twenty-one, popped past the downstairs door and climbed the stairs. He bought a single ticket, not too unusual Doug thought, probably a hustler looking for a pickup. But this guy behaved differently - really strangely for an older dude. He didn't approach a single girl, just hung around the band's platform listening, nodding, moving from one foot to the other, and scratching his head. At the beginning of the last intermission he walked over to Doug and without introducing himself began, "Hey buddy, it'll be quite awhile before these guys sound anywhere near pro. Whaddya say my boys, Marvin's Movers, make the music for you next week. I know you've heard of us." Doug hadn't. "I can use the trombone, and the bass maybe - not too sure he knows what he's doing, but there aren't many basses around."

With time for only one rehearsal, and even without its usual drummer, the merger came off pretty smoothly. Players, let go and disappointed, were promised free tickets and a chance to sit-in for an occasional play-along. The marching band drummer would stay on until Marvin's man got back from up north; his parents had driven him to Los Angeles to compete in the all-teens-welcome Gene Krupa Southern California Drum Contest.

By mutual consent, his and director Marcelli's, String left the high school orchestra. He knew he would miss being a part of something he had never before experienced, a complete merge with others, a giving up of self. Surrounded by peers fused to a single goal, eyes fixed on the hypnotic baton, he'd be lifted to some other dimension, as if carried away by Grace Church ceiling-beams come to life.

Marvin's Movers weren't all that bad. Marvin's exemplar, Glenn Miller not surprisingly, was imitated shamelessly, right down to his theme song, "Moonlight Serenade." With the return of the boy Gene Krupa had judged 'best teen-aged drummer around,' a dramatic shift came about in the group's music, a greater vibrancy and intensity. String had trouble believing that boy - center stage, just to his right - the boy whose drum sticks flew at light-speed - snare to cymbal - cymbal to tom - tom to tambourine, to woodblock, to cowbell, whose feet thumped the hi-hat and big bass drum pedals with metronomic precision, the boy who would tell him about paradiddles, flams, and ratamacues - was George, George Talbott, the boy he had admired in junior high but had never met; the jitterbugger he had envied, the boy whose thinking had so impressed Miss Perry.

One Saturday at the club the unbelievable happened, unbelievable to almost all but String. A muscular young man, wearing full dress blues with the single red-edged yellow chevron of a private first class in the U.S. Marines, pulled a bright yellow, stretched-out convertible, a Lincoln Continental, to the curb almost directly in front of the hall. Once he'd squeezed it miraculously into the parking spot left by a much smaller car, he hopped from the driver's seat, took on the stairs three steps at a time, where, at the top, he said a few words to Doug, and without buying a ticket walked straight to the stand with an air of ownership. There he leered up at Rosalie, Marvin's vocalist, as she tried to finish her song with as much Marion Hutton style as she could command.

> Tell me darling is there still a spark?
> Or only lonely ashes of the flame we knew
> Should I go on whistling in the dark,
> Serenade in Blue

"There's always a spark, honey," the twenty-five year old marine kind of chuckled, looking more at the growing crowd on the dance floor than at Rosalie. When he jumped onto the bandstand tossing his coat to Marvin, George stood and handed him his drumsticks, butt end, handle out. String was flabbergasted. George whispered "Buddy Rich" into String's ear as he stepped off the stage. String shrugged, having never heard of the man billed often as "the world's greatest drummer."

Rich played with the band until the following intermission. It didn't go too badly until the last number when he jammed down on the bass pedal with such intensity the leg-spikes on the big drum popped out of where they'd been wedged into the floor, and the big drum shot forward, stopping only in time to avoid careening off the stage. String didn't know how to compare Rich with George, but had to admit the man who'd played with jazz greats Joe Marsala, Bunny Berigan, and Artie Shaw, and who'd left Tommy Dorsey the year before to join the marines, did a pretty freaky single-stroke roll - amping up to a volume-screaming hand-blur of incredible speed. He also agreed with the two comments Marvin made of him when he left: "Don't mess with him; he teaches Judo up there at Pendleton north of Oceanside," and, "He thinks his shit smells like ice-cream."

After that night, George talked differently to String, like a mentoring older brother - though his use of 'brother' as comradely address wasn't new. The teaching began casually, first about jazz, then classical music, then onto subjects in realms beyond String's prior breadth.

"Listen to this, Brother String," George volunteered one evening after the group had broken from a short rehearsal. He began whistling, "feu, feu, fa, feu, fa, fa." Then showed String how to play a little riff on his bass, da dum dum dum dum. "Those are parts of a tune composed by one of your fellow bassists, String. His name's Bob Haggart. He plays for Cosby's Bobcats. He wrote the music, but the band's drummer, Ray Bauduc, does the whistling, and during part of the score he plays on Haggart's bass." George reached over with his sticks and did a little roll on String's highest pitched, or G, string, then hummed more of the melody until, together, they managed reasonable facsimiles for parts of Haggert's tune, "Big Noise from Winnetka." George was exhilarated. He went on in the charged mood to explain how other drummers had influenced him: his hero, the now dead Chick Webb, the early bebopper Shelly Manne, and last year's national Krupa contest winner Louie Bellson. String responded with an unemphatic, "Oh?" Aside from Buddy Rich, the only direct contact he'd had with any big band member occurred at the Hollywood Palladium with three other Kings, on a night ending in a sleazy downtown L.A. hotel. The four stood in the famous ballroom looking up from beneath the stage, listening and cheering. The only instrumentalist whose name String knew was the guy out in front with the trumpet, Harry James.

It didn't happen overnight but the two became friends. It was as if String lived in two worlds, the world of George, and the world of school and the Kings. As with other friends of String and Carolyn, the house on Pershing Avenue became a kind of retreat, a second home for George. He would sit at the piano in the living room, or chuckle, amused and approvingly, over archangel Gabriel still soaring protectively above String's bed. Neither he nor Rose knew it, but much had to do with her, with the way she welcomed teens, chatting with them as she chatted with peers. Her grimaces went unseen when he struck the keys of Carolyn's little spinet with a force more suited to a concert grand, as did her retreats to the kitchen - pulling behind her the thick swinging door - trying to block all sounds of one of his long tempestuous creations.

"Do you remember that one, Brother String?" George asked, swiveling from the bench toward his friend, sprawled out on the yellow overstuffed chair to his left. He'd just finished playing a composition of his own. "I'm not sure," String weaseled, he couldn't tell one from another - George's originals or those attributed to famous composers - whether he'd heard it before, or it was just being faked. Like Rose, George simply shared what he wanted you to know. He had no capacity to judge his listener's comprehension, to filter or dumb down. This day it was about the wonderful goings on in classical music: Schoenberg's atonal and twelve-tone scale - a revolution right up there at UCLA - Schnabel's performances, and Prokofiev. "Did you know when Prokofiev was a kid he got piano and composition lessons from Reinhold Gliere?" he asked. String didn't.

Irv had changed the family name before String's sophomore year - turned it from Jewish to Irish with, literally, the stroke of a scalpel. He changed Rose's and his legally, through the courts. For his kids there would be no such heritage paper trail, no knowledge of any less-than-American past. He sat to the left of the fireplace braced against a straight-back chair from the dining room, Carolyn and String's birth certificates laid out carefully atop the pull-down desk at his front, and meticulously picked out race altering parts of their names with a letter opener shaped like a doctor's tool. "Keep this to yourselves," he cautioned. String honored his father's wishes to the best of a fifteen-year-old's ability, telling only four friends. When he did, he shared it as a joke. "I'm a German, I'm a Jew," he would say, slapping his left cheek with the palm of his right hand. "Take that schweinhund."

String strongly identified as German - his remembered love for Grandma Ambuehl - the tools he now shared, carved with Grandpa's $\mathscr{P\,A\,A}$ - his mother's native language - his dad's discard of family and past. It wasn't often on his mind, but when it was, it puzzled. How could they just march into other countries? How could they march people into chambers and gas them to death – people - girls like, like Mitzi Shiller? How? How?

George began explaining Alfred Korzybski's general semantics, and in return String spoke of things troubling him: the war, poverty, population growth, and his latest peeve, "the flagrant mixing up of political with economic systems!" Even his social science teacher had that wrong, speaking of communism, fascism, and democracy as if they could be compared. George and he did listen to one another, but much passed by like an arm-wave between north and southbound traffic. Not that String didn't think about Korzybski, as much as he could absorb. He liked the quotes: "When in perplexity, read on," and "God may forgive your sins, but your nervous system won't." They made sense - kind of - a lot more "Oh! Yea!" than "Whatever you say it is, it isn't," and all that stuff about the "is of identity." But Korzybski didn't compare in relevance to the stuff he'd recently started reading, Huxley in particular. Slowly, haltingly, he'd been pouring through his third Huxley, *After Many a Summer Dies the Swan*. Forget literary merit, he couldn't get enough of the man.

After an evening together, they'd walk back and forth for hours, from String's to where George lived on Bancroft Street - back and forth about a mile each way - talking and walking until eleven, twelve, or even later - until one or the other would say goodnight at his own front door, leaving the other to walk the final mile alone. George had started putting his own thoughts on paper, essays on science, or philosophy, or the philosophy of science - notions largely incomprehensible to String - painstakingly typed, with five onion skin copies, on $8\frac{1}{2}$ x 11 inch bond. He always gave String one of the carbon copies. When handed the first, String reacted, "That's so great, Brother Talbott. I don't know how you can do that. In social studies we've been told to write an essay about what it's like to live in our families, about the relationship we have with our parents and our brothers and sisters. I don't know how, how to say what's really in me, what I really feel about something that close? I wish I could get it all out, you know, kind of like lie down on a piece of paper and have a steam roller roll over me, press it out of me. Be there, all of me, on that paper." George looked surprised. "You showed me a poem you wrote for English class, Brother String. Maybe you could let your thoughts flow, like you did with it, let them flow with more definition, sharper, less obscurely." String thought for a minute or two before replying, "No, it's not like that could happen. Except for directions, ... , you know, like recipes for cooking,

I could never see any difference between prose and poetry. Who knows what's sharp or what's obscure? Maybe that's the problem - my problem."

George opened String to an undefined world, one that could be tight and structured like a mathematical model, or floating free, empty and limitless; a world where every past belief could be challenged, where old rules were gone and none replaced them. Korzybski showed George the problem with language itself, how words shaped, twisted one's thoughts; how logic, Aristotle's in particular, erred. A few years later, *Worlds in Collision*, a book by the Russian-Jew psychiatrist Immanuel Velidkovsky, would teach him that one could refute all of known science. Meanwhile, he wrote and spoke of how the world looked to him - and String listened, enthralled - but would remember less of his friend's sophisticated theories than of his dancing and drumming, and the lightning-shooting Tesla coil he had in his Bancroft Street garage. George showed him that big coil only once. He ran a battery to a Ford trembler - a small wooden-boxed coil used to set off a model T's spark plugs - sending high voltage through the Tesla coil's primary windings. It came to life, illuminating the garage's dark interior with a series of spectacular three-foot-long electric sparks. He laughed uncomfortably while disconnecting it. "Probably caused static in every radio in the neighborhood. If you had a radio on at your house, a mile from here, String, I think I could send you a Morse code message." He laughed again, this time amused over what he'd said.

String's daily life - centered around home and school - remained unaltered by exposure to the contemporary intellectual happenings and beliefs George provided. Shortly after five, every evening but Sunday, his family began dinner around the walnut dining table. Irv, when home, sat at its head on the only chair with arms - his back to the window facing Pershing Avenue. Rose sat opposite him, closest to the kitchen, with String to her right facing sister Carolyn. Occasionally, in the middle of a meal, Carolyn would peer directly at her brother's face, then spontaneously erupt into fits of uncontrollable giggling, initiating a reciprocal response from him and enraging their father - all actions occurring for reasons no one understood. Since being recalled to police duty, Irv spent a great deal of time away from home. Rose, upset and frowning, once complained to Guido, "String's dad's never around anymore," evoking from her suave young confidant, "Why do you care? He'd just be asleep on the front room sofa if he were."

At school Robbie pushed String to find a date for the junior prom, implying it was his duty as president, and suggesting he ask the pert little second cellist, Ellen. "I know she likes you," he said. "I used to see her look at you when you were still in the orchestra. I'll be taking Thelma, and getting my brother's car. We could double date." Guido pushed equally hard for him to take political action for Ed, a King member who'd been suspended for a week, accused of being one of those responsible for climbing the University Heights tower at the corner of Howard Avenue and Idaho Street - less than four miles from school - and painting **LABA** in white, 17-foot-tall letters just below the top of its water tank, 125 feet above the ground. Ed told his buddies: "It wasn't me, and anyway, **LABA** means **L**et **A**merica **B**e **A**ggressive." No one ever confirmed or refuted that assertion.

In contrast to the nebulous cosmos of George's imagination, established traditions and beliefs shaped the molds from which the Kings were poured. None still attended church, yet memories of its art, vision, solidarity and collective moral credo merged with local advertising and pop culture to build them a stable universe. Movies: *For Whom the Bell Tolls*, *Mrs. Miniver*, and of course, *Casablanca*, gave them their vision of war. Their hearts went out to *Bambi*. Radios and spinning 78s: Miller's "Chattanooga Choo Choo," "Moonlight Cocktail" and "A String of Pearls"; Jimmy Dorsey's "Tangerine"; Woody Herman's "Blues in the Night"; Harry James' "Sleepy Lagoon"; and strangely enough - in semi-arid San Diego - the misplaced nostalgia of Bing Crosby's "White Christmas," provided them with fantasies and escapes. All of them believed that science, engineering, and the technologies they engendered, would make the world a better place, would, in fact, be mankind's savior. Several suffered that perennial teen malady, "idealism." It ranged - high to low - from flighty, emotional Guido, past String and the serious, pragmatic Doug, through Robbie, to worldly Max and indifferent, if not callous, Carl.

One afternoon, after being let out early from Chemistry,

String got the attention of both Doug and Guido. "So this general sci teacher at Roosevelt, Miss Perry ... Winifred," he smiled. "She had this Petri dish she spit in." After monitoring their expressions he added, "Yea, it was pretty yucky," and went on, "she kept it around quite a while to show us how the crud living in her spit grew. It finally stopped and she took a cotton swab, ran it around in the dish and then into a different dish. Nothing grew in the second dish - those bugs were all dead. That's what's happening here on earth," he went on, raising his voice theatrically. "There are about two and a third billion people around right now. Less than two billion when we were born. That's a growth of more than three hundred million in 15 years. Before that, it took a century and a quarter to make enough babies for the race to grow by a billion - like about a third as many people born each year as now. Man, we're gonna eat up all the earth's food just like Perry's slobber ate what it had. Guess that'll be it."

String had intended to go on, share his thoughts on how communism could be just as democratic as capitalism, when Guido picked up on the drama, cut in, and began one of his not uncommon rails against social injustice. This time it was poverty. "We already do let people starve. What's wrong with us? How's letting people go hungry so different from outright killing them like the Nazi's are doing?" "Quite a bit," Doug interrupted, "it's a matter of intent." Guido went on, "Half of us here in the U.S. earn below the poverty level." Doug first frowned, then smiled, "42%," he said. "What?" "Not half, 42%." Guido couldn't be quieted, "Well, where my father lives it's over half."

Guido, reared like a prince, had no personal knowledge of poverty. His immigrant parents settled first in Mexico where, during prohibition, his dad, Señor C, created a prosperous liquor trade. He now owned and managed a brewery in south Tijuana - the site of his major residence - and two nightclubs in the tourist strip just below the border. Guido attended public school, San Diego High, only because of his personal insistence. All his prior teaching had been by private tutors, or at prestigious Catholic institutions, places hand-picked by his parents for their reputed academic, cultural and ethical excellence. Many of his summers had been spent traveling with his mother and governess to his parents' ancestral lands outside of Trento in northern Italy.

String spent several days of his first spring break at San Diego High as Guido's guest in a little cottage on the brewery property behind Señor C's ornate casa. The good papà forestalled many of their anticipated plans, giving specific instructions to his bouncers to bar them access to either of his clubs, the infamous Midnight Follies in particular. They did have complete run of the manufacturing plant, but without samples. Lengthy discussions became a major pastime.

Guido had much to share, both of his lonely childhood and of his beliefs. He told String a harrowing story of once walking into a Catholic school kitchen for a late night refrigerator raid, seeing one of the nuns lying on the ground, legs up, feet against the rungs of a stool, heavy black skirt thrown up over her thighs, and thrusting the handle of a broom in and out of her vagina. It was an image String couldn't completely visualize - not yet sure what his favorite movie stars actually did following the fadeout from a kissing scene. And on matters of more global interest, Guido didn't discriminate: Italy, Mexico, France - he spoke of them as if they were as good as the United States. "Where does it come from, this best business," he'd say. "You're born where you're born. Does that make it best?" String couldn't help himself from countering. "San Diego's a better school than Hoover, everybody knows that." He knew Guido's response before it came. Might have said it himself. "So why's your sister, Carolyn, going there next year, and what about your friend George? Thought you told me he was smart." String needed to change the subject; he interjected, "Wish we'd brought the car." They both laughed. It was their secret, a bond between them.

Soon after becoming friends, Guido had stumbled onto an *Evening Trib* ad for an eight-year-old Chevy 'smart coupe.' Its listed price, a doable $25.00 - 35 times less than a new one off the showroom floor - burned into Guido's brain. He had to see it. He called its owner; he called String. They'd meet on 28th Street two blocks south of where he lived. The clean appearance of the bright, azure blue machine, parked at the appointed spot, surprised them both. Next to it stood a young man in bell bottoms and navy jumper. A white braid stripe around the shoulder seam of his right sleeve, and the two stripes around each cuff, identified him as a seaman 2nd class. "Hope we didn't keep you long," Guido began. "Nope, just got here mass-elf," he answered in a slow southern drawl. The three squeezed into the single front seat and the sailor drove them on a twisting loop around a number of neighborhood blocks. The anxiety of the three appeared equal, an owner anxious to sell and two teens, undaunted by a bit of *harmless* exhaust smoke, anxious to buy. Even so, and with the two maintaining the best poker faces any fifteen-year-olds could muster, the price proved nonnegotiable. "Shipping out on the old Saratoga in a few days, drather drive this here baby off the old wharf next to her than give her away for nothin." SOLD! Each half-owner chipped in a requisite $12.50, rode along to Harbor Drive where the seaman got out and String took over - a skill he'd learned from Irving almost two years earlier after a prolonged struggle over bicycles - and drove the two of them back to Guido's. He would later teach his fast-learning friend how to drive.

Guido told his mom, Mrs. C., that String was sixteen years old and had a license, and String gave Rose similar misinformation about Guido. Rose made a single, puzzled-brow wrinkled response: "Pretty little for sixteen, isn't he?" The trick became 'turn taking.' String parked at Guido's and Guido parked at String's. 'The blue smoker,' as the Chevy became known by Grey Castle associates, served its owners well - even after they became properly licensed drivers. In it, and on a ride to Hoover High for the game - a big yearly football rivalry - String got a first and unexpected acknowledgement, perhaps, of his masculinity. Like with some circus clowns, passenger loading always presented an impossible to ignore challenge. The record to beat, for a successful carry over a meaningful distance, remained at seven. On this day only a comfortable five crammed their bodies into the cab: Guido drove, Max sat next to him, Cathy on his lap skirt up - both straddling the gear shift lever - and String by the door supporting class-vamp Molly. She curled her head down, mouth close to his ear, and whispered provocatively, "Is that a pencil in your pocket, or do you just like me sitting on your lap?" It took String awhile to comprehend, and to laugh. It would never have entered his consciousness that Molly's line may have been lifted from similar ones titillatingly made by busty comic actress Mae West.

They'd arrived at the game early that day to accommodate String's need to serve as team manager, the politically correct term for water boy. Pursuing football's least glamorous calling grew out of his growing desperation to acquire a letterman's sweater sporting the coveted S. Earning one by running was problematic. Could he really run or had his Uncle August's early words simply and unsuitably fused into his subconscious? He never trained; his athletic dad told him runners got troublesome, oversized hearts; his team captain would a year later write in his senior yearbook: "To the laziest cross county man, ... ," and the chance of his lettering at track next spring were equally bleak. He wasn't fast, couldn't get out of the blocks for a sprint - the longer the distance, the better he did. But now, at almost six feet tall, a junior and sixteen years old, he still weighed under a hundred pounds. He'd be classified B, not varsity or even JV, and not allowed to run any farther than three laps, 1320 yards.

For the Kings, that day at Hoover became a day of pride. The team's new halfback, Kris, made an unbelievable leaping catch then weaved his way past bewildered opponents. He made a touchdown. He was a King. Kris had, at the term's beginning, transferred from Santa Clara High, made friends with Max and joined as its final member. At least one letterman, and a celebrated one, would grace club meetings. But the ride to Hoover, the ride with Cathy sitting on Max's lap, had drained String of much of the group's shared joy. Max just wasn't a fitting companion for sweet Cathy. String had no idea what they did in private, but he did know Max shouldn't be trusted with Cathy. He hated seeing them together. A hay ride had been planned for later that year. String had talked with Cathy about it and she'd told him: "I'm going with Max, but you know, it would be great fun if you'd come too. My sister, Sandy, likes you. Why don't you come with her? Sandy really likes you, and she's only two years younger than we are." Two years - an impossible barrier - how could she expect him to go out with a kid. He heard his mind mumbling: "God, it's a generation." Maybe so. No one in his circle would ever learn that on the 11th of the past January, a few weeks after he and

Guido had purchased the Chevy, the seaman 2nd class, its previous owner - a scant three years String's senior - would, along with five of his shipmates, drown in a flooded boiler room aboard the USS Saratoga, after she'd been torpedoed by the Japanese submarine known to the U.S. Navy as I-6.

And the eyes of them both were opened, and they
knew that they were naked; and they sewed fig leaves
together, and made themselves aprons
Gen. 3:7

On one of those walking back and forth nights - String's house to George's to String's to ... - George managed to morph the conversation from jazz to physics: "Kind of like drummer Moeller with Krupa's drumming, it's not as far-fetched as you might imagine to suppose that Newton actually formulated a pretty good approximation of quantum theory." String zoned out at the subject change. He didn't know or care much about the historical niceties of drumming, knew less of modern physics, and had entirely different things on his mind. His abrupt switch lacked any of his friend's subtlety. "How come we have to work to make someone else rich when other animals can just move around and grab what they want?" he blurted out between Kepler and Bohr. "Oh Brother String, what's going on for you? We all work you know. Aren't those animals working? Isn't looking for food working?" String sighed, "I guess, Brother Talbott. Mom watches the birds around our house, not many 'cause we don't have any trees, but they seem so free, so into it. They don't have to look at a watch to know what to do next. Sophie gave me a leather bound Bible on my last birthday - kind of making up for the one I didn't get for a perfect ten year attendance at Grace." He chuckled. "I just kind of scanned through some of the early stuff. Stuff I may have read before, Moses' stuff, I guess. I'd always thought that Genesis stuff between Eve and the snake had to do with sex; now I know I was wrong. May be the most insightful stuff in the whole damn book. That guy's not talking about sex at all, but about what we know about what's going on. Do you know what I mean - the difference between how we think humans think, and how we think other animals think? I guess it'd be called self-awareness. When they ate that apple, God really shoved it to them; let 'em know what was in store ... . Those little birds don't know they're going to die." George looked at him; String had gotten his friend's attention.

"I just saw in the paper that a guy in Tibet, Tenzin something or other, was made - they called it "enthroned as" - Dalai Lama; 'cause they said he reincarnated from the Dalai Lama before him, a guy who died in '33. Do you think he really believes he reincarnated from some other guy?" George threw back the ball, "How would you measure that, Brother String, and do you think it's not possible to be another person's reincarnation?" String laughed, "Some argue we think and do what we do because of heredity; others say it's because of what we're taught. I don't know why we think we know anything. You've told me about a lot of great theories, but at bottom isn't it all just a big mystery?" He stopped for a long, uninterrupted while. "I guess believing whatever we believe is no crime, ..., unless, maybe, ..., it's believing that we're a super race and it's OK to get rid of anybody inferior."

Few opportunities remained for the two to explore their world together. George would graduate from Hoover when String became a senior, and Marvin made no effort to keep the band alive. Occasionally, he'd get a pick-up combo to play one of the drinking clubs, and all but once thought String looked too young to risk taking along. Each band member earned 15¢ on New Year's Eve, 1942-43, the last time they played together at The Loft. Apart from the tiny crowd, the night remained memorable only because Doug flooded the stage with light after String shouted, "Oh my God, my G-string broke." It had. The literal gut-snapping pop of his instrument's highest pitched string made itself clearly heard between "Sentimental" and "Journey," as Rosalie sang: "Gotta take that Sentimental Journey, Sentimental Journey home."

Robbie's determination to remain an upper-grader, to graduate with his original mid-year classmates, brought an inadvertent finale to String's formative San Diego High School years. Robbie would attend summer school to make up the needed credits. For something to do while wearing his sweater with its junior varsity **S** - football's Coach Peterson had given the large varsity **S** to the other manager - together with his friendship for Robbie, mixed with a bit of guilt over the bike swap, String chose to take the classes with him. He had no intention of graduating early, retained aspirations of becoming student body prexy during his senior year, looked forward to taking fun classes like radio shop - maybe get to go on-air with the teacher's amateur station, W6KSE - and, sweater in hand, no longer needed to run. At the one meet where he did run the three-quarter mile 'B' event, a single slower runner saved him from the complete embarrassment of last place. He'd led the pack for the first two laps after which, breathless and stiff, he quickly learned what it meant not to have trained.

Late one evening, the second week after the beginning of his first semester as a senior, Irving shattered String's calm with the simple statement: "I'm meeting with your principal tomorrow." "W h y?" came quickly back in a long drawled-out, squeal of a response. The tone of Irv's mumbled, "Tell you after I see him," made further inquiry inadvisable.

Crime and punishment on Pershing Avenue varied over the years, both in what constituted an offense and in the retribution exacted. Rose may have been the more frequent leveler of charges, but Irv served as unquestioned executioner. Both kids could remember the long leather razor strop hanging by its string loop from the twist latch on the ironing board cabinet across from the kitchen table. It hung there only when one of them had misbehaved. A push at its free, its handle-end, caused it to swing back and forth, to signal its anger. If the strop ever did strike a threatened rear-end, time and infrequency blunted all memory. A subtle change seemed to occur in the enforcer after his fast-growing son topped his own five-foot-ten. Stick-figure body notwithstanding, height seemed to pose some kind of menace. It played itself out only once, late on a weekend afternoon. Irv's fist was closed, but String didn't know whether he'd been hit, lifted or thrown - he sailed, feet off the ground through the hall, from in front of the bathroom to just short of the dining room phone stand.

Their quarrel, a frequent one, had been over bicycles; a

father's sincere concern for his son's safety; a headstrong adolescent striving for a childhood like 'all the other kids.' String's beg for a bike always met with Irv, the policeman's, response: "I pick em up in baskets every day," a platitude used second only to, "Clean your plate, people are starving in China." Irv contended cars were far safer than bikes, and tried - as soon as his son turned fourteen - to get him an emergency license. Teaching driving, hearing his gears grind their laments to his student's shifting, required a patience never previously demonstrated. He did it. String learned well, then failed the test. Unknown to his father he owned half a car before he got the Schwinn.

The night after convening with principal Aseltine, Irv shared with String what he considered the good news and the bad. "Dr. Aseltine says you want to be a martyr." From the way the words tumbled out, String wondered if his dad had any idea what that meant. Irv went on, "He agreed not to take any major action against you for the turmoil you created ... ." "Turmoil!" String blurted. "BE QUIET - Yea, the turmoil he said you created last semester. He said that up until then you'd been an excellent student, so you'd only lose a few little privileges - like lunchtime passes." Irv saved what he thought best for last. He prefaced it with, "There's some great news he and I worked out together." Then, "Because of the units you accumulated in summer school, you have almost enough to graduate; he'll see that you get to do just that - and a half a year early!"

String's head swam. What could he say? Aseltine had really played his old man; made him think he'd bestowed an honor on his kid - when, in fact, he'd given him the boot. Until then, String hadn't given a lot of thought to the past semester. Now it played in his head like a term paper about a B-movie. The track meet and the junior prom aside, most for him had been what would then have been called "swell." Like the race, the prom had been more suffered than enjoyed. He danced with his date infrequently and awkwardly, deserting her on occasion to play bass with the band. By contrast, he remembered with some pleasure surviving the short motorcycle ride across University Avenue, and, of course, the so called "turmoil" creating assembly he'd sanctioned.

But for the unforgettable terror it engendered, the short motorcycle incident wouldn't deserve recounting. Max had made the purchase earlier in the week, and today rode by a few of his fellow-King homes to show it off. Its exhaust-pipe rumble brought String and Guido to the Pershing Avenue curb where, both agreed, it was a 'nifty' vehicle. Max explained how it worked; how to shift, steer, and give it gas. He then made an extraordinary offer, "Would either of you like to try it out?" String couldn't refuse. After a satisfactorily smooth start, and almost to the intersection of Wightman Street - the first block from home - he realized Max had not mentioned brakes. Arriving a block later at the University Avenue boulevard-stop-sign found him amazed at how much distance could be covered while simply gasping and pondering. Traffic on that thoroughfare flowed in either direction. Unable to stop, he swerved first left then right - mindlessly - accelerating where he had to - avoiding the path of equally frightened drivers - before managing a squealing weave onto Oregon Street. Two blocks farther on he discovered the appropriate levers and executed a slow, triumphant ride home. On returning, he nodded to the machine's owner, summarizing his ride with, "Great bike, Max. Thanks."

Reflecting on the assembly always began with a, "Why me? Why not Guido? It was all Guido's idea." Doug's response had been, "Maybe so, String, but who told everyone in the auditorium to take the day off - to just walk away from school? That wasn't Guido." String looked away; the accusation both troubled and amused. Guido had been needling him for weeks to do something, to win some sort of a reprieve for Ed over the **LABA** incident. "Talk to Aseltine," he kept up. "Make him do the right thing." Then finally one day he came up with, "Why don't you call an assembly, take our grievance right to the Junior Class?" String kind of liked that. He considered it within his purview as class president to hold assemblies and, given proper office permission, it might have been.

The Kings left the event's direction to Guido, their self-proclaimed theatrical-adept. Guido tackled the assignment with enthusiasm. Carl and Kris would pull String up into the flies - the space high above, out of audience sight. Then as the curtains parted, he, Guido, would stand center stage welcoming the crowd of juniors packing Russ Auditorium, while having String slowly lowered, ever so dramatically, to land and deliver their important message of "justice for Ed." Acrophobic String demurred. "You want me to hang up there with those curtains - with all that scenery and junk - forty feet in the air? You've got to be kidding." Peer pressure can be redoubtable. At eleven-thirty on the appointed day, two-and-a-half hours before showtime, a few of the Kings put up flyers or made surreptitious classroom announcements.

String swung for a seeming eternity - wet palms grasping, thighs clamped together above his sandbag seat, tightening, squeezing against an inch-and-a-half thick manila hemp rope, his only support from a dizzying drop to the floor below. Guido's words: "Don't worry, the counterweights will make it easy to move you up and down," didn't help. Only downward movement averted imminent panic. Feet touching wood, and happy to have survived, he peered out at the scant handful of students scattered about in the massive, twenty-five-hundred seat theater. They appeared more stunned than amused, a state unchanged by his spirited pitch to garner help for the revocation of Ed's unjust punishment. Now he felt stuck. Little time had passed and he'd said his piece. He could only ad-lib, ramble on. "Remember when our school letters, SDHS, were burned onto Hoover High's front lawn," he began. "At least we didn't get blamed for that one ... " No reaction, nothing, he could have been putting on a risqué comedy show for the College of Cardinals. "Might as well take the rest of the day off," he shouted to the small audience. "Sure, go on home. That's a good message ... I'll ... I ... ," he waved and walked offstage.

It pained String to accept that this, the fall term 1943-44, would be his last. George had left, the band had dissolved, what had he but school: the Kings, the girls he idolized, a student-body office to preserve his persona, provide his plumage. Would it be fair to run for top job - not that he thought much of fair - if he were only to be there for half of it? He'd run for Activity Commissioner, not a much thought-of position, but a bit of an epaulet to wear along with his sweater. More troubling were thoughts of what next. How, after being exiled, could he still hang around? Should he enlist? His dad would go crazy, wants him to go to college, probably San Diego State. No, no good, he had to get away. Did Cathy, or even any of the other girls, think guys should join up? Would they like them better? He'd never heard anyone speak of patriotism or, except for Carl, actually fighting, but in San Diego everyone loved a sailor.

The semester rolled along well enough. String did win the election; became Activity Commissioner. A hollow victory since one of the "few little privileges - like lunchtime passes," taken from him by Aseltine, included the privilege to attend assemblies; assemblies he would now be obliged to organize. He did get a reprieve to play the role of Satchel Moyer in the senior class production of *Best Foot Forward*, even asserted himself over Guido's aesthetic objections and wore corny, Rose-made underpants. In radio shop he took and passed high on an exam for admission into the Navy's radar training program. He looked forward to its physical scheduled for the week following Halloween.

In the mid-forties, Halloween observers celebrated in a wide variety of ways - from the true trickers like guys who dis-assembled sheds and rebuilt them atop three-story dwellings, through window-soapers and TPers - to the little kids, or even bigger ones like String as Little Red Riding Hood, happy with treats. This Halloween he, Doug, Guido, Carl, and Max were just hanging around near Pershing and University Avenues, checking out the action. Carl had picked up a pint of cheap gin from a guy outside a liquor store near Thirtieth Street. The others had tried it and declined more than a sip. Carl pretty much polished it off before passing out in Max's car where Guido and Max attended him. They'd seen Carl get sicker on a previous occasion; had whisked him off to Mercy Emergency and called his parents. This evening they diagnosed him as fit to sleep or puke it off.

Doug and String were wandering along mid-University, laughing at how they used to put two-headed framing nails on the track and pick up the tiny swords formed by a train rolling over them, when three younger teens pulled the power line of an approaching streetcar from the cable overhead, bringing it to a jerking halt. Within seconds, and still preoccupied watching the conductor and motorman fussing with the stopped trolley, Doug uncharacteristically froze as the big right hand of a Man-in-Blue wrapped itself around his left arm. He looked toward String to see him being similarly grasped by a giant of an officer, then paled, any fear he'd been experiencing turning into hopeless dismay. His idiot friend was staring directly into the monster's eyes wearing a stupid, comfortable grin. Neither officer seemed amused. "You used to play tiddlywinks with me," String began. The officers glared threateningly. Doug closed his eyes. Undaunted, as with an old friend, the lad who'd grown up around cops went on, "I'm Irving's kid."

Following all around introductions, they walked the half block to a parked patrol car where, once police obligations had been fulfilled - sobriety and guiltlessness assured - reminiscing began. It had been eight years. Officer Cavanagh, one of String's favorites, looked no different. "Remember the little tin steam-boat you and my dad brought me?" Cavanagh's face lit up. "Did it run by lighting a birthday candle under a little boiler?" "Yea, yea. You filled the kitchen sink with water and ran it around there. I had trouble getting near it." Giggle. "It was my favorite toy, next to the erector set I got when I was eleven. I couldn't get near it either. Not for a long time. My dad and the minister's kids, Pastor Damshroeder's kids, played with it most all Christmas."

Guido drove String to the Naval base for his physical. They wouldn't let him in - he could park and wait in the lot outside the guard-gate while String walked to the dispensary. It wasn't far. The exam, given by the two petty officers, second- and third-class hospital corpsmen, felt more like a warm body assessment than a real test of fitness. The last, the eye test, would be a typical chart read - String figured a standard Snellen. It didn't much matter. Without glasses, his 20/200 vision would allow him to see only the big **E**. Once seated and glasses off, the senior petty officer placed the chart on its stand and barked, "Read me the line with the smallest letters you can see." String's mumbled response, "Only the E," evoked unexpected, sarcastic, almost sneering laughter from the two men; followed quickly with another, snickeringly bellowed order,

"Put your glasses on." As the chart cleared for Sting revealing the large top letter, an O, that same corpsman disappeared into the medical duty officer's adjoining room where more chuckles and a hardy, "Send him on in," could be heard.

"Thanks so much for applying, son. Can't tell you how much your patriotism is appreciated, … , ha ha," he couldn't help another little giggle; a laugh reaching out like a slap across String's face. Clueless, the Commander continued, "Might have to have a guide dog for you here in the Navy, son, ha ha." Guido, watching his friend open the car door, could almost make out the reddened cheek, the sting that hadn't gone away. Cautiously he ventured, "Didn't go well?" "It wasn't failing that hurt; it was listening to the prick with the gold braid laugh about it."

Except for again double-dating with Robbie and Thelma - this time to get to and from the Hotel Del Coronado - his senior prom went nothing like the junior one, the one inflicted on second cellist, Ellen. From first walking into the lobby and spotting Edward G. Robinson getting into an elevator - smiling at him and being thrilled when he smiled back - to giggling in Robbie's back seat going home, they had fun, a lot of fun. Why did he never get girl-nervous around her? Well, almost never; he did spill milk at dinner on an overnight stay at her Alpine house, and smoked, actually enjoyed, his first cigarette in the backseat of a streetcar on an initial visit to her earlier home in the city. And why did he never notice her prettiness, the equal of any girl at school? It may have been because she lacked both fragility and temerity; if he could do it, sweet Alice could do it. Prom night she climbed and beat him getting over a fence, her beautiful blue formal tucked round her waist, so they could stick their feet into the off-limits hotel spa.

Rose and Irving watched their son with pride, the first from either family - they didn't count Irv's nephew and two nieces in New York City - to graduate high school. Back on the familiar stage in Russ auditorium, the stage he knew intimately - floor to fly - Dr Aseltine smiled, and without the slightest hint of recognition, handed String his diploma.

Chapter 13

Third Aside - Berkeley: A Lump, Chips, and Regrets

But whoso committeth adultery with
a woman lacketh understanding:
he that doeth it destroyeth his own soul
Prov. 6:32

It must have been after midnight when I slid, slithered a better verb, into bed next to a sleeping Joan. I stared up at the ceiling, rigid, stiff, all I wanted was a shower - an alteration in ritual that couldn't be risked - get the oppression off me, wash it away. Joan had told me I'd become too dependent on her for recreation, amusement. She encouraged me to do things on my own, meet with friends, go out by myself. Sexual liaisons, I'm sure, hadn't been her intent.

I'd met Naomi on a bus from Berkeley to Livermore, less than a year after getting a PhD and three years following my hiatus from the lab. I'd been rehired at LLL by a group researching operating system security, something I knew a little of from the Gordo time-sharing project of six years before. I would have preferred continuing to fiddle with small interactive machines, the subject of my dissertation, but my only other job offer - for substantially less money - came from a Bank of America data processing team - not one located in the posh, five-year-old, heyday behemoth, San Francisco financial district's 555 California Street, but one far more representative of the company's slide from glory during that mid-seventies recession, in an older office building on the corner of Market and Van Ness.

My association with UC Berkeley had started concurrently with Ronald Reagan's in 1966, eight years earlier. Mr. Reagan began his by trashing the University as a way to win votes for the State's upcoming gubernatorial election. Mine took root as a lecturer in the Department of Electrical Engineering and Computer Sciences. I'd followed up on Sid's directive to call the department chair about a teaching position. It turned out to be remarkably simple. The slightly-built, bald, round-headed professor I met, while quiet and dignified, evoked in both appearance and intensity the caricature of a matured leprechaun. He conducted an amiable, no-nonsense interview; asked what I had done, nodded, inquired as to Sid's health, nodded, told me what and when I'd be teaching - furrowed his eyebrows and cocked his head in wait for my nod of agreement - and wished me well. I don't remember ever seeing him smile, then, or in the future. I do remember, at a department seminar several years later, staring at him spellbound, as he translated into English a Russian mathematician's incomprehensible proof of some obscure theorem. They told me at the main office outside of his that I would be sharing a room on Cory Hall's third floor with another lecturer. I was thrilled.

Computers had triggered interdepartmental races within academia; where and who should teach about them, and what should be taught. Our chairman had wisely overseen the department's name change the previous year, from Electrical Engineering, EE, to Electrical Engineering and Computer Sciences, EECS, its competition - the Department of Mathematics. A physicist wag at LLL asked me, "Will you also be teaching in the Department of Slide-Rule Sciences?"

The course I had agreed to teach struck me more as background material for a short sci-fi work, maybe Arthur Clarke's *The Nine Billion Names of God*, than an undergraduate introduction to computers. My relationship with machines had always been nuts and bolts: registers, bytes, bits, cores, and codes - not esoterica, not hypothetical automata, Turing machines, or recursive grammars. The little book, translated from Russian, I'd been asked to teach from covered exactly those rarefied topics. It led me to expect a small class, a few geeky kids. Not so. I walked into the assigned room, found myself behind an imposing lectern looking down from a high auditorium stage onto over 125 expectant faces - to begin pontificating on information I knew little of.

Near the end of my first teaching quarter, Reagan took his oath as 33rd Governor. His two campaign themes, "send the welfare bums back to work" and "clean up the mess at Berkeley," had won the hearts and minds of the California electorate. Three weeks later, University President Clark Kerr - a once *Time* magazine cover choice, acclaimed internationally for reshaping higher education in the Golden State, creating the 'multiversity,' opening it up to all - was fired by the Board of Regents, including its newest member, the governor. Kerr took the heat for what came to be known as the FSM, the Free Speech Movement. Even FBI's Hoover had coaxed him to stop it, have his subordinates deal severely with the protesters. This counsel from the director would later be understood in a broader context. J. Edgar's animosity toward the man of letters had been festering for eighteen years.

The FSM itself - beginning with the specious banning of posters, easels and tables from the plaza fronting Sproul Hall, through the arrests, the sit-ins and the Joan Baez appearances, to the incarceration of 814 students at the Santa Rita jail and their subsequent release with faculty-provided bail money - happened two years before I got to Cal, and, while difficult to describe, fits easily into the decade of the sixties: the decade of the sexual revolution, *Hair*, the pill, Freedom Summer, and the summer of love. On a day only three months following Lyndon Johnson's tough won Civil Rights Act, photographer Steven Marcus, himself a student at the time, captured the most memorable expression of that campus chaos with his snaps of a police car, a milling mob of two to three thousand young men and women, and two young men - one standing atop the car, the other alternately peering out its left rear window or sleeping across its back seat during the 32 hours the crowd held it surrounded and motionless. The man inside, Jack Weinberg, a former UCLA grad student in mathematics, had been arrested for passing out literature from the civil rights organization CORE, the Congress of Racial Equality. On top, shoes off to keep from scratching the car - some had already taken a collection to pay for any damages - Mario Savio eloquently addresses the crowd, becomes its ad-hoc leader, talks of a short-term understanding with Kerr, and concludes with the appeal, "I ask you to rise quietly and with dignity, and go home." They do.

By the time I got to Berkeley the cause had changed but dissent persisted, and more confrontationally than during the largely polite FSM-university exchanges. In the last half of the sixties, tables popped up over an ever changing panoply of student vexing issues: throwing out the ROTC, freeing imprisoned Black Panther Huey Newton, gaining more rights for women, stopping local military recruiting, keeping Dow Chemical - maker of napalm - off campus, 'saving' People's Park, even changing, 'reconstituting,' the University itself. Now it's the war in Vietnam. Clark Kerr was purported to have quipped, "Where do they get the time?" Three years will pass before half a million citizens vent their anger in the nation's capital, but Berkeley students had already been on the move - marching with Students for a Democratic Society at the Oakland Army Terminal, listening to faculty teach-ins like those started at the U of Michigan, burning draft cards in front of their local board - a short stroll from campus - and organizing 'Vietnam Day,' a symposium drawing unanticipated thousands to ponder the conflict's ethics.

I'm embarrassed to admit I personally witnessed little of that early activity. Cory Hall sits at Hearst and Gayley, the north-east tip, kitty-corner across campus and about as far as possible from where most of the action took place - that open space inside Sather Gate between Sproul Hall and the Student Union - a sizable separation in distance, a far greater one in temperament. None of my principal associates at Cory, engineer aspirants or non-tenure-track faculty, were likely purveyors of political strife. Looking back, ambition probably accounted for my conflicting behaviors. Even so, it seems strange to have participated in Livermore's anti-nuke gatherings, been thought suspect and photographed by right-wing John Birchers at the Lab, while, during the same years, remain a serious, uninvolved pencil-behind-the-ear techie at Berkeley. Of small relevance here - but even more curious - is that another uninvolved faculty member of the time, a twenty-five-year-old assistant professor teaching math in now-gone Campbell Hall, a short walk across Hearst Mining Circle from my office, would be found responsible, fifteen and eighteen years later, for two bombing injuries, one serious, in that same quiet, restrained Cory Hall. He'd be called "The Unabomber."

Over time my assignments better matched the subjects I felt qualified to teach: data structures, machine organization, operating systems - stuff engineers might really use. It began to be fun. I swaggered a bit, simultaneously feeling like the naked emperor. Clothesless because many around Cory called me doctor - or professor. I was neither. After tracking down the faculty member responsible for admissions, and stuffing his mailbox with requested information, he set up a formal appointment. It was brief. I sat in a straight-back chair across a cluttered oak desk from a man who looked more like an NFL tackle ready to show his stuff than a scholar sizing up a potential colleague. He asked me nothing, looked up from my papers, stared into my face for awhile, then announced, "If you came to apply as an undergraduate, I'd tell you to try elsewhere." Then, rotating his big head side-to-side a couple of times, added, "You haven't even had a course in drafting." I think I heard a sigh before he lowered his eyes back onto my transcripts and concluded, "But I don't know how I can keep you from enrolling as a graduate."

> ### *If there has to be a bloodbath,*
> ### *then let's get it over with.*
> Ronald Reagan - *San Francisco Chronicle*, May 15, 1969

The students in my operating systems class, twenty-six guys and one young woman, were hunkered down at their desks taking the second scheduled midterm of the Spring quarter when Reagan got up-close and personal. Hazy, cloudy stuff wisped its way past our open classroom door in the old wooden Naval Architecture Building near Cory. I walked over to close it, felt my eyes sting and looked out to see a canister rolling toward me; farther down the hall stood a slight, gas-masked figure wearing some type of military apparel. I teared quickly, closed the door, told the class what I'd seen, and asked who wanted to stay and who wanted to leave, an absurd question for a bunch of engineers who'd just studied for an exam.

No one put a hand up for leaving, but the door proved to be an inadequate protector. In a short while, and against vigorous protests from my wet-eyed charges, I insisted. Class was over for the day - a day ending, not far from the other end of campus, in over a hundred injuries and one death - a day named Bloody Thursday.

This time the struggle concerned a 2.8-acre piece of land three streets south of Lower Sproul Plaza, and a quarter block east off colorful, commercial Telegraph Avenue; a neighborhood of small, single-family dwellings when first eyed by the university as an apt site for offices, parking and student housing. For eleven years it remained a wish. Then, after acquiring sufficient funds and with plans simplified to sports field and parking lot, a purchase made through eminent domain forced eviction of the residents - the bulldozing of their homes. Money ran out before the project completed, and the razed plot - abandoned throughout the winter - became a murky sea of rubble-dotted mud, a place to dump unwanted cars. Merchants from 'The Ave' got together with other locals to find a solution. Without concurrence from the school, they decided on a park, enlisted both community and student help, and in less than a month voiced their praise for the now tidy, if not pristine, space: paths, garden, trees. During the cleanup and planting, the university announced another reduction in plans - no parking lot - a playing field would be enough. Chancellor Heyns promised to take no action without a warning. It proved too much for the governor to ignore; a singular opportunity, a campaign promise to fulfill. Heyns had said a warning would be given, not the governor. He'd let his constituents know how to deal with a direct leftist challenge. All stops are out as he declares the campus "a haven for communist sympathizers, protesters, and sex deviants."

Sixteen months later with coursework completed, I had a choice: get the Master of Science degree by writing a research thesis or by reporting on a project I'd hope to pursue for a doctorate. What would you do? Even if I later failed, I'd have the M.S. sans thesis; besides, an appealing project really did exist - a cheap little machine, all my own. After summer break, I registered for classes and picked up my diploma at the departmental office. There in that frameable certificate - affording me 'all the rights and privileges thereto pertaining' - I read in bold black letters across its lower left corner the reproduced signature of a man not considered a great admirer of the institution over which he presided: *Ronald Reagan*, GOVERNOR OF CALIFORNIA AND PRESIDENT OF THE REGENTS. The man had struck again; his signature would be with me for life.

That year, 1970, and the one following became pivotal for me, as well as a major bump in the university's ongoing student restlessness. I left the Lab for a programming job on campus; we bought a lovely old house in north Berkeley; our kids played a role integrating Berkeley public schools; and Joan found a lump in her left breast. At UC, the reaction to events may have been unique, but turmoil erupted nationally after Ohio National Guardsmen shot and wounded nine students and killed four others - one, at least, while simply walking past 'the commons,' a place on the Kent State campus where protesters gathered after Nixon announced that American troops had entered Cambodia. Demonstrations rocked 700 or so colleges, and a student strike of over 4,000,000 - high schoolers on up - shut down more than 450 campuses.

The cry on the Berkeley campus was "RECONSTITU-TION." I don't know if I ever knew what that really meant, even after traipsing up to the Greek Theater along with about fifteen thousand others two days after the shootings, and listening to it explained by Political Science Professor Wolin - later Emeritus Professor of Politics, Princeton University. In retrospect, I think I took it all a bit opportunistically, opting for pass-fail credit in a rigorous, and particularly difficult, recursive functions course, and getting through an information retrieval seminar with a term paper titled "Information Retrieval and its Relevance to a Reconstituted University." The paper proposed a number of shockingly radical notions - like outlawing live lectures, restricting faculty to data-base enhancing research, and asking students to refuse degrees - which leads me to doubt any of the Cory Hall elite hosting that class ever looked at it. I do know at least one person later read it. I know because I'd submitted it for inclusion in the Association for Computing Machinery's National Conference to be held in Chicago the following year. Its rejection letter came back bearing one reviewer's scrawled comment: *"If this student had been in my class, 9 would have failed him/her!"*

It's just not possible to exaggerate Berkeley's uniqueness - neighborhood to neighborhood, block to block, street to street; it's all different, changing from the heady hills where rock climbers first practiced for their assaults on the mountains of Yosemite to the narrow spit poking west past the shoreline, presenting its marina to the blue bay. A single salesman we felt some loyalty toward showed us over seventy houses. He didn't seem to hear us. We bought the first one shown us by a second realtor. The move from Livermore changed my visual experience of the outdoors, from Polaroid-like snaps of brown rolling hills to intense Fuji-color emulsions of the world beyond campus. Standing on our new back porch, a story above the house's finished basement, the backyard looked to be a fairy forest - flanked left and right by a tall, old redwood and an ancient, slanting sycamore, before rolling down invitingly to Codornices Creek, its eastern border. Surprisingly, its cost was modest; the neighborhood middle class.

Berkeley felt good to Joan and me. We made our place pretty, we built bunks and desks for the kids in upstairs rooms, we painted walls and ceilings, bought bright furniture from a store on 'the Ave' - Telegraph, and we dined, visited friends, and played together. And in Berkeley, age didn't excuse anyone from being an active progressive. Our seven- and nine-year-olds dutifully hiked the two blocks to Hopkins Street every school morning, where the bus they boarded angled southeast to its end on San Pablo for another short walk to their designated grade school: forgotten, decaying, old Franklin Elementary. The city, the first in the nation to desegregate its schools without being ordered by a court, did so by implementing two way bussing - black youngsters were to be hauled east to the affluent hills and white kids west to the neglected buildings toward the bay; a leak from a sink in our daughter's class dripped its way to the room below. I don't know if their black classmates missed the busses heading east, for if any other white-skinned kids, beside ours, attended Franklin, I never caught sight of them.

My new job, located in a commercial building near Berkeley High a convenient mile-and-a-half from home and about a mile from Cory, provided me a lot of flexibility. I could float easily between teaching, classes, and work. The work itself, senior programmer for a research group ostensibly building a failure-proof machine by duplicating much of its hardware, didn't much excite me. Particularly because my specific assignment turned out to be the coding of a programming language created, unnecessarily, to implement this project and no other. If I had to write code, I liked front end design, stuff that made a user's work more intuitive; not builder's tools or gritty unseen layers down in the muck. Besides, while I designed well, I wrote pretty sloppy code, about like what you get in a system sold by Microsoft. It wouldn't have occurred to me at the time, but the project likely also raised many 'reconstitutionalist' eyebrows. IBM had financed it and our boss, a former employee of theirs who'd ushered in the money, had, without a PhD or academic experience, been rewarded with a tenured faculty position.

Before that first Berkeley year ended, good news preceded bad, followed by tears. With a tiny - but later meaningless - touch of fortune, Joan avoided a procedure common in those years: the one step - a patient under anesthesia would have her lump biopsied and, if deemed cancerous, its soft, encircling breast removed, there and then. Go to sleep with a lump, wake up without a breast. In Joan's case, our primary care guy cut out a small sample of the questioned tissue right in his office, and sent it off to the lab. He was an internist, but practiced like an old-fashioned family doc: handing out financial imperatives along with medical ones, freezing away skin tags or unsightly lesions without asking, doing minor surgical chores without referrals, and caring, always seeming to care. Joan picked up his upbeat call a few days after the biopsy. He told her the pathologist had found nothing. A couple of weeks later he called again. This time I answered. He sounded a little conspiratorial; a second pathologist had looked at the sample and it didn't look good. I'll not give him a unique name as I did for MDs in a previous chapter, only say I did get to know him later and liked him; liked him for all the reasons mentioned above, and for the way he spoke of his own dozen kids. I think Joan first liked him as well; liked him before he recommended the surgeon who tore off her breast, tore it off without mercy, tore it off along with all the muscle, lymph and tissue mass on her left chest and under that arm; performed what he called in sanitized doc-speak a 'radical mastectomy'; sent her home with a weak, long-useless arm, hanging limply alongside a flat half-chest: flat and hard as an archer's shield.

Joan had for several years been on 'the pill.' What role that played in her cancer I can only guess - thinking back to our earlier talk of the toll artificial hormones exacted on many post-menopausal women. The pills at the time Joan took them had five times the estrogen used today, and they remained on the market until pulled from shelves at FDA request seventeen years later. The site of Joan's operation and recovery, Alta Bates Medical Center, took us about as far south of campus as our Colusa house stood north. The kids and I tried our best to enjoy the neighborhood nearby; ate Chinese, poked around the shops, and got ice cream a few times at a, then, always-crowded parlor on Telegraph just south of Ashby. I took Joan a large black and white poster: a scrawny, pale cat with dark paws, ears, and tail, dangling from front claws wrapped tenuously around a thin branch. A caption, below and to its left, read, "Hang In There, Baby." The nurses helped me attach it to the curtain track by her bed. I got a number of goodwill strokes from them and from other patients. Joan smiled at it - a weary, half-hearted smile; I don't believe it much amused her. When she returned home, I took a formal leave of classes. She spent the next several months walking her left arm up walls - the fingers of that hand moving like little legs - until partial arm strength gradually returned. How do you show comfort? How do you show sympathy? You don't. You say really dumb, stupid things, ... : "I like you better this way." ... "Why?" ... "Cause we're more the same."

We old computer junkies, guys and gals who grew up programming ancient IBM-700 series machines, knew what those devices looked like inside - what everything did, how it ticked, how data moved between memory and registers, how numbers got worked on by processing units, how stuff got into and out of it - all of that structure now called machine architecture. We had to know because we wrote machine - or later its more readable form, assembly language - code, code that the computer's hardware interpreted directly. We sometimes thought in hexadecimal, but mainly in octal, number systems that let us condense our picture of the machine's binary guts. What we didn't know was how to build one - how that maze, those thousands of components engineers managed to wire together, made up that architecture, made the logic inside glow hot with vacuum tubes, made memories first of dots on cathode ray tubes, Williams tubes, then later out of little magnetic rings called 'cores.'

Then came integrated circuits and everything changed. It didn't come overnight. In the U.S. it took more than a decade from inventing the transistor at Bell Labs to cobbling a few together onto a single chip, a chip first of germanium at Texas Instruments, then of silicon at Fairchild Semiconductor. By the time Reagan's facsimile signature appeared on my MS diploma, you could buy, in what's called Transister-Transister Logic, TTL, a complete arithmetic logic unit on a single piece of silicon. It could add, subtract, compare magnitudes, and do a bunch of logic functions. Within three years Texas Instruments began distributing a large, fat, bright-yellow, hardcovered, 640 - growing later to 832 - page book the *TTL Data Book for Design Engineers*. It showed how to hook up hundreds of such chips, all with different functions. Now we could do it; we old-time programmers could build our own machines - hypothetically at least. It might take a little engineering to know where to stick a capacitor or a resister, but even that would be made pretty simple a short while later with publisher Sams' release of the *TTL Cookbook*.

To this day, people ask me who invented the personal computer. The simple answer is no one; integrated circuits made it possible - possible for almost anyone. "What about the book *How I Invented the Personal Computer?*" they go on, adding that it's about a machine made by Apple. I tell them, "I haven't read that book, but guess the author meant the title as a joke."

The first Apple sold in mid-1976, quite a while after a bunch of other PCs were either around, designed, or already on the market. Like Henry Ford - who never laid claim to inventing a car, just a better way of putting one together - Apple had a talent for marketing and an abundance of enthusiasm. The DINKIAC I, my entry into the world of little computers, got its first formal introduction in Atlantic City at the American Federation of Information Processing Societies' 1971 Spring Joint Computer Conference. I thought the man who critiqued the talk crazy for writing, " … it is the reviewer's opinion that the problem of extending computers to the consumer level market is not as strongly related to cost as it is to the question of what you do with it if you get it." Not so inapt a question at a time when even illustrious John McCarthy considered them toys; championing for a future that belonged to time-sharing.

What could you then expect from a machine of your own? You couldn't get on the internet; you didn't have much of what could be called an operating system - we'll look at CP/M and DOS later - and my paper foolishly left out anything about application programs. I wrote that the Dinkiac could be used like a desk calculator, but didn't think to add you could make it look like any calculator you wanted, have separate programs for every calculator on earth if you wished. In those days most of us never thought of programs as having any monetary value. They were free; only hardware cost money. Further back, at the very time Joe B.'s program tracked Sputnik, the U.S. Department of Defense created ARPA, the Advanced Research Project Agency. They gave it a single goal: avoid future technological surprises - like that Russian satellite. A decade would pass before that mandate changed, and, as we dreamed of owning our own machines, ARPA began ARPANET, the internet's progenitor. By the time a modem could be bought and jammed into a slot on a PC with a standard motherboard to - maybe - gain trickling phone access to that fledgling universe, the Dinkiac would have been six years old.

Unlike colleagues forming Silicon Valley start-ups, I made no money designing the never-built Dinkiac I. It did bring other rewards. It became the basis for my dissertation, for a patent drawn up without charge by an attorney interested in new technology, for a grant proposal to the NSF - National Science

Foundation - with the attendant possibility of a tenure-track faculty offer (forgive me reconstitutionalists) and, for a source of personal amusement. The NSF concluded my faculty advisor, an automata theorist, and I - neither with hardware experience - were unsuitable candidates for the large at that time, $207,600, I had requested. Happily, the time they took before sending a rejection kept me favored, for many months, as a potential source of departmental revenue.

'Lowest-possible-cost' and 'off-the-shelf-parts' became the main mantras dictating Dinkiac design. To avoid high memory costs it was to have a virtual memory - like a time-sharing system. Somehow, while I knew of three-year-old Intel's microprocessor, the first ever, built that year to - strange as it sounds here - power a Japanese calculator, I completely overlooked how they and competing companies would soon and significantly drop memory prices, bringing them in line with their other integrated circuits. For computer history junkies, the Dinkiac's entire review, taken from Computer Reviews of the Association For Computing Machinery, October '71, is given below:

6.2 COMPUTER SYSTEMS

Author (Univ. California, Berkeley, 22,070 Calif.)

The DINKIAC I—a pseudo-virtual-memoried mini—for stand-alone interactive use. [in Proc. AFIPS 1971 Spring Joint Computer Conf., AFIPS Press, Montvale, N. J., 1-9. See main entry CR 12, 9 (Sept. 1971), Rev, 21,789.]

This paper is an interesting exercise in "cheap-cheap" computer design. The author outlines a processor containing four magnetostrictive delay lines with a capacity of 1,024 16-bit words for primary memory, a small (7 rows of 12 characters) CRT, a key-board, some lamps and switches, and a tape cassette used as secondary storage.

Because of the relatively small primary memory, the author chooses to consider the computer a paged machine, with each delay line corresponding to a page and with the cassette tape containing up to 128 additional pages. Page swapping is under software control, although the author gives a brief description of an originally planned (and rejected on the basis of cost) automated page swapping control.

The bulk of the paper is taken up with a description of a simulation that attempts to justify some design choices (page size, delay line lengths, etc.), and to quantify the performance one could expect if such a machine were available. As the basic instruction rate is determined by the delay line frequency and the optimal placement of data with respect to the instructions referring to them, performance is strongly related to the page fetch/swap delays and the pattern of branching associated with a given program.

The author concludes that a machine such as he describes could sell for under $3,000; if so, it could replace all current desk calculator applications with a completely general purpose computer that offers the same functions (and speeds) at the same or lower cost, and that will provide, in addition, a single-user computing experience similar to that obtained from interactive working. He envisions it primarily as a conversational Joss or Basic machine, although he speculates that use of the cassette tape permits inexpensive specialization by providing tapes for desk calculators, preparing Federal income tax, and the like.

Perhaps it is unfair to place undue emphasis on this aspect of the paper, except that the author himself raises the question: what good is an inexpensive, low-performance, general-purpose computer?

The real question of utility of this approach hinges on the truth or falsity of the assumption that, given a choice between a desk calculator and a computer for the same price, most people would buy the computer. This reviewer would surely challenge that assumption. There is a greater difference between even an advanced desk calculator and a computer than price alone would indicate. While it is difficult to put precisely into words, the difference is that the functions performed by a computer must be preplanned to a greater degree and at a more elementary level than is required by a calculator. Thus, in effect, the appeal of the design in this paper is to the professional programmer. To him the critical issue will be whether or not the 500 instructions per second execution rate is fast enough for him to do anything interesting with. To anyone else, the considerably greater inconvenience and difficulty of using the computer may prove a deterrent.

Further, it is the reviewer's opinion that the problem of extending computers to the consumer level market is not as strongly related to cost as it is to the question of what you do with it if you get it. The author alludes to the capability of the machine to specialize in dedicated applications such as desk calculator, Federal income tax, and the like. The machine would be a clear choice over a desk calculator only if the variety of these applications were quite large.

The paper is, however, well written and quite interesting. It is recommended to anyone interested in the current limit on low-priced machines based on standard, available hardware.

The reviewer's name has been deleted from its place below the text. He may not wish, in today's PC world, to be associated with: " … the question of what you do with it if you get it."

> *Now the works of the flesh are*
> *manifest, which are these;*
> *Adultery, fornication, uncleanness, lasciviousness,*
> Gal. 5:19

I don't know it you ever really leave the Lab. There's a you're-one-of-us feeling about the place, a feeling that overrides the clutch in your gut when you think of its major undertaking: better and bigger bombs. I felt that cozy pull when they issued me a new badge, my ticket to pass an always alert guard, a guy scrutinizing us - the badge and me - like two wanted felons, despite having waved us by a zillion times before. While the job would be all new and different, my return played out like a homecoming; tramping familiar grounds, gathering supplies from the old stockroom, reconnecting with friends - and foes. I'd been hired into the RISOS - Research in Secured Operating Systems - project; another program sponsored by the Defense Department's ever-expanding ARPA. Over Sid's objections - he wanted me to come back as a temp - the group's Principal Investigator rehired me as a full-timer, meaning if ARPA's funds dried up, the Atomic Energy Commission would have to pay my salary. I got started there as soon as my degree's completion requirements had been verified, months before being officially hooded at the Hearst Greek Theatre. By that time I'd been pretty much integrated into the group, acquired a brilliant young partner, Rick - a recent top-of-his-class, PhD graduate in engineering from the University of Hawaii - and had started submitting technical papers, based, most often, on Rick's ideas.

I can't recall when I started riding the bus, transportation provided by the university to get staff between Berkeley and Livermore. It had to have been after June 15, '74, the day my advisor failed to show up so a friend, a junior faculty member, draped the bright blue and gold hood over my head, transforming me into one of the favored - one, once again, with all the rights and privileges thereto pertaining. This time, like chiropractors, dentists, and physicians, my rights included the 'right' to be called doctor. I'd make that clear to my MDs' receptionists, imagining they'd now summon me with, "The doctor will see you now doctor." Three things that occurred on that bright, sunny day in late spring continue to remain vivid: Rick's wife, Susan, brightening my hood in Hawaiian ceremonial fashion with a lei of pink and white orchids; Joan taking super-8 films of our kids wearing my gown, arms stretched straight to their sides, leaping off the front porch, zigging around the yard, looking like bats; noting my new diploma bore a second, never-to-be-destroyed copy of our governor's signature. "There you go again," Mr. Reagan.

I would board the usually empty bus on Hopkins, about a half block north of where my kids took their school shuttle. It would weave around, picking up a passenger here and there, before stopping by Lake Merritt where Naomi joined me. Our encounters could be made to read like a romance novel. I'll begin that way, but the complicated, unflattering truth requires far more probing. On my first bus ride, she sat directly across from me, looked over, smiled, opened a book, and read. From that day on she simply sat on the bench next to me, talking as if we needed no introduction. Her chatter began casually enough, increasing gradually from the personal to the intimate. She'd look up at me with her beautiful young eyes and comment, "My brother-in-law wants me to sleep with him," or, with a self-pleased little grin, "I'm doing kegels."

What was it I then wanted, and why must I write of it here? If you feel burdened, dumped on by my guilt, then, please, skip ahead to the next scene break. For me it's a story of the times, an account of rationalizing, of stupidity, of how men thought - think. Not all men, maybe not even most, but those whose actions altered their lives. Were we, Naomi and me, as dime fiction would have us, 'drawn together with a fervor akin to nebulae swirling together, forming ever larger masses, becoming stars'? Not even close. Together, away from her apartment, I felt only an anxiety bordering on terror; would we be seen together? Once, a few weeks before Christmas, we went to check out some new exhibits at Lawrence Hall of Science in the hills above campus. We'd been there less than half an hour when I remembered Joan's mention of possibly buying a Mushroom Kit and a Prism-Light Crystal at its gift shop, presents for the kids. Naomi - puzzled - couldn't guess why I rushed her out of there - pulse pounding. Even physically, sexually, we never much matched. Her petite, and visually lovely lips felt awkward, missing and wanted, against mine, their more ample pursuers. I had no experience of our mouths coalescing, binding, tickling our passion. So much for the romance image. In what's to come - either here, or later when I write of my marriage's disintegration - it's important to limit lines of explicit sexual content, like the ones above; to refrain from soliciting interest with shock, ala Howard Stern, or by encouraging clucks of disgust.

In the 1979 movie *Manhattan* a party guest tells Woody Allen (Isaac Davis), "I finally had an orgasm, and my doctor said it was the wrong kind." Allen replies, "You had the wrong kind? I've never had the wrong kind, ever, ever. My worst one was right on the money." I feel compelled to admit that my experience conforms with Mr. Allen's, romance or no romance. I'd often looked at women with desire, even made office remarks that could today get me cited for harassment. In back rooms at parties, I'd touched, kissed, rubbed against the wives of a few colleagues, but in seventeen years of marriage had not stepped over the line drawn with the narrow courthouse definition of fidelity. I clung to an image of the world that differed from the real jungle we live in; saw it as did Anais Nin with her naïve, imaginative notion that multiple partners wouldn't alter her person; her sexuality wouldn't, to paraphrase, "wash away her genitalia as if they were soap." She, as I, failed to acknowledge that we were people, humans, not bonobos, not little chimpanzee-like apes who could call upon sex anytime, anywhere - and with any other - to relax, resolve conflict, show affection, garner social status, just get excited and enjoy. Even today I'd argue for the superiority of bonobo sexual behavior over ours. Saying that necessitates repeating: we are not bonobos. We're people, humans, a species whose actions might hurt, can hurt, do hurt - cause pain, sometimes great pain. Neither Ms. Nin nor I accepted the complexity of a simple screw.

Justification abounded. The greater part of the sixties had passed us, Joan and me, quietly, and in Livermore; the decade that had, as mentioned before, blared out its message of sexual revolution with *Hair*, the pill, Masters and Johnson, the summer of love. I restate that here as an observation, not a witless excuse. Also - whether true or imagined - when struggling for and after getting the PhD, I found myself an occasional and flattered recipient of suggestive remarks from young, attractive women - a complete reversal of the past. But my main prompting likely derived from a less obvious motivator than anything so far considered: the machinations of a distorted, latent-infantile intellect. In this four decade later retrospective, I see myself then as a fruitcake. I lived with the recurrent notion of fusing, exploding, melding into another; being absorbed in a sexual odyssey of colliding galaxies; finding a woman, a Joan of Arc who would forsake the siege of Orléans and live for me, for me alone, for our ecstasy together. Was that union sexual only? No! It was an affair far more Hollywood.

Except for getting a funky little roach holder from Naomi, Christmas passed that year much like any other: a tree by the front window wearing old family ornaments and topping out about a foot under the eight-foot-something living room ceiling, sheltered an early morning flurry of gift exchanges - mostly for the kids, and the afternoon replayed Thanksgiving's food-centered activities. The tree remained decorated and unmoved when, in mid-January, Joan walked toward me from the hall that opened between the living and dining rooms. The children had left the night before to enjoy a weekend with Ernie's family at their Lake Tahoe cabin. I'd been shuffling through notes for Rick, and had just gotten out of a chair on the far side of the dining room table. She looked directly at me, unsmiling, hazel-green eyes fixed long on mine, then asked - in uncharacteristic monotone, "Am I the last to know?" My eyes dropped. I looked where they fell, staring at her feet, seeing them unflatteringly wrapped in bulky sheepskin slippers, a holiday gift; trying without success to choke back an irritating half-giggle, one that forced its way out whenever embarrassment paralyzed me. I sank back down into my chair - acting stupid, uncomprehending, unknowing, dumb, ... , then defensive, ... , then quiet. ... . Relieved? ... ... Had I hoped she'd find out?

Joan and I were talkers. We talked our way through almost everything that had to do with our lives together: what to buy, how much to spend, who wore what, what we thought others thought - on and on. With Joan that's just who she was - open - Joan being Joan. For me, it's not clear how much the need to persuade, to get my way, influenced what I said. If I did talk only to manipulate, I didn't know it, and it didn't distract from the warmth, the closeness, talk brought me - an intimacy greater than any I experienced outside of bed. Now it stopped. How could it not have? Time had to pass. Time after my exile to the guest room, then the family room down in the basement. Time until Joan grasped what she needed to do next.

She'd been a student at Antioch College in Yellow Springs, Ohio, the only school then with a work-study program. The work credit she'd earned came from counseling disadvantaged pre-teens. Counseling had always been an interest, now she wanted to be counseled. She surprised me by joining a group that met weekly in a sprawling College Avenue house, across and down the street from the Julia Morgan Theater. Surprised me because it went by a name I found impossible to associate with her, 'Radical Psychiatry.' To me, radical meant political. It did. Its founder had taken the name from a group at an American Psychiatric Association meeting in Florida opposed to the Vietnam War. Now, with that conflict ended - the last of the CIA station contingency recently plucked off a Saigon rooftop - Berkeley seemed quieter than I could ever remember. Radical psychiatry didn't mean marching or burning draft cards, but sitting around on the floor, five or more in a circle, working with each other and a therapist, talking out problems that troubled. Some also tried bodywork - yelling, deep breathing, pillow pounding - practices Joan would later lead - to our daughter's eye rolling - in my now permanent basement retreat.

Life went on. Chatty talk began again, emerging, slowly, gradually, from the curt one-liners of daily necessity: "Your laundry's still in the dryer," "I won't be back til after ten," "Did you feed Fritz?" Fritz, our three-year-old keeshond, did cause a bit of extra talk during that monosyllabic period. He'd spend many daytime hours straddling the lowest major limb of the old sycamore, hanging, dangling all four of his legs over it like a contented, digesting leopard. He'd get there by running up its slanting trunk. One afternoon he followed our children into the front yard and there, without provocation and for reasons no one has yet ascertained, bit the leg of our next door neighbor's eleven-year-old daughter. It may have been a trigger. Within a few weeks, Joan persuaded me to join one of the Psych groups; not hers, that would have been considered improper, too much concentrated power. I would go on a different night.

Although hoped for, it actually startled me when Joan began speaking directly of our rift; surprised me even more when she ventured, timidly, "You'd like us to have an open marriage wouldn't you?" A book by that name, *Open Marriage*, had received considerable press in those heady post-sixties days, growing out of a misreading, by many of its over one-and-a-half million purchasers, that it advocated sex with multiple partners, a claim unsupported by its authors, Nena and George O'Neill, who wrote, "We are not recommending outside sex, but we are not saying that it should be avoided, either. The choice is entirely up to you." I understood Joan's question in its popular sense. Is that what I wanted? Did I want a marriage with each of us having other partners? As usual, her query came well ahead of any clarity I had about where my actions should take me. Naomi and I had stopped meeting; I'd been seeing Grace, a young woman who worked with her. Grace had walked up to within bumping distance of me one day, looked up, and with her mouth an inch or two from mine, introduced herself.

A paper I wrote for RISOS gave me a temporary reprieve, more time to think. I'd based it on some clever ideas of Rick's about using 'flow models' to check a system's security. The Canadian Information Processing Society accepted it for their 'Computer Pow-Wow,' a conference to be held that summer in Regina, Saskatchewan. Schools would be out; I made arrangements for my own vacation to coincide, convinced Joan it would be a wonderful experience for all of us, and we were off: Berkeley to Yellowstone Park to the Province of Saskatchewan, back west across Canada to Victoria B.C., and home - three-thousand-six-hundred and eighty-two miles on the old Delta 88 Oldsmobile odometer.

While the open marriage question never had to be directly answered, the trip would be, sadly, our last major family outing. On the ferry ride back to the States from Vancouver Island - a bouncy, blowy passage across the Strait of Juan de Fuca that pleased no one aboard over the age of twelve - and while Joan and I stood clutching tightly to a rail near the ship's stern watching the Olympic Mountains leap up and down on the horizon, I suddenly, all sense possibly jarred from my head by the motion, blurted, "Shit, I forgot to bring anything back for Grace." I got no response from Joan at the time, only a long enigmatic look, one that could have meant anything from amusement to bemusement - or simply musing. Later, as we approached Port Angeles seated in the calm of the mid-ship lounge, she offered, "Why don't you see if you can find Grace something in this little port town? Probably a lot of gift shops around." "That's OK with you?" I mumbled. "Sure, why not," she shot back quickly, matter-of-factly, like she'd just suggested a chew-toy for Fritz. It overwhelmed me. Why? Because of her abrupt change in tone, one of acceptance, not a heavy acceptance, like Kübler-Ross's last stage of grief, but an almost joyous one. "You're OK with Grace?" I pressed. She smiled, "We'll see how it works."

I saw Grace only once after giving her a hand-crafted drinking glass, cut and twisted from a brown beer bottle, that I'd purchased at a place on the corner of Front and Lincoln in Port Angeles. I gave it to her wrapped together with a can of Pepsi, a drink she never seemed to be without. She didn't thank me much for my thoughtfulness, but it's unlikely the twisted glass could alone have been responsible for severing our connection. A few weeks later I unwittingly broke a major Radical Psychiatry rule, ending up in bed with a fellow Tuesday-night-session attendee, Betty, following a dinner of honey-almond lamb topped off with a cigarette she'd fashioned of cannabis sativa leaves. Epicurean components of the evening took place at El Mansour, a newly opened Moroccan restaurant on Clement Street in San Francisco's Richmond District, only a short walk from her apartment. The reaction to our naive and excited sharing of the night's events, from both the group and its leader, shocked us. We continued to see one another, but not in group. Sexual intimates, like married couples, could wield too much power, gang up on others in the circle. My association with Betty, while lasting far longer than with either Naomi or Grace, had no sense of permanence, just another in a line of disjointed, stumbling interactions. Serial monogamy stands out as a particularly bizarre constant in these goings-on, for except in my own marriage, being with someone new happened only after parting from another. Little else remained predictable in my post-Naomi days.

Talking with, seeing Bill again, hearing him laugh as he's greeted on the phone with my expected, "Fuck J. Edgar Hoover," ranks high among the benefits brought me by returning to the lab. Despite his own wealth of technical knowledge, insight and ideas - a movie he'd created the previous summer while on temporary loan to MIT took viewers down Boston Streets, traveling close to the speed of light, letting them see the effects of Einsteinian relativity on the signs they passed - he'd be there to listen, to umm, to nod and to praise specific details of any work you had to offer. He did this with a broad smile on his handsome face when commenting on the Dinkiac's small instruction set, "Yeah, I could write worthwhile stuff with these ... ," and went on, "What'd you plan on for an operating system?" "Not really anything, Bill," I answered him timidly, "just punching everything in at the keyboard." "How about I introduce you to John Torode and Gary Kildall," he countered, "or do you know them?" "No not really, I may have met John on campus, and I've heard a little of what Gary's working on, but ... ."

Gary and John had been classmates at the University of Washington, getting PhDs in Computer Science. They'd both headed south to teach, John at Berkeley and Gary at the Naval Post Graduate School in Monterey, right next to Pacific Grove where he'd later start his company, Intergalactic Digital Research. He'd received a contract with the Lab licensing the use of CP/M, his Control Program for Microcomputers. Octopus time-sharing honchos wanted it to monitor programs in that network. CP/M was the first ever operating system for microprocessors and Lawrence Laboratory the first to license it. Gary needed to get it, and the controller for the floppy disk it ran from, operational. Bill led me to where he sat, hunched over and frowning at a pile of printouts on a low table temporarily set up between one of the Control Data STAR computers and a row of tape drives. He didn't appear annoyed by the interruption, answering my very broad questions about his work with the softness of a teacher to a poorly-informed student.

Those of you who still use an operating system with a boot component called BIOS need to credit Gary with that name and its purpose. "I wrote the system in three parts," he told me. "BIOS, the smallest and only part that has to be tailored for different machines, checks out and starts things up, you know, loads the system from the disk. Then there's CCP to process console commands, and the Basic Disk Operating System itself, BDOS, the file system, and ... ." Bill interrupted, "You've seen GORDO, Gary, this is the guy who ... ." "Oh sure," he laughed, "would you like to look at some of this code?" I demurred, but did query him about the floppy disk, "I hear you're working on controller hardware ... ." Another interruption, "Oh, John Torode's doing that. We can ... ."

> *Let us not be desirous of vain glory, provoking*
> *one another, envying one another.*
> Gal. 5:26

Thinking of that time, thinking of BDOS and the system calls it provided - to move data, to read and write files, to get status information - I'm caught up in the turbulence, the intrigue, the fourteen years of bitterness and haranguing and the ensuing four decades of commentary in journals, *Forbes*, *Bloomberg*, blogs, a book chapter, even a PBS series - over the alleged, possible, probable misappropriation by Microsoft's Bill Gates of that small piece of software. In 1992, the University of Washington invited Gary, as a distinguished graduate, to attend its celebration of their computer science department's silver anniversary. He'd been among that department's first to earn a doctorate. For keynote speaker they chose not him, but Harvard dropout William Henry Gates III. Not long after, Gary wrote a short memoir, *Computer Connections*. In its appendix, and remembering that DOS's first 26 system calls worked the same as CP/M's, he called it "plain and simple theft." On a more personal note, he wrote of Gates, "He is divisive. He is manipulative. He is a user. He has taken much from me and the industry," and elsewhere, "Well, it seems to me that he did have an education to get there. It happened to be mine, not his."

It's doubtful even Hercule Poirot could piece together the story that unfolded between and around these once friends, Gates and Kildall. It all began in 1980, six years after I'd met Gary at the Lab. Even more of a mystery to those who lived through those times was seeing Microsoft, a company of two people with nothing more to peddle than an interpreter for the trivial programming language BASIC, become bigger than International Business Machines - IBM - Big Blue - the biggest of the big; it's like a kid with a lemonade stand outselling Walmart - and all because of this same little piece of code.

To briefly outline that cloudy tale, told so many times before, it was Gates, himself, who sent IBM to met with DRI, Digital Research Inc. - by then the shtick 'Intergalactic' had been struck from the company name.

Did Gary meet with them?

Gary said he did, Gates appears to have been complicit with journalists who say no, reporting Kildall was out joy-flying in his private plane when the IBM reps showed up.

Did Gates have an alternative system to sell IBM?

Not at the time. He bought QDOS, Quick and Dirty Operating System, from Tim Paterson.

Was Paterson's QDOS copied from CP/M?

That's the sixty-four thousand dollar question, and what Sir Harold Evans alleges in his book, *They Made America*. Paterson sued Evans and his publisher, Little Brown, for defamation. The judge threw out the case on a number of counts, observing, "truth is an absolute defense to a claim of defamation."

Did IBM offer CP/M to its PC purchasers, as an alternative to DOS?

Yes, in return for Gary's release of liability. They charged $40 for DOS and $240 for CP/M.

I gave no thought back then to any of this and, like most PC buyers, too much of a cheapskate to pay the extra two hundred dollars for an elegant product over one that mostly worked. If I have any gripe with Microsoft, it's not over what it may or may not have wrested from others - actions seen in its spate of litigations, huge cases against the United States or the European Union to smaller players like Novell, some won, some lost - and not because it brought about the fall of companies creating software superior to its own, like the word processor Wordperfect, but because Microsoft took away something dear to me, the precious hardware lying buried, layer under layer, below its sloppy code. Little by little, with each new Windows release, DOS disappeared, became harder and harder to access, until only a monstrous system remains, a system reproducing and spewing files wherever it pleases, burning up memory like worthless trash, sending its daily warning "New updates are available," hoping they'll stamp out yesterday's bugs.

Not long after Gary had CP/M ready for use with the Octopus, I left the Lab for good. Well, not really for good; I got a consultant's badge and came back whenever I could convince someone I might have information they needed. Two reasons prompted that resignation: a tenure track faculty offer from the department of electrical engineering at U.C. Davis, and a growing agitation - a work-interfering helplessness - over what I'd set in motion, the disintegration of a family, mine. Joan soldiered on, patiently and caringly, with a rarely shattered outward calm, but when that poise faltered, it didn't just dissipate, it exploded - dramatically. One weekday afternoon, I'd come up from my dungeon living space leaving two acquaintances - actually business partners - working on the hardware for a tape system we hoped to market. Joan asked me a reasonable question about plans for the evening, who'd be with the kids, that sort of thing, and I can't remember any of the words that came before it began - our shouting, yelling, screaming, turning us into two cats on a fence - out of control. My associates appeared from below and glowering at me nonstop, made their unescorted exit out our front door.

The cassette storage device being developed in that basement space demonstrates my second failure at market prediction. Memory did not become a cost consideration for personal computers, and neither would the price of a floppy disk. I'd left the Lab in mid-spring, in time to get my head together before the June 2nd start of the Davis fall quarter. Shortly after, I got a conference call from two very persistent men at IMSAI - Information Management Sciences Associates, Incorporated - a personal computer maker, the favorite of many hobbyists. I never learned where they got my name. They asked if I'd do a little software clean up for them, told me I'd be well compensated. Nothing, at the time, could have gotten past my 'please leave me alone mood'; all their talent at persuasion blocked by an automatic "No, no" to commitment. I asked for a return number; told them I'd get in touch. Less than an hour and a half later, a half hour before dinner, a non-stop ringing of the front door bell startled, jarred, forced me to answer. I found the IMSAI duo standing there, smiling broadly, holding up a quite nice-looking machine, an IMSAI 8080. Who could refuse it? I did do a little work for them, met two of their engineers, and the three of us quit to form our own, one-product company, Micro Designs Inc. Our product: cassette drives that differed from all others. They had randomly accessible data blocks, yep, like floppy disks, and they would be much cheaper. My job, provide an operating system - how about CP/M?

Joan had had enough. Unbelievably, I didn't know it was coming. She invited the four of us upstairs one afternoon, to the dormer den between the kids' bedrooms. We sat on cushions already there, in a kind of irregular circle, looking back and forth at one another, the seriousness of the gathering apparent. "I'm going to move out," she began, "I just want everyone to know, and to be able to have a say." I said little. Our daughter decided she'd go with me to Davis, when I left to teach; our boy, not yet twelve, would follow his mom. Joan's plans followed a gut-searing struggle with what to do next. She'd been forced into a 'Sixties' vision of relationship, unaided by upbringing or a polygamous nature, to face the bitterness of being regarded, at forty-three, an 'older woman' - old in a world of 'young bucks' her age or older. When, one day, she did inform me she'd be spending the night with a friend in the city, in San Francisco, I passed the night lying stretched out, rigid, stiff in that bleak basement room - staring at the ceiling, unmoving, cold and afraid - a night with no end. How could she be with another man? She had reached out to me earlier with a proposal, "I've gotten to know someone who teaches sex play to couples. Talk to her, go see her, it might give us a ball, a toy to play with." I met the woman and asked her about some issues I'd been having with Betty. ... .

Chapter 14

The Unknown Years - College

*To give subtilty to the simple, to the young man
knowledge and discretion.*
Prov. 1:4

The war was over for String. For everyone else it had been
over for 3 years, 5 months and either 5 or 24 days; depending upon whether you believe World War II ended when
the Japanese surrendered in fact, or when they did so formally.
The pundits remain out on that.

In the months before the U.S. joined them, the Brits began
singing one of that war's most enduring tunes, a tune recorded
by most all the leading pop bands and singers of the time -
Kaye, Miller, Kyser, Dorsey, Smith, Crosby, Lynn, Francis, and
on and on. Sappy and bright "The White Cliffs of Dover"
assured us of Jimmy's safe return.

> There'll be love and laughter
> And peace ever after
> Tomorrow
> When the world is free
> The shepherd will tend his sheep
> The valley will bloom again
> And Jimmy will go to sleep
> In his own little room again

So, too, would String sleep again - now conflictedly - beneath Archangel Gabriel; all cozy and weird, warm and weird.

A soldier home from the wars. A boy or a man? A man whose soap and cigarettes, and infrequently charm, had rewarded him with hours, nights, of unsanctified connubial joy; a joy now so foreign at 3691 Pershing Avenue. Would his sister Carolyn, his mother Rose - in the front bedroom across the hall - be unapproving, be appalled? He imagined so; in truth, he didn't know - or even bother to rationally consider.

A bed remained where his father, and before that his sister, once slept. It had no bedding except for a spread matching his. The room now belonged to him alone. Rose and Irving had divorced while he'd been serving with the Allied Military Government's Army of Occupation along the Morgan Line in Venezia-Giulia - Italy's most northeast corner - and although it never occurred to him, less than 160 miles east of where his friend Guido had spent many of his childhood summers.

String's discharge from Fort Ord, on California's Monterey Bay, brought a kind of circular closure to his life in the military. There, at that same base almost five years earlier, at age 17, he'd raised his right hand to be sworn in as a private in the United States Army - not the Army of the United States - not the draftee army - but the United States Army, the army of regulars. His serial number would begin with a "1," not a "3." He executed that simple, all-binding gesture with a near audible sigh of relief.

He'd been attending the University of Southern California. A proud Trojan his letters home would claim. Even a belt buckle to prove it. In the first of those five letters, the one dated March 7, just seven weeks after receiving his mid-year diploma from Principal Aseltine, he wrote:

Dear Mom, Pop, Carolyn, Sophia, Pepper (and all others interested in great literature,)

a'm I tired!!! What a day. In fact, what two days. Yesterday I went to English 1st period. (8 o.c.) English was fine! Yea fine, I am in a class with foreigners who can't read,

write, or speak English _either_. Second period
I went to German and spent a full 45 minutes learning to grunt; and I do mean grunt.
Third period I had Chemistry and started out
by finding I should have enrolled in another
lab class. (twenty more bucks, wow). Fourth
period I went to Man & Civilization and am
now working on the same stuff contained in
the first few chapters of, _The Outline of Histo-
ry_, (how about that pop) Mother, you would
just love the part on _evolution_ were working
on now. Then I went to lunch (what a relief)
and then to phy. ed. where we were yelled at
by some punk ensign.

Today I started school at 9 with trig. (the
advanced stuff) Boy is it fun [here he's drawn a
little spiral turning clockwise from the inside out] This
whirling represents my head. Then to phy. ed.
where I nearly killed myself. we took various
exercises to see which strength group we are
best suited for. This is a very good idea, or-
dinarilly, _but_ I am not suited for anything.
(Oh well, thats life (expression)) I might get
assigned to ping-pong after all. Then third
period to Man & Civilization again and
thats my school up to date. [here there's a crude
desk sketch piled twice its height with lines captioned "My
home work for 2 days"]

This afternoon to top off the aches of our
muscles from gym and add to the muddle of

facts in our brains, Noam and I went to the Museum, where I spent about 3 happy hours (I almost dropped with exhaustion) looking at rare musical intruments and bells. (Mrs. Bell would have gone mad)

My Books came to around 17 dollars. My new lab fee was 20 My round-trip train ticket was 4. My total account now amounts to exacly $2.44 and three San Diego street car tokens. I'm sorry I went broke so soon, but I think (I sincerely hope) that this will be the end of my (main) expenses for the semester. Please Remitt (If you wish itimixed account of my spendings so far will be glad to send same)

I'm ready now to drop now so I think I had better go to bed (Noam''s already there)

So, So long for now XXXXX Lots of Love Everybody
X String XX

His other letters have a similar upbeat tenor. In one he drew a likeness of his Trojan buckle, guiltily admitting it had cost a dollar twenty-five, not counting the dollar for the belt essential to its proper display, and several times he expressed a seldom verbalized caring for his father, twice asking solicitous questions about an upcoming oral exam for police sergeant. Irv had scored second in the written. Nowhere does one read of String's daily terror: his inability to exist within his agreed-to allowance, his fear of academic failure.

College hadn't been a must for String. The Navy's radar training program had fizzled, but his need to get out of San Diego had not; it hung tenaciously, threateningly, overriding all his other concerns. Why? He couldn't answer that. He knew only that remaining at home felt fatal, deadly. A dread enhanced with each encouragement from almost everyone he knew, "Attend San Diego State," they advised, "Robbie'll be going there." But Robbie wouldn't, didn't. He'd been summoned by AAFTC, the Army Air Forces Training Command, to start pilot training at an airbase southeast of Los Angeles. Then, an offhand remark by a boy he hardly knew changed it all, assigned his future to happenstance.

Noam, one of only four all-A students in the mid-year class, could be looked at and not seen. Short - sure, slightly framed - sure, neither attractive or unattractive - sure, but none of those particulars accounted for his almost complete invisibility. Only two attributes gave him substance, cloaked his ghost: he spoke with no apparent fear, and he liked to talk dirty. But for the latter, String might never have remembered him from one hall passing to another. He had once tapped String on the arm, winked, and offered this terse philosophical imperative, "If you ever get the chance, take it." A joke or sage advice? No smile or other facial clue gave a hint. String laughed, shrugged, and patted him on the shoulder. That may have been their single encounter before Noam blocked String's exit from Russ Auditorium late on a Monday afternoon following a graduation rehearsal. "I need to talk with you," he announced authoritatively, his face blank, routinely enigmatic. He reached up, grasped a nonplussed String by his right elbow, and led him to a back row seat.

"I'll be going to the University of Southern California," he announced. "Be starting the Spring term in March. My folks found me a nice room on West 35th Street in L.A., 616 West 35th. It's just a couple of blocks from campus. The room's pretty big, has a couple of beds and desks, and the old bitc..," he stopped himself, "the old lady who owns the place throws in a free breakfast. Not a big one, just juice and rolls, that sort of stuff. It's not to late for you to enroll," he went on, "share the room with me. We'll share the rent." String stared at him - incredulous.

Selling Irv proved easier than expected. All his talk of academic excellence, getting a better education there than he could at State - just extra sprinkles on the frosting. Irv knew how hard paying for it would be, but he couldn't tackle pride as it ran down the field, ball in hand. His little Snoozer, off to college, and accepted at such a prestigious school. How could anyone not want that?

Settling into Los Angeles life, meeting his landlady and her only other tenant, a dental student who would later show him how to cast gold to make jewelry the same way tooth crowns were made, moved along smoothly, fun even. And being on his own in strange new surroundings, bright, friendly South Central Los Angeles, didn't scare him. It would be more than two decades before the Watts riots, the time when that neighborhood burst into flames and a shopping center across the street from campus became rubble and ashes. Even then - thanks to the rapport it had established with the growing black community - the University of Southern California remained untouched.

The morass String faced settling into appropriate classes contrasted sharply with that easy relocation. Did advisors for incoming freshmen exist at U.S.C.? If so, he never found one. How could one get into a good school in the '40s so easily - having an acceptable high school GPA and enough money to pay the tuition, pretty much the only imperatives - while getting into the right classes be so difficult? He poured through bulletins, the university catalogue and, well, guessed. Except for enrolling in five academic courses plus gym - three of them tough fare for even talented students, eyebrow raisers for slow readers - he'd made only one calamitous choice: spherical trigonometry. He'd taken trig in summer school with Robbie, done well in it. Now he wanted to take the next step up on the math learning-ladder; he knew nothing of the proper rung, analytical geometry. The bulletin listed trig as spherical trig's single prerequisite. Great, he'd gotten an 'A' in trig.

In his last letter from Los Angeles, April 3, 1944, he first lets everyone know, " ... that I am still living, but broke," and later, " ... Right now I am trying to prepare for my five-week exams which start tomorrow." Is he worried? What can one read into the largely glib letters he sends home? He raves about the candy and cookies, all the food boxes, that arrive from his mom and Sophia. He thanks them over and over. Even speaks of eating a whole box in one short sitting. Nowhere does he share that he eats all that is offered by his landlady, Miss Troy,

in her continental breakfasts, or that he has found a nearby
restaurant, a one-of-a-kind Denny's-like place where big meals
are cheap. A long curved counter dominates the diner's rear.
He sits, each night, in the last stool at its left end, where counter meets wall, and forms a protective niche. He eats quickly,
greedily, and leaves without tipping. He feels some shame,
more from having no money to be gracious and give than
from the stiff itself, ignorantly believing one need not tip at a
counter seat. Night after night he's served by the same frowning, always courteous, young woman. He once wonders if his
dad would have flirted with her, left her a generous tip, even
though none was called for.

Twice he writes of maybe joining a frat; Noam has already
started pledging. Later he dismisses the 17-dollar-a-month
idea, even if membership were to include free lunches. He
describes an off-campus philosophy lecture series he went to,
enjoyed, and thinks of attending again. The spiral drawing and
the cited remark about his whirling head is his only hint of
academic challenge. References to Man & Civilization take a
casual, hard to swallow tone, as if he chats, buddy-buddy, with
the professor. In the coming German mid-term, he claims to
expect at least an A-, and gym, too, now looks up; he'll be
getting into a goof-off class thanks to a Dr. Belford note that
he suffers from chronic sinusitis.

*I returned, and saw under the sun, that the race
is not to the swift, nor the battle to the strong,
neither yet bread to the wise, nor yet riches to men
of understanding, nor yet favour to men of skill;
but time and chance happeneth to them all.*
Eccles. 9:11

Here, there's a major disconnect. String's next letter home
- ten short days after writing of his up-coming mid-terms - is
not postmarked Los Angeles, but Corvallis, Oregon. "Free" is
written where a stamp usually sits, and the return address after
'Pvt. name and serial number' is S.C.U. 3900 - Co. B., Oregon
State College. It's a short letter, scrawled wide-eyed, awed over
his trip north from Fort Ord through, in his words, "hail-
storms (perhaps not hail), rainstorms, snowstorms (no kid-

den and heavy.) In spots up to four feet." He's made a sketch of his "Pullman" conveyance, a boxcar turned sleeper, tells of stopping to prevent holding up civilian trains, and of his travel companions, specialists in the Navy's Ship Repair Unit on their way to Farragut, Idaho.

The letter we never see is the one delivered to him around 3:00 P.M. on the third of April, minutes after he's posted his "five-week exams which start tomarrow [sic]" message. It arrives, forwarded from San Diego in an innocuous white business envelope bearing a return address, The United States Department of War, and begins, "Congratulations you have been accepted … ." How could it be real? A return form requires both his and a parent's signature, and provides a timetable. He was to have reported at Fort Ord that very day.

Recalling the test taxed his memory. He'd taken it right before his senior year. All the boys took it, were told it was for some sort of army college program. Before now he'd given it no thought. That other one, the one for the Navy's radar school, that was the one he cared about. This letter called the program A.S.T.P., Army Specialized Training Program. He had been accepted into its reserve.

Flurry doesn't describe the state of String and his father's activities over the next two days, nor does chatter convey the onslaught of messages received by their uncensoring brains: "I'll forge his name if he won't sign." "I don't want him in the military." "In three months I'll be eighteen and can sign for myself." "I can leave San Diego and be up there before it gets dark." "I could fail the eye-test again." "I wonder if we need to call the school." "We have to call the army." "… ." "… ." …

In the end, a kind of pragmatic reason triumphed. Triumphed wordlessly. The knowledge each held remained private, locked and unshared. String knew how bleak the odds of enduring on his allowance looked, as did the certainty of getting a passing grade in each of his subjects. Irving knew no more money was to be had - unless, maybe, if he made sergeant; his current commitment already a burden. Of all the participants party to ending String's civilian life, none showed greater resilience, did more to accommodate, than the United States Army. They called from their Los Angeles recruiting center late Wednesday afternoon requesting he report there

ASAP, bringing with him all signed and relevant documents.

A little later, a grim-faced Irving pulled his car up to the curb in front of the San Fernando building at Fourth and Main, lifted his son's small travel bag from the back seat, clutched hands with him briefly, and watched as he walked into the lobby of the fading, old eight-story building. String spent little time at the center. A young lieutenant looked over his papers, smiled, made a phone call, and introduced him to a much older man, a corporal, who walked with him the twenty minutes to L.A.'s Union Station. There the corporal handed him a ticket, showed him where to wait for the train to Salinas, and told him, "You'll be picked up there by an army vehicle and taken to Fort Ord." He arrived at that post two days before the Jewish Passover, on Christendom's Maundy Thursday.

While the first of the thirteen letters String wrote to his family from Corvallis told only of his trip north, the second, sent three days later, provides so much detail on what he finds when he arrives and what he expects his future there to be, it's best read as written:

April 16, 1944
Corvallis Oregon

Dear Mom, Dad, Carolyn, Sophia, Pepper & Everyone else in the land of Sunshine

Rain!!! That's all its done since I've been here, but that's life. I'm beginning to get writers cramps. Yesterday I wrote Carl, Robbie, Doug and Max. Today I wrote Guido, and when I get through with this one to you I will write George and Noam.

Getting started is worse here than it was at

S.C. I'm still not registered properly. They put me in a slow section. So I (check that) told them I was smart, so they have to reregister me in the fast group tomorrow. We are grouped accordingly to a ability at mathematics, and right now we are working on beginning algebra. So when I told the Prof. that I had been taking Sperical Trig, he was impressed. (although I've forgotten all the simple algebra I ever knew)

I'll get my uniform tomorrow, but I'm sort of afraid to, because I gave the captain all my measurements about a size too small, except my hat size which I gave him two sizes too big. But I'll just wait and see how it turns out (, and ~~pray~~).

There is a great, manpower shortage around here. There are 3.1544117647 + girls to every one boy. (It took quite a while to figure that one out). As a result of this manpower shortage when I went to church (Yes, I did go to church) this morning I got into a conversation with the minister. Would I make a better Sunday school teacher, or boy scout troop leader? I think I'll take the job teaching. By the way the name of the church is Grace Lutheran.

Some fellow named Barton advertised for a base fiddle player for the local swing band. It seems that it's a Union Band but there is a clause in Union code stating that if there is no union man available a non-union man may accept the job. These fellows get 8 bucks a night, and a bass is furnished. Guess whose trying to get the job.

My stys busted upen yesterday morning, and are all better now. But this light in my room isn't so hot, and I think that's probably what makes me sleepy so quick when I write at night. So I guess I'll get me a good desk lamp. I keep plenty warm here, for every room is fited with a steam heater. Since I was so late here I got a room all to myself, with the rest of the fellows down the hall. This and the fact that there are only four other fellows on this the fourth floor makes studying much easier. All the other floors have about 15 fellows in them.

I splurged and went shopping yesterday. I got a wastepaper basket, some towels, some washrags, some wooden bookends, and and an officers garrison cap with a two-toned brass emblem. Boy! is it flashy. Were're allowed to wear just about any type of dress uniform when we go to town. (which is seldom.)

I'd sure like to have you send me about three towels (the Y.M. type), some clothes hangers (I tried to get some all over town with no luck) and a shoe ration coupon. I'd like to get a nice pair of dress brown shoes. The kind they furnish us are big high top <u>lead</u> shoes.

I'm going to send my clothes home Saturday. We are allowed off the campus every night til after 10:00 P.M. and on Saturday at noon until 7:30 P.M. Sunday. But that's O.K. I wouldn't have anything to do anyway.

I was furnished everything I need so I guess I'll send my slide urle and stuff home too. The one they furnished me isn't as good as mine, but it is good enough, and I'd hate to lose mine. The one they furnished me is a K&E polyphase and costs about 10 bucks. They also furnished me 13 books, including a nice atlas and a good Websters Collegiate Dictionary. (But I also got such books as the <u>Soldier's</u> handbook.) etc.)

The campus up here is much prettier than U.S.C's and the Student Union Building has one of the nices lounges, dance halls, etc that I have ever seen in any school.

The only thing that's been hard for me so far has been getting up at 6:30, washing and dressing, being at assembly at 6:40, Returning straightening up my room between 6:50 and 7:00, going to breakfast at 7:00 eating, getting back, making my bed (The army's way) and getting to role call and marching to class by 8:00. But I guess I'll get used to

it. What I can't get used to is saying no &
yes sir. I keep saying O.K. - The fellows who
have been in the regulars and then have come
here say that they write the joke column "This
ain't the Army" about this place, because
there is so, so little disaplane. I was talking to
the Col. (He's the C.O.) and he said he can't
tell what the army's going to do, but as he
understands it if we get recommended grades
we have a chance of coming back here after our
basic training. Anyway he says the little drill
and military training we get here will give us
a big edge on the fellows just going into basic
from civies.

The food here is excellent and if we are not
full after eating everything on our trays we
can go back and get a complete refill. We can
do this and get as many refills as often as we
like.

We have that same awful gym here that we
had at S.C. but here it is only 3 times a week
for two hours a shot. But there is a consula-
tion in the fact that we eat 6 times as much
when were finished.

There are 120 regular army A.S.T.P. fellows here, 47 of us reserves, 8 officers, and 5
non-commissioned officers, and I am the only
one here that has not had my immunization
shots. But I guess they'll shoot me one of these
days

I am enclosing in this lengthy letter some post-cards showing snaps of the college and town; the arrow pointing to the room on the men's dorm really is my room.

Well that's about all for now I have to do a little algebra yet tonigtht.

Oh! by the way they had a mixer dance last night and a Soroity here invited our Co. to open house today. But I didn't go because I would have been the only guy in both cases not in uniform. But I'll go next week-end. Oh! you should see my hair. They didn't order us to have them cut, but I thought it would be better if I got a nice sensible short haircut, just long enough to part and comb. and does it look awful.

Well that's all for now.

All my love to all of you,

String

This, and subsequent correspondence, comes from a young man who sounds increasingly pleased with himself - comfortable enough to compose a couple of letters while attending algebra class. Little remains of the slick, self-effacing humor sent from Los Angeles. His second letter accurately predicts some of what will come, misses completely the surprising re-awakening of interest in physical activity - yes, gym - he will boast of being among the fastest quarter-mile runners in his company and, even quirkier, of beating several classmates in a climb up a knotted rope to the gym's ceiling; it doesn't touch on what will become a recreational passion, and omits any mention of his unit's interplay with history - either locally or in the world.

He does write of playing a few times with the local swing

band, earning nine dollars a night, a dollar more than anticipated. If he ever taught Sunday school, it's not confided to the
folks at home; they're told only the big news, that Pastor Wes,
as he calls the Grace Lutheran Church minister, has won him
over and he's finally become a Lutheran - not a crusading Missouri Synod Lutheran, his mentor having been ordained by the
gentler, Scandinavian, Agustanas. The confirmation would not
be without effort for the church's leader. The heavy burden
of accepting Jesus in a formal way couldn't be done without a
wrangle, that back and forth harangue so much a part of String's
connection with his father. He continues sending encouragement to his dad, supporting him on his Sergeant's quest. One
passage absolutely gushes: "... the most wonderful father, the
swellest fellow in this big old world of ours - you pop. -..." Now
it's Pastor Wes' turn to be verbal sparring partner.

> **So God created man in his own image,**
> **in the image of God created he him;**
> **male and female created he them.**
> Gen. 1:27

"That is all so much nonsense, Pastor Wes," it began. "God
wouldn't have looked like a puny human. He could look like
anything he wanted to look like. How about a bighorn sheep?
If I wanted to look good, that's what I'd look like. They're
so beautiful. I could watch them for hours climbing around
on their wall, their fake concrete mountain, behind Roosevelt
Junior High. You can talk all you want to about the Sistine
Chapel, sure it's great art, great looking people too, but ... ".
Pastor Wes worked his way through all the boundaries of rhet-
oric - " ... the Old Testament writers meant to establish how
men were the earth's caretakers, String ... . It's allegory,
String, allegory ... ." - before finally understanding nothing he
said would, could make a difference. If String agreed to accept
Jesus and the doctrine of the church, so be it. He did.

Several times, and enthusiastically - gripped with a fervor
for hitchhiking - he wrote of adventures on the open road.
Thirty-two years would pass before Sissy Hankshaw, Tom
Robbins' heroine in *Even Cowgirls Get the Blues*, would hit the
concrete with her gigantic thumbs, and another three before a

Guide, *The Hitchhiker's Guide to the Galaxy*, would be published - eight, even, before its author, Douglas Noel Adams, was born. But no time was ever better for holding up a thumb by the side of the highway than during the years of World War II. A lad in uniform could pretty much go where he wished, even more than simple travel if he followed all invitations. Not so for String and his Company B buddy, Phil. Many of their noon Saturday to seven PM Sunday off-duty passes were obtained with a specific preplanned goal, a destination, a distance, what new had to be seen. They pursued their plans obstinately, declining all alternatives, even those that had them staring slack-jawed at one another: "I'll be leaving this route in about eighteen miles. Let me take you home with me, cook up a nice Sunday dinner. Both my pretty daughters will be there. They're about your age. .... "

Two trips stand out, the failed attempt to reach a snowed-in Crater Lake, and the winning of 'the Canada bet.' Not a lot can be said of the attempted lake exploit. After dropping to its south and finding rides east to where a southern approach could be made, they found ever deeper snow and traffic trickling to naught. One last ride - on the back end of some sort of garbage conveyance - brought them to a stop at a group of sheds, an operation whose purpose they never learned, and left them to mush ahead on a blanketed road disappearing as quickly as the falling sun. The time to retreat had passed. Luckily, Phil's understanding of outdoorsmanship surpassed his partner's. He found an abundance of covered, but yet dry, shrubs - manzanita, huckleberry, buck brush - and created an inferno on the huge white canvas surrounding them. Both marveled at a night of toasty sleep, interrupted only to throw on another bush or two. Next morning's arduous trek back to the major roads had its upside: not one of the grateful, patriotic citizens who gave them a lift seemed offended by their disheveled, their very dirty, appearance.

A lot more planning went into the Canadian trip. Phil and String were heard talking of it at lunch, and a couple of classmates looked at them and quite spontaneously began laughing. "You're talking maybe 800 miles. How many rides you going to get at night?" "Wanna bet we can't make it," String snapped, perennially quick to confront a scoff, if more temperate at the sight of a clenched fist. That, and other small wagers, mandated the undertaking. It was a must do, and a must do soon. They set the date for May 20, a predicted no rain day. On the Tuesday before, Company B stood in ranks at parade rest waiting for the quartermaster to arrive with their much desired summer khakis. Winter wools irritated, not as scratchy as the church pants String wore as a child, but enough so to welcome the summer dud's arrival. Then, concurrent with their handing out, the deluge came. By the time the lads had been called to attention for dismissal, they each supported heavy loads of squishy tan fabric, their future 'Uniforms of the Day.'

Saturday arrived sunny, as predicted. Once back from their last morning class, the anxious travelers - reputations were on the line - rushed through lunch, grabbed previously packed gear, and picked up weekend passes that read: "to Seattle, Washington." The trip proved itself a rush in at least two meanings of that word - non-stop moving, and an emotional upper - uniformed kids on a lark, proving their prowess while proudly on display as defenders of democracy. Canadian border guards winked at the "to Seattle" passes. Kind townspeople in the little town of White Rock, BC, the first settlement north of the U.S., seemed to intuit that success lay in the proof. Cards appeared from boarded-up shops. Mail went out from a post office closed until Monday. At the American border, two patrol members met them with similar compassion, if less jocularity, than their Canadian counterparts. Both examined the military passes, looked at one another and shrugged, before the shorter agent issued the edict, "OK, get south as fast as you can." All in all, the near 800-mile journey took 39½ hours, getting them back, not at the seven pm curfew time, but at around three-thirty the following morning. They went straight to bed without turning in their passes, falling out for roll-call at the usual oh-six-forty-hours. "Sorry, we forgot," would have been their defense had they been asked why the passes had not been turned in. They were never asked. The ASTP had managed, outside its known curriculum, to teach the circumventing of army rules, even the elements of gold-bricking; lessons which would serve those troops well in their coming assignments.

Company B always marched to and from classes. They

fell in line randomly and marched two-by-two - a column of twenty-three with a single follower at the rear. This day on the tramp to second period chemistry, the lanky, well-built young man directly to String's front stopped suddenly, pointed to the damp soil just right of the path - String doesn't recall it ever not being damp - and shouted with an odd intensity, "Look, Tricounis." The forefinger of his right hand remained aimed unwaveringly at a series of footprints in various states of preservation. "Corporal," he yelled to the non-commissioned officer at the group's side, "permission to break ranks." "You all right, William? Look like you're seeing a ghost." Permission wasn't granted, couldn't be late for Chem. After lunch, young Willi led a group of his followers back to the spot, dissecting the best preserved of the prints, dent in the mud by dent. "Lucky it didn't rain much. This one's still pretty intact," he began. "See down the middle of the sole and in front of the heel, those were made by Mugger nails, and you can make out Tricouni nails all around it. The heel's smudged a bit, but I think it was surrounded with Clinkers." String wasn't among Willi's disciples. Climbing mountains had no more appeal to him than being hauled up on a rope above the Russ auditorium stage. He did like to watch when a bunch of his buddies descended to the ground - one after another and also on a rope - from the hall window next to his room on the fourth floor of beautiful Weatherford Hall. William "Willi" Unsoeld would be up there coaching them, teaching them to rappel. String knew little else of Willi aside from their age difference, and envied him for that. Willi wouldn't turn eighteen until October; a shoe-in for at least another quarter at OSC. Nineteen years later, at the heart of the cold war, President John F. Kennedy awarded Willi Unsoeld the Hubbard Medal, National Geographic's highest honor. He had been among the first Americans to ascend Mt. Everest, and he had done it the hard way, ascending from the thought-to-be unclimbable West Ridge. It would be one among many of his lifetime achievements.

" … You are about to embark upon the great crusade to-
ward which we have striven these many months. The eyes
of the world are upon you…I have full confidence in your
courage, devotion to duty and skill in battle. …"
Supreme Commander of Allied Expeditionary Forces,
General Dwight Eisenhower, June 5, 1944

String celebrated his birthday on a Friday that year. Now eighteen, he'd be leaving after the term's end, a week away. Seventeen days earlier, on the night of June 6th, the Colonel called a general assembly of all ASTP members. They listened enrapt to reports of the landings at Normandy, and to a repeat of the message given the day before by the man String would one day stand before, General Dwight David Eisenhower.

The path of no resistance appears to have been String's choice - eat mom's food, and go to school expense-free with a small kicker-stipend courtesy of the G.I. Bill of Rights - the bill that changed the perception, or had it been a reality, for most Americans - only the wealthy go to college. Properly called The Servicemen's Readjustment Act of 1944, the Veteran's Administration now writes of it:

> "Before the war, college and homeownership were, for the most part, unreachable dreams for the average American. Thanks to the GI Bill, millions who would have flooded the job market instead opted for education. In the peak year of 1947, Veterans accounted for 49 percent of college admissions. By the time the original GI Bill ended … , 7.8 million of 16 million World War II Veterans had participated in an education or training program."

San Diego State would do for String, a few Kings would be there, and what the heck, a school's a school, Trojan buckles a forgotten memory. He'd come to think of college as a kind of hospital for the drifting. A place where one could search out what life meant. It's less clear why he chose to live at home. Sure, it cost less. Was there more? Did he still need that unchecked, pervasive giving from his mom? He would have denied it. Yet on his first trip to the refrigerator after returning home, he spotted the Moët & Chandon champagne he'd been given before leaving for Italy over three years earlier; a gift from a recruit he'd helped finagle a weekend pass. "It's good stuff," the recruit had told him, "be sure you keep the cork wet." "Of course," he'd answered, oblivious to his benefactor's meaning, but repeating the admonition as he handed the bottle off to his dutiful mother. There it stood, center shelf, a washcloth wrapped carefully over its thirsty stopper - a cloth she had soaked anew each and every one of the past 1,202 days.

Doug became String's major back-to-school guide. Except for being even more than ordinarily self-absorbed - goldenhaired Donna had him spinning, and he'd been campaigning to become student body president - Guido would have competed harder for that honor, always seeing himself as his friend's indispensable advisor. His two distractions were not unrelated. How could Donna remain noncommittal if he became campus big man? Guido's folks had sent him to live with his dad in Tijuana away from military service as soon as he'd turned eighteen. Near the war's end he enlisted in the U.S. Army, earning dual-citizenship and some G.I. Bill time. String never learned how he managed to spend his short service time as a clerk for a Camp Callan anti-aircraft artillery unit near La Jolla, only about 11 miles north of his mom's home on 28th Street.

Curiously, Doug also spent much of his naval career south of the border, actually in Mexico City, but not as a military attaché, as a deserter. Right after graduation he had followed his father, lost at Pearl Harbor aboard the USS Arizona, into the Navy, only to be denied every request for combat duty; an armed-forces family member death policy both compassionate and maddening. Action oriented Doug re-acted - stuck his navy blues in a duffle bag, put on a three-piece suit and took off for the big city to the south where he stayed for about nine months with another former-high-school friend, Mexican citizen Mario Reynoso. Then, just as impulsively, he flew back to San Diego, put on his bell-bottoms, walked into the Naval Training Center's main gate at Barnett Street and Rosecrans, and on into the brig There he served four months and twelve days, had a brief sexual affair with his female service-provided mental health therapist, received a court martial review for extenuating circumstances, and was honorably discharged. When he took on String's guidance he had only a year left before graduating with a major in sociology.

Doug demanded much of his ward. It all began with Shakespeare. "I'm going to audit an English lit class I took a couple of years ago," he announced with some enthusiasm. "You have to get past the prof's mannerism - he kind of blurts, spits-out, a loud **ptdauh** before every paragraph, but he really brings an author's words to life, plays in particular. Matter of fact he may be directing some classics this year. I'll check. Think there's one scheduled before classes begin." There was. The drama department would be presenting *King Lear*. "I'll take you with me," he told String, "but you've got to read it before we go. Won't mean anything to you if you don't. I'll loan you a copy - comes with a few notes and some of my scribbles."

His next directive, talking his adoptee into joining him in an upper division political science class, Comparative Government, became String's college ethics' awakening. The instructor liked him: this young man fresh from the cold war front - this straddler who'd had one foot in communist Yugoslavia and the other where he could watch the exile of King Umberto II, allowing the launch of a new Italian republic. String, in turn, wanted to impress. What overtook him on the first midterm exam can only be called terror. Not one question elicited a response. His desk, second row back in the small, tiered classroom, looked down on Doug to his left and immediately below, to his right, sat the class wiz, that polite, friendly guy who answered most every question asked in class, and always correctly. String's eyes followed the man's hypnotic pencil, and his brain turned the words they formed into his. He shared his shame with no one. He began studying. He didn't much like to study, but it beat the unendurable pain of cheating.

Guido hadn't completely given up on mentoring. String still read Huxley - *Time Must Have A Stop* and *Ape and Essence* the latest, before Guido began telling him what books he had to read. W. Somerset Maugham's *The Razor's Edge* topped the list. Apparently, finding salvation and making it with Donna weren't incompatible goals. He'd been making progress with her even though he hadn't won the election, and although always having some excuse to leave early, the two would often show up together at the Friday night pinochle games the remaining Kings still hosted. It would be Carl and Doug, String, Guido, and occasionally Robbie - all but String with a girlfriend or, in Carl's case, wife. He had married and would soon be recalled by the marines and off to fight again, this time in Korea.

The four Kings now attending San Diego State didn't seem much changed from their high school days, five years back. Robbie was a senior by the time String returned. His pilot training unit had been dissolved near war's end, and he'd served as part of a military police unit before being discharged. Because his short time in service hadn't earned him much college under the G.I. Bill, he'd lived on unemployment compensation during his second school year, another benefit of that same act. He would report to the California Department of Employment, and, based on that police experience, seek work as a security guard or private cop, jobs impossible for him to get - California law then prohibiting anyone under 21 from carrying a handgun.

He still saw Thelma, and one day - in the manner String had come to expect of Guido, not him - opened up about their courtship. "Haven't actually had sex with her," he kind of blurted, "too afraid of getting her pregnant." His eyes dropped, "I've been eating her." String looked puzzled. "You know, licking her clitoris with my tongue." It came out more testily than intended. Didn't his friend remember when they used to ink their corduroy pants in high school with "Eat Me" and "I'm on the Menu"? "Clitoris?" String mumbled. "Her vagina, String, her pussy," Robbie managed, his voice fading. String reacted with an abrupt, "Oh!" and wanting to say something to even it up, offer some sexual secret of his own, recounted a never before shared incident he'd almost erased from memory. "I don't really know how I let it happen.

I was in Sausalito, in uniform, walking by a beautiful sailing yacht. I think it might have been a schooner. Anyway, it was docked right alongside the road, and there was a party going on onboard. Some dude standing back by the wheel, yelled at me, 'Come aboard Sergeant, have a drink.' I did, had several I guess. Then he asked me to go to San Francisco with him, said he had some girls coming to his apartment. Like I said, I don't know how it happened, but no girls showed up and before I left he had me in his bed and had sucked my ... ." String paused. "Should I say, ate me? I think I just felt silly, giggled, when it happened." After that exchange Robbie seemed to shy away, their long closeness a question.

English, a first semester class he expected to hate, became one of String's favorites. Once again he had failed an entry exam - reading slowness and spelling the reasons given - and told to take the bonehead course; and once again he'd ignored that order, this time signing up for Freshman Composition. Its instructor, Dr. Fulman, about the same age as his military vet students, had just graduated UCLA after finishing his PhD thesis, *Shakespeare's Concept of Death*. He had a talent for getting his charges to write thoughtfully. String ended a short fictional, suicide-themed story with one of Guido's poems. Fulman's note on the returned paper referred to the poem as "a lamentable doggerel." String loved him for that. And Freshman Comp's rewards didn't end in class. Its star pupil would become a close friend. He had never known a man quite like Chet, two years his senior and a decorated marine hero from the battle at Saipan in the Pacific's Mariana Islands, and he would never be told the whole story of how Chet had volunteered to clear a cave of holdouts there, two days after the Japanese formal surrender on the ninth of July, 1944; how he had taken a grenade to the head and lay without consciousness, all unknowing, until waking to the care of his future wife, nurse Jean Sullenburger, at the Navy Hospital just north of San Diego High. String knew only of his friend's hair, black on the right side, and completely white from x-ray radiation center to left ear, of the glass eye he could pop out on that side of his face, and of his writing. He wrote smooth, funny prose, reminding one of Garrison Keillor's *A Prairie Home Companion*, about his own hometown, Troy, New York - more jagged and urbane than Lake Wobegon - where his wit played with the lives of his telephone-book reading brother, and his bother's companions all employees of Cluett Peabody & Company, the maker of Arrow shirts.

Chet and wife Jean shared a little bungalow in an eight-unit court a couple of blocks up Park Boulevard from Grace Lutheran Church. String became an all-but live-in guest at the place. He'd drive Chet to and from school, talk with him, and listen to his endless accounts of Troy, the shirt factory, and of Jean's hometown Piqua, Ohio, and they'd end up at the Peanut Inn, a tiny bar on the south-west corner of Park Blvd. and University. There they'd drink a beer or two, eat peanuts, throw the shells on the floor, and hang around until Jean got off duty from the Ear, Nose and Throat clinic where she now worked as head nurse. String wondered - always - but never asked why, right after high school, Chet joined the marines. He thought it bizarre when strangers called him and his military-veteran buddies - Doug, Carl, Robbie and Guido - patriots. Is that what Chet was, a patriot? The concept befuddled him. It existed outside his knowledge of reality.

After a year-and-a-half at State, summer sessions included, String felt OK about his academic record; probably not good enough for a top med school, but pleased with his A in Physics-2A. He'd managed two other A's, counting the Comparative Government theft, eleven B's, and a single C from second semester French, a class he attended - as he had 'French A' - in the seat next to Robbie's love, Thelma. String didn't know if Robbie had shared their 'genital eating' conversation with her. If so, no indication of it appeared in her behavior towards him. In fact, it was in French B that she knit him a pair of tan socks with yellow beer mug patterns. The mugs bore his initials, and foam, created of white angora wool, spilled from each stein rim. Thelma knitted throughout all of her classes. Her eyes remained fixed on the chalkboard and teacher, while her hands never stopped moving, the needles they held clicking constantly. For reasons unknown, no instructor ever complained. She left school, after marrying Robbie, with all A's and a life-time supply of toasty wearing apparel.

Between classes, String spent much of his time sprawled out on a chair behind one of the round, umbrella-shielded tables outside the main cafeteria sipping coffee, looking over notes, or talking to anyone nearby so inclined. Late on an autumn afternoon soon after the start of the new school year while he sat thumbing through a just purchased Comparative Anatomy text, a pleasant looking if otherwise nondescript, middle-aged woman pointed at the chair next to him and asked, "OK if I sit there?" "Of course," he answered, smiling without looking up. She took a number of papers from a worn briefcase, arranged them carefully in a row to her front, and slowly began marking them with a variety of colored pencils. "What's so funny?" she asked, her concentration interrupted suddenly by a loud guffaw from String. He couldn't answer. Besides it being embarrassing, who else would think it funny? He'd been reading his book's chapter headings, and struck by the one titled "The Evolution of the Penis" recalled the author's name, Libby Henrietta Hyman. 'Wrong spelling, should have been hymen,' he'd mused. "Oh, just thought of a joke a friend told me," was the best he could do. "Want to share it?" "No," changing the subject seemed his best option. "I see you're correcting papers. Are you a professor?" "No, I work for the State - California - review curricula for education departments. What is your major?" String laughed, "Wish I knew. Guess it'll be physics, but I'm not sure why." "There's only one extremely important occupation right now," she responded quickly, "teaching - and teaching in the elementary schools is the most important." They talked on until the sky began to darken, String and this engaging lady from the State, who spoke far more eloquently than he had expected by her appearance. He never saw her again or ever learned who she was, but she had forged new meanings for him, new life purposes. Within a month he'd withdrawn from all his classes and applied to the college's Department of Education for a degree leading to an elementary school teaching credential.

He met the ed department's application denial with disbelief, anger, and arrogance. How could he not be accepted - he must have more to offer than the average grammar school teacher. Strangely, the department's evaluation of him didn't differ appreciably from his own. He simply had too much academic aptitude, made particularly evident by his A in physics, and would quickly be bored. Were they correct? Yes or no, winning an appeal proved fairly easy; it led String to wonder about his own time at school, what had he learned during the early years? Did he want to teach simply to find out what he'd missed? The question cropped up now and again, but remained moot for now, his concentration fixed on getting into elementary-school-practicum prerequisites: classes in art, music, p.e., and how they might/could/should be presented from kindergarten through the sixth grade.

Apart from the joy of finding himself in class after class mined with attractive young women - only three other men made up their lockstep study group - the courses themselves became life changers, shifting him from science hopeful to aspirant artist. The music classes weren't the challenge. He regressed to high school clown days, used his male counterparts - two of them enormous football players - to play straight men to his antics, and put on programs that had his teacher howling, calling in associates to enjoy the fun. In one presentation - after raucously banging out "March Slav" on the piano, huge football tackle "Big Dick the terrible cat" Ortega, yelled out, "How would that sound on a Chinese oboe?" "Glad you asked," the now slapstick comedian responded, and pulling a cheap double-reeded instrument from a pocket inside his jacket, squawked out Tchaikovsky's main theme.

In art, not 'Crafts for Elementary School' where most of his associates were known, but in Design, it differed. These were talented students, gifted young men and women who could make a portrait look like the model they drew it from; he called his attempts, "Van Gogh on bad drugs." Early in the term, Design Professor Ernie deLindstrum assigned highly structured projects. In one, students were to provide him with patterns from nature. String found himself baffled to have received best in class praise for an arrangement of seeds, tree bark, sand and pebbles glued to a stiff mat-board backing, while hearing a couple of the young artists admonished for their inked renderings he greatly admired. An even greater shock came following completion of the classes' first open effort: a still life in any media of choice. On manila colored, heavyweight paper in thick layer over layer water mixed acrylics, he splotched out what might pass for an assortment of orange and yellow blossoms jutting awkwardly on fat green-black stems from a darkly stained, brown bowl. Disbelief, mixed with an emerging "Do I do art?" confusion, a self-image enigma overtook him during deLindstrum's critique. There it hung on the front wall, his with the work of two others; Professor deLindstrum leaning over it, pointing, "I want you to look carefully at this," his lecturing began. "It looks, in its shapes and texture, much like a Cézanne."

A similar metamorphosis took place in the craft class where, not only did he also do well, but fell in love with its instructor, Cheryl Fann. Tall and thin matching a high cheek-boned face under dark, long black hair, and with piercing dark brown eyes above a contradictory smile that could melt, equally, people or steel, she enthralled him on first sight. He saw her as an incarnation - the sexiest possible - of Charles Addams' nameless *New Yorker* cartoon, a character later adapted for television and known as Vampira. In addition to her craft class for her elementary school hopefuls, Mrs. Fann taught other, more sophisticated art: painting and life drawing. String followed her like a puppy, would have done her every bidding. For her crafts class he used the garage of his childhood, filling her task requests with unexpected, unconventional items: a Calder-inspired sculpture of gut, bass-fiddle strings and wood for one. In return, she did think well of him, felt he had a certain ability, made him her teaching assistant, introduced him to locals in the art world, and gave away - with his permission - the bass string mobile for display in the La Jolla living room of a wealthy patron.

> " *It was the best of times, it was the worst of times, ... - in short, the period was so far like the present period, that some of its noisiest authorities insisted on its being received, for good or for evil, in the superlative degree of comparison only.* "
> Charles Dickens

This too-often quoted, misquoted first sentence, first paragraph from *A Tale of Two Cities*, Dickens' story of turmoil in the late seventeen hundreds - before and during the French Revolution - was, as he points out in its final clause following the dash, as relevant in 1859 when published - String's grand-

father, Peter, was six - as during the bloody years of the narrative. So also were events 'the best' and 'the worst' in the last year of the nineteen-forties and the ten that followed, a decade giving us: the Korean War - our first "Peanuts" cartoon - J. Edgar Hoover and Senator Joseph McCarthy's suppression of political dissent - increases in middle-class home ownership - a revolution in China - the opening of Disneyland - a revolution in Cuba - the first organ transplant - the start of H-Bomb construction - Rosa Parks' refusal to give up her bus seat - the execution of atomic spies - a polio vaccine - the issuance of ID cards in South Africa to identify their bearer's race - middle-class college degree increases - a report claiming cigarettes cause cancer - the funding of NASA - a revolution in Hungary - a U.S. court ruling that racial segregation is illegal
... .

Until that tumultuous moment when the sirens screamed and the dozen or so cars, all flashing blue lights, surrounded the art complex, most of String's life could be said to have fallen into the 'best of times.' He was with Cheryl in the big gallery room - its large plate glass windows overlooking Mission Valley - hanging pictures she had chosen for a major student exhibition scheduled for display the following week, when three U.S. Marshals, guns drawn, blew into the room from its only outside door and, followed by a legion of equally armed and colorfully multi-uniformed law-enforcement agents, shouted, "Hands in the air, Mr. ... ." Beautiful Vampira first thought it an elaborate hoax, then realized it had to be beyond the budget of anyone she could envision. Her makeup, her inherent artist, pushed to take it all in. She stared inscrutable stares at String, at the Marshals, at the weapons, at the horde of officers surrounding them, before exhibiting disbelief by using the muscles of her long, flowing neck to rotate her pretty head - side to side. "Mr. ... , You are under arrest for Conspiracy to Commit Espionage." With Miranda rights a decade-and-a-half in the future, nothing more needed saying.

Accompanied, front and rear, by cars from the local police, the California Highway Patrol, and the San Diego County Sheriff's Department - all sounding sirens at their deafeningly loudest - String and his Marshal captors caravanned slowly through San Diego's city streets to the tarmac of the Lindbergh Field runway. Today, a prisoner would be taken across the highway to San Diego's International Airport and put aboard a special Justice Prisoner and Alien Transportation System (JPATS) plane, a plane used only to move federal inmates. No such system existed when String boarded the four-engine propeller-driven Douglas DC-6 airliner to be flown - with stops in Los Angeles and Chicago - to New York's LaGuardia Airport. As policy then required, two of his arresting Marshals stayed by his side from departure to arrival. Conjecturing on String's state - either of mind or well-being - during that flight, is an impossibility. A 25-year-old, savoring, moment's before, a quiet life and modest, well most often modest, dreams, flying 2,971 miles at an average speed of 311 miles per hour - close to ten hours not counting stopover time - shackled to older men he had never before seen, saying goodbye to no one he knew save an attempted shoulder shrug toward a fantasy love last glimpsed through flooded eyes. The day was Tuesday, May 1, 1951 - mayday!

Chapter 15

Fourth Aside - Exile in Davis:
Hope and Tears

*How shall we sing the LORD'S song
in a strange land?*
Ps. 137:4

A couple of weeks before classes began, I attended an on-campus dinner for new faculty. Chancellor Meyer hosted, moved from table to table - each set with bottles of red and white wine - uncorking, pouring, greeting every person in that very large gathering. His strong preference for red wine, almost trivializing the whites, led me to incorrectly infer he had majored in enology. He shook my hand and welcomed me as graciously as possible, but after he moved back to the head table, I found it difficult to remain unaware of the contrast between my appearance and the young, clean-shaven lads, and several lasses, surrounding me. Age could not be held responsible for all of it. I blended in, unnoticed, at Berkeley, just another Grigori Rasputin look-alike - one with bushier, darker, shoulder-length brown hair and a matching beard that dropped to below the knot on my tie. At Davis I stood out, even my black, horn-rimmed glasses shouted.

The department chair must have found me a challenge as well. I'd be only one person up from the bottom of his faculty ladder, but he needed me to teach upper division courses - material for a recent computer science option - not the large introductory classes typically assigned green faculty. He accommodated me a bit, wrangled me a private office from mechanical engineers on the floor below, but I believe my appearance wouldn't allow him to trust me. On my first teaching day he stopped me in the hall to ask how class had gone; then accused me with, "You weren't even there," totally unaware my classroom had been switched.

As regular faculty I became privy to all the ego-sparring and petty jousting of university life. No disrespect directed here at the gifted scholars and dreamers scattered about in campuses around the world, or even at the bright, hardworking teachers and paper creators I worked with. It's the institutional structure, the baronies, the tight little power groups struggling one against the other; the pressure to achieve, to write, to get name recognition, to move up the ranks, become famous in some obscure field. I heard a couple of senior co-workers laughing about that very thing one afternoon following a salary/promotion meeting. "Well, now he's a full professor - 'world renowned' - before today nobody knew him outside of Bainer Hall." I sat through a number of those meetings during my stay at Davis. First there'd be a business session. I remember the one when the chancellor lectured-on about how we were already pushing him beyond reason, " ... forget Silicon Valley," he'd said, "only medical school faculty makes more than you electrical engineers." After the business part, we'd take a short break, then get right to it; send out the person deemed lowest in past-achievement-points, then talk about him or her. Were there any outstanding qualities, problems? What had been published? What did students think? These staff evaluations never took much of my time; I was the second to be excused.

Today I regard my Davis years, before taking the chancellor's inadvertent advice and heading for Silicon Valley, as those of a person misplaced. I taught to students who wanted to learn what I had to offer, with little tolerance for anyone taking a class solely to fulfill some graduation requirement. I used textbooks I liked, not those written by fellow faculty members. The research I began had more to do with the occult than with engineering. If I'm to take any job credit, it would be for putting together the school's first microcomputer teaching lab. The department bought me a few IMSAI 8080s. I had them modified, their top panels partly cut away to allow direct data-bus access. Students would design and build circuit boards, programming them to perform some unique and, hopefully clever, task - a model railway switch, a traffic light, ... Intel gave me a lot of chips and provided great product literature. Unofficially, I used the school's computer complex to get CP/M ready for Micro Designs. Beneath all the activity, and beginning during my third quarter, an intermittent weighing down, a report-to-next-report anxiety, made itself felt. Joan's cancer had metastasized.

What about our children, Joan and mine? Every parent needs to gloat, to repeat a child's bright remark, reflect back on all the clever - or side-splitting - things said. I'll not do that here, hard as it is to refrain, nor will I say anything of their schooling, who lived with whom, or of their shufflings back and forth between mom and dad. Admittedly, my parenting may have been even worse than my uneven teaching, but our daughter and son always came first with both Joan and me. Freeing them from participation in this story is the simple act of a protective father.

Relocation introduced me to a different kind of space, a city of young people - each with two bikes and a swimming pool; a university where no one yelled, "Pigs off campus." Pigs lived in sties literally one stone's throw behind my Bainer Hall office. What moving hadn't altered was my pursuit of some nebulous, ultimate, life-fulfilling union. I looked for it everywhere: in art, in literature, in the Unitarian church, doing the 'Dances of Universal Peace' with a group calling themselves the Sufi Order International. But mostly I looked for it in women; looked in lust from my loins and in awe and expectation from behind my eyes; moved from date to date, from an infrequent one- or two-night stand to another, from women everywhere: a weekly hot-tub group I'd connected with, assistants and secretaries from every academic department, and from friends I knew in Sacramento. When I was alone without a woman I thought of them, when with a man I talked of women.

Bill became a required confidant and advisor for me, grasping affairs of the heart with the same keen perception he'd shown over computer esoterica or the notions of Einstein. Whenever the need for clarity overwhelmed me, I'd motor to the Lab - I still had a consultant's gate crasher's pass - or meet him for lunch in Berkeley or Walnut Creek. This day, a no class day, my head wouldn't stop grousing over last night's date. The theme, an oft-repeated one, had to do with being told by one woman what every woman thought and wanted. I called Bill, greeting him as I always had at the Lab, with a "Fuck J. Edgar Hoover," and asking if he had a little hang around time. He had. With traffic heavier than expected, the more than eighty-mile trip from Davis to Livermore took a little over an hour and a half - time I used to replay, more than once, every detail of the preceding night.

I'd been out with Wendy, a secretary in the departmental office of Mechanical Engineering, just down the third floor hall from my own. I liked Wendy for more than the obvious - her bounce, her good looks - there was something retro, kind of Berkeley about her. I learned, again, of a recently opened restaurant, and we went to dinner there - a new Greek place, the Symposium Restaurant & Pizza House on 8th Street, had their Pikilia Platter for Two, downed it with a liter, maybe a liter and a half, of house red, and got all goo-goo towards one another. Probably the wine - not the food combination Wendy attributed it to, or my conclusion of a cosmic phero-mone leak - brought on the mutually amorous reaction leading to a blouse and shirt unbuttoning frenzy at her apartment, the one closest to the restaurant. The party stopper came about after I put a gob of spittle from my mouth between the thumb and index finger of my left hand, rolled it around slickening her now braless, left nipple, expecting that delightful tissue to firm up all hard and yummy. Not so. Her whole body firmed up - tensed - she jerked back, pushing me away with surprising force. It wasn't that reaction that made me crazy, but her com-ment that followed, "What are you doing? No woman would want you to do that!"

We met in Bill's office, squeezed in even more tightly than before by a number of electronic gadgets recently added to his already large collection. Aware of my agitation, he skipped the usual explanation of how each of them worked, gave a half-smile, nodded, and quietly pushed the all-inclusive ques-tion, "OK, Buddy, tell me what's going on." It was unneeded encouragement; words gushed out of me like water from a run-over fire hydrant, not the words I'd run through on the way over, but a mixed jumble of complaints, a combination of many relationship frustrations. Caused by what: shallowness, disconnected sex, my performance, my partners? I didn't then confront it in any specific way; now I consider those exasperations all self-directed - feeling honored as I did by any woman who shared my bed. The long ramblings Bill listened to started with, "Help me out Bill, God-damn-it, what's it all about. Why can't I seem to find someone to hang around with for a little while at least, that likes it like I do, gets it off with me? When I'm with someone who does, we find something else to piss one of us off. What about company too? And I really freak out when I'm told how 'all women hate it when a guy does such and such,' like 'tries to get a bunch of fingers where his cock should go, sucks a toe, spits on a nipple,' you name it. How does she - they - know; I'd like to know. How does she know what all women like or don't like? Has she talked to every women on earth? ... ."

Bill listened as he always did, his Buddha face betraying no judgment. After my diatribe, he remained silent for a long while, simply staring at me. Then, "Um, do you take part in those conversations, say anything back?" It seemed like a strange question, "Yea, sure," I answered. "Do you, like, argue about what no woman wants?" he went on. My brain blanked, "I guess," was all that came out. "Why can't you just ask them what feels good to them, and do that?" I didn't answer, and that phase of our interaction ended with his, "Do you want to be right, or be laid?"

Lyla marked a turning point - not a long-term relationship, but a pleasant, profitable one, and a lead-in to the three that followed, and were. As I drove to Berkeley early on a Friday afternoon, there she was, thumb out on highway 80, a little before the on-ramp from Pedrick Rd near the Dixon 76 service station, less than six miles southwest of campus. Her Harley Sportster had broken down; she'd pushed it into the station for safe-keeping, hoping to hitch-it to her sister's in Richmond before dark. With hair obscured by a plain red-and-white checkered bandana, matted from the weight of the previously worn helmet now hanging by its strap over her left shoulder, wearing a drab suede jacket above oil-splotched Levis, and carrying a soon-to-be-trashed saddle bag, she presented tough; a cyclist riding for cheap, gutsy, transport - not a cute biker chick. I stopped to offer her a lift, as I would have, at that time, for any female hitchhiking solo. My first surprise, after she got into my Opel Kadett, came when she identified herself as a Davis grad student. The second came later, at lunch. I'd left without eating, and the sight of the popular roadhouse and amusement center ahead reminded me. "I'm stopping for a sandwich at the Nut Tree. Want to join me or get back on the road?" I asked. She gave me the first smile of the ride, lighting a mainly hidden, finely-featured face. "Sure, I'd like to get something to eat," she answered quickly, more enthusiastically than the extended offer. Bag in hand, she left for the powder-room as soon as we were seated, returning in an amazingly short time - touched by the wand of some fairy godmother; golden hair falling over the shoulders of a lovely regal neck above a short, slim body clothed in a simple loose-fitting, though non-obscuring, knee length, tank-tunic dress of pale green rayon.

If Wendy was retro, Lyla was pure country, gifted with such feminine skills as food canning, car repairing, clothes making - the Nut Tree outfit for one - even ear piercing. I know of the latter because I once mentioned it might be nice to have an earring, and she took on the task immediately, cutting an Idaho potato in half intending to hold the flat, fresh side behind my ear and coming at me with it and the action end of a size 14, $2\frac{3}{8}$-inch yarn darner needle. I demurred and she retreated, reluctantly. Why she pursued psychology as a major or had such a strong and insightful interest in the paranormal, extrasensory perception in particular, to have been accepted and mentored by Professor Tart - world-renowned in that field and for his work on the nature of consciousness - I never learned. Whatever the reason, it turned out to be a godsend for what I, if not my department, considered quality engineering research.

Lyla and I collaborated on two projects. I'd hired Ralph as a research assistant - known on campuses as an RA - to help set up and run my microprocessor lab. RAs receive a small stipend for their efforts. Ralph and I made a deal. I agreed to pay him only after he promised not to come into any space I was in charge of, except as data for Lyla and my first paper, "Electronic Equipment Failure in the Presence of Certain Individuals."

When Ralph entered my lab, every IMSAI computer - known for reliability - broke. What became of him after he received his BS degree, with honors, in Electrical Engineering is unknown to me. Our paper referred to him only as 'Student Y.'

Astrology had, at that time, a large, shallow following. You couldn't go into a bar without being asked your zodiac sign. "I'll bet you're a Scorpio," may not have often scored, but it was a less offensive pick-up opener than "Hey, can I buy you a drink?" So, what about astrology? I had a friend who called it "playing tennis without a net." I'm not sure what she meant, but whenever someone asked me what I thought of it, that's the quote I'd repeat. Lyla had reservations. "You fill the bill of your sign perfectly," she told me. That got us started. Who was it that assigned attributes, specific personality kinks and behaviors, to each of the astrological signs? Lyla would find out. She'd ferret out those traits, the ones most highly-thought-of astrologers agreed to, and together we'd write a questionnaire asking for a birth date, then fifty 'would you rather' questions like "Would you rather be seen with (a) a sailor, (b) a policeman, (c) a school teacher," and so on to see which of the twelve zodiac slots each respondent best fell into, then correlate that with the given birthday sign. My task was to write two computer programs: one for a list of potential test takers, the other to perform the statistical analysis. I used a canned package, SPSS, Statistical Package for the Social Sciences, for the later. For the other I hacked into the University's data base and plucked out, randomly, the names and class locations of 100 students in each zodiac age group. Tart's importance on campus made it possible for Lyla - without boring or bothering him about it - to distribute the questionnaire, along with a research permission agreement, to participants in departments scattered all about the school. We ended with a reasonable sample size of 858, and SPSS correlation coefficients let us know how poorly they fell into their intended categories; hence the submission, for possible publication in pop magazine *Psychology Today*, of our second paper "Astrology Apology."

We hadn't met on campus, I had no teacher-student power over Lyla - working as she did for an MS in a different department. What caused me anguish was the great difference in our ages: early twenties to, well, earlier fifties. The gap never left my consciousness. It kept me from even trying to connect in any long-term way, a state of mind conveyed without any need for the extrasensory, Lyla's ordinary perception more than enough to sense and dislike, to pull slowly away with little resistance from me. Looking ahead, way ahead, my next eighteen years were blessed by the serial company - with a gap or two that will become apparent - of three wonderful, totally different women, and, sadly, understanding nothing of commitment until the third, the very last. Her age, only two years greater than Lyla's, although we'd met much later in her full life - after kids, divorce, the whole bit - gnawed at me, rankled. I hadn't sought permanence; yet my sense of being discarded, cast aside after several togetherness years, brought back, finally, far later than it should have, the pain of having a life-affirming ally rent, ripped away, any dream of perpetuity ended; a pain not experienced since breaking up in my early years with a treasured love, a love doomed by the solemnity of youth.

*And had suffered many things of many physicians, ... ,
and was nothing bettered, but rather grew worse,*
Mark 5:26

Back to Davis, fresh pain, an entirely different source of pain, presented itself when Joan's cancer first returned. With no apparent cough or struggle to breathe, either then or later in life, I don't know what prompted her to be medically evaluated. She reported her findings cavalierly, or so it seemed coming from someone with her taste for the dramatic. "They ran some tests," she told me privately, after a kid exchange, "and I got the same old pushy, intimidating 'you're a bad person if you don't do what we say' stuff I've always gotten from those arrogant ... , from MDs. I guess they have ears to stick pencils behind." She went on with a smirky grin, atypically caustic, "Or maybe the only thing they can hear is what comes through a stethoscope; listening to what patients have to say is beyond them."

Joan had decided, early on, to forego further treatment from the established medical community; alternatives were a possibility. She couldn't tolerate much foreign stuff in her body - a glass or two of wine ok, not so with grass, or most medicines - a situation responsible for ongoing struggles with her growing array of interested healers, not only oncologists, even a dentist later got into the act wanting to pull all her teeth. Before her surgery she'd informed her surgeon - written down - the medications that made her sick, only to have him treat her with them while under anesthesia. She'd been pressured, and refused, to do post-op radiation; now they chided her for refusing chemo, a cure she learned of while sitting for hours with a similarly affected friend, watching her as she transitioned from nauseous-and-bald to dead.

The five-year survival rate for Stage II breast cancer is 93%, at Stage III it's 72%. From the underarm muscle and lymph node mass they excised when, more than six years earlier, they cut out Joan's breast, I have to assume they considered it Stage III. Now, with metastasis, she'd hit the final plateau, Stage IV, and the odds givers put her chances for making it another five years at 22% - with or without treatment. She needed the 'legitimate' medical establishment to keep her informed, to let her know what had spread, and where. The rest she could do, and did do, on her own. Early on she braved hot-tubbing in the company of men and woman she scarcely knew, shamelessly baring her disfigured torso. It was a statement. Later, after the release of Samuel Epstein's *The Politics of Cancer* - a book the University of Illinois professor of environmental and occupational health wrote on the fundamental causes of the disease's rapid escalation: pesticides, growth hormones (even in milk), nitrosamines, preservatives and many other food additives - she championed his message, spoke of it wherever she appropriately could, and modified conflicts with it in her own eating and drinking habits.

After four years at Davis, I too had decisions to make. Tenure, a very long shot, would require a major makeover, almost a personality change. I'd have to learn to teach compassionately, get decent student reviews, use books my colleagues wrote, do accepted research in computer engineering, maybe even shave. After reviewing that list, my choice wasn't so hard. I cut my hair but not my beard, got a job in the Palo Alto research facility of transistor design pioneer Fairchild Camera and Instrument Corporation, bought a funky old house on the Los Gatos side of the Santa Cruz mountains, and bailed. The move refreshed like a reprieve, left me feeling freed from some nebulous constraint - an Iowan heartland perhaps - central California's *American Gothic*.

Soon after the move, I sent Joan a gift for her upcoming 46th birthday, and think of it now as a fulcrum, the cusp of a slow thaw. She wrote of her appreciation, made me a big brown corduroy pillow for my own soon-to-come natal day, and when we next met, we talked of many things besides the usual lengthy critique of our children's well-being. City life, she now lived in San Francisco's Potrero Hill, began to burden. "I'll not let this illness dictate my life," she repeated, but its consequences couldn't, wouldn't be ignored. Even in that neighborhood, touted as the quietest and sunniest in the city, life was city life - full - too full of city energy, sounds, pollution - not the place for meditation, for unique diets, for healing. She'd learned of, and practiced, Vipassanā, insight meditation, at the Zen Center on Page Street off Laguna, and had started a self-cure regimen in earnest: juice cocktails - wheatgrass - awful tasting stuff, pressed, squeezed and downed.

I took her to the Sathya Sai Baba Center, a basement room in an old apartment building on Ivy Street in the Western Addition's Hayes Valley. Why? To find her a miracle, I guess, get her some all-curing vibhuti, the sacred holy ash of burnt cow dung. Sai Baba, his devotees said, just held out his hands and out it came, dropping from his palms. They, millions of them, called him God incarnate; others called him trickster, magician. I'd been poking around the religion stacks at the Los Gatos library, and wandered into the mysticism section where Howard Murphet's recently published book *Sai Baba Avatar*, got my attention. I pulled it off its shelf, popped it open and ouch, a face jumped out, came to life, stared at me: a pleasant, round, tawny-hued face above a red gown - framed by the black afro of all afros, a mane that tripled the volume of an already huge head. The face didn't change expression. What had I really seen, a picture, or a smiling God? Happenings like that, strange experiences I took to be mystical, had both thrilled and disconcerted me a number of times in the past, once during Sufi dancing when an amber bead came to life.

We went to the center together several times. It amused me to learn Sai Baba was younger than me; I fancied telling friends I was older than God. Joan also found something to smile about at the meetings. "Have you watched how all the women compete for Dr. Conway's attention, his favor?" she asked me, chuckling. "Just like the way the faithful ladies, the stable ones, ladies the church always counted on, tried to out-do one another to please Pastor Boling at the old Presbyterian church I grew up in. Guess I expected it would be different in a non-Christian church, especially with the Indian women."

Along with the humor, we felt joy in our attempt to worship together. We spoke of Joan's future, her need to get out of the city, find a place with fresher air. I shared details of my place in the hills, how it had a basement unit beneath the main house - a bath, a kitchen and a private entry. I took her for a visit, and while she saddened at the thought of moving more than an hour's drive from her large number of acquaintances - people I knew little of: meditators, friends - some from radical psych days, supporters, fellow cancer sufferers including two terminal she'd been learning to coach - we agreed, she'd come live there, not with me, but privately in the unit below. It could be just the place to get well. She'd stay until she got rid of the cancer; juices and meditation were working, and she had other options still untried.

Joan had a few good weeks in the little studio, then the rains came. When they fall in the Santa Cruz mountains, they fall with fury. Water made its way down the chimney into the basement fireplace, through the crawl space to its opening behind the bath, turning a warm cozy space into an environment, while still livable, more suited to a camper than a convalescent. She moved upstairs to the spare bedroom; we'd have to share the bath. It was when passing her there that I first saw the large open sore, the ulcer on her neck, always before covered by one of several attractive scarves tied beneath her still radiant red hair. We never spoke of it.

In time, I became an accepted part of her treatment program, helping press wheatgrass and other juices - carrot juice once turning her skin to a glowing orange, accompanying her for medical updates and, most importantly, listening. Every health care worker we encountered had advice, wanted to work on her. They, the tooth-pulling dentist and the chemo-thumping MDs who harangued and scolded her, brought blood to my face, enraged me. She flowed with it, showed no upset, got the information she needed and moved on, continuing to softly pass along her message: "Look at cancer's causes, think for yourself, don't give your power away to medical authority." She took off one day with a girl chum from the city. "I'll be gone for about a month, … be living at La Gloria Hospital off the old Ensenada Road south of Tijuana," she told me, "learned of a treatment they do down there. Sounds a bit … um, nutty, but I'll give it a try. It's to cleanse, get rid of toxins, they have you do enemas with coffee."

My work life now centered on Fairchild and, unlike my partners still trying to keep the company alive, I no longer gave Micro Designs much thought. We'd had our heyday a few years earlier, sold a few of our tape-drives, got a new product write-up in the July '77 issue of *Kilobaud* - it even had a picture of me with one of the devices on page 81, in the magazine's coverage of the first West Coast Computer Faire at San Francisco's Brooks Hall - at the time the biggest computer show ever. Most well-knowns in the personal computer world were there; among them Steve Jobs pitching the Apple II, Gary Kildall for Digital Research, and a co-inventor of the microprocessor, Intel's Marcian (Ted) Hoff. As earlier reported, I'd once again misjudged the market, first memory, now mass storage. Floppy drive prices dropped over eight hundred dollars the year we incorporated. How could a one-product enterprise compete with firms making faster machines to serve the same purpose at no greater cost? We had a kind of weak excuse; this all took place when cassette storage sales led floppy disks by 73 to 22 percent - five years before IBM introduced its first PC, a machine still sporting an almost never used cassette port. It's likely I was one of a very select number of early computer entrepreneurs losing money in a Silicon-Valley-type startup without ever recouping. Maybe the only one.

Therefore my heart is glad, and my glory rejoiceth:
my flesh also shall rest in hope.
Ps. 16:9

Joan returned from Mexico too thin, but otherwise looking great - upbeat and energetic. I'd missed her, missed her ambivalently, in the way my continuingly perverse character dictated.

These days are difficult to write of, serious days, days I in no way mean to treat flippantly. I'd gotten into an alliance, occasionally sexual, with Bonny, my immediate boss' secretary, an extremely good-looking ex-contract flight attendant. In those days hostess requirements included 'young' and 'gorgeous.' She told stories of dealing with aggressive males: handing off shaken, unopened cans of Coke, spitting into soup. Our association at work came to be dominated by boss confidentiality. She knew every specific of the plans to get rid of me, and had sworn to share none.

Except for the Lab at Livermore, I'd never lasted more than four years at a single job; so it was at Fairchild where I'd settled into a holding pattern, our honeymoon together long ago over. The Vice-President of Research had become my enemy - in honesty, enemy is too strong a word; I doubt Tom Longo ever gave me that much of a thought, more like a casual "Get rid of him" toss of his head. Human Resources chose a gentler manner of execution than I had anticipated: stripped me of management authority and offered a probationary position designing circuits. Negotiations with Berkeley ended in an Acting Assistant Professor agreement for the following semester. I told Bonny I'd give her a call, packed up my things, and quit.

More and more, Joan shared her fears with me. We'd sit together, often late into the night, in the small front bedroom overlooking the magnificent redwoods carpeting the hills of Chemeketa Park, where she'd talk of death, of the terror it brought. I listened without responding. Sometimes we'd hold one another. Once we came together as the still married couple we were, on my part awkwardly, unable to sync head with body, not sensing, not appreciating, or sadder, not able to want reconciliation.

Joan no longer shielded her neck with a scarf; the wound had healed, disappeared. Today that seems natural enough; early menopause had begun cutting off her body's estrogen. Did she make a connection between menopause and her seemingly improved health? I didn't. I declared her healed, and spoke to her of our agreement, reminded her of her intent to move once she had beaten the cancer. I hadn't lied, I did think she was well - even so what had been accomplished? How much stupider could my actions have been? She found a home to share in Aptos, south of Santa Cruz, and left. My promised call to Bonny was never made.

> *The Council of the Royal Society is a collection of men who elect each other to office and then dine together at the expense of this society to praise each other over wine and give each other medals.*
> Charles Babbage,
> Inventor of the Programmable Computer, 1816

Moonlight consulting had become a part of my life before leaving Fairchild. Most of it for a Psych Prof from the University of Illinois wanting to build, then peddle, a Vagal Tone Monitor, an instrument of his design that would quantify variations in heart rate between breath cycles. Its primary, while not universally peer-accepted intent, was to non-invasively measure the response of the parasympathetic nervous system to a variety of psychological stimuli.

Wiring circuit boards, creating software, and assembling a machine to the shrink's specs at the little house in the hills, while commuting twice a week to lecture again at Berkeley, brought a measure of fulfillment but, more and more, my bills were being paid by credit card - one of many cards, shuffled cards, one paying off another. That, and zero in bank balances, encouraged me to either find new employment or get real about consulting. Syva, a medical diagnostics company and subsidiary of the pharmaceutical corporation, Syntex, gave me a start at their Palo Alto research center - planning software for a proposed automated blood typing system. Not enough of a start, though, to stop hoping for greater cash flow, for work more to my interests. I decided on a Pacific Grove trip to see if Gary Kildall had anything for me. Even though I hadn't spoken with him in maybe fifteen years - not since lab days - I knew from headline articles in geek newsprint what he'd been doing at Digital Research. I called. He agreed to see me.

Guiding my car west by northwest - at little more than walking speed - past attractive, ever the same, Victorian store fronts all hailing Pacific Grove's downtown, I found a parking spot at the curb directly in front of 716 Lighthouse Avenue, where Gary had arranged for us to meet. It wasn't the ornate old mansion friends had told me served as DRI's main quarters; that building was across the street and a tenth of a mile farther west, toward the shore. I'd stopped at a unique three-story structure, three boxes one set atop the other, each considerably smaller than the one below. Once inside, I was directed through the busy lowest floor - cubicles protecting workers, men and women, staring into computer screens - up a flight of stairs past fewer people, also at terminals, to a ladder leading into what looked to be the bridge deck of a large ocean liner, a box kept bright by windows on all four sides. Gary sat behind the room's only desk, a huge one, and faced an equally impressive screen. He looked up, greeting me warmly, dispelling quickly the intimidation I first felt thinking myself in the presence of a super Mickey Mouse playing his role as sorcerer's apprentice.

Gary asked what I'd been doing since leaving Lawrence Livermore, then shared a bit about his own current interests. In a short while it became apparent I hadn't the talent to contribute more than many of his employees, and I cost more. The conversation shifted to CP/M and how we'd used it at Micro Designs. It embarrassed me to finally realize we should probably have paid something for its use. "I thought everything done for the Lab was in the public domain," I stammered. He didn't seem to give it much thought, laughed it off and asked, "Did you call it DOS?" "No, COS," I answered, "Cassette Operating System." He seemed relieved, pleased even.

Just now, thirty years or so later, right after writing the above three paragraphs, I Googled his name, Kildall, hoping to learn what buildings DRI had used for office space, when coincidence - if you believe in such a thing as coincidence - distracted me with a message at https://www.**ieee**.org/, website of the IEEE, the Institute of Electrical and Electronics Engineers, a group calling themselves "the world's largest professional association dedicated to advancing technological innovation and excellence for the benefit of humanity." It announced an event planned for the 25th of April 2014, just a month away. The IEEE would be honoring Gary's work with a plaque to be installed in the sidewalk fronting 801 Lighthouse Avenue, DRI's company location in the '70s. At 2:00 PM, two hours prior to the plaque's unveiling, a celebratory program of friends, former Digital Research employees, and bigwigs from the IEEE and early computer days would be held in the Pacific Grove City Chambers at 300 Forest Ave.

Gary would not be in attendance; he had died on the 11th of July 1994 - three months short of twenty years before the scheduled occasion - after a never satisfactorily explained accident in a Monterey biker's bar. In spite of believing, without reservation, that Gary earned and deserved any and all credit received, I couldn't help being reminded - as Joyce and I sat through the encomiums of the IEEE narrators - of the quoted rants, the tirades, the " … praise each other over wine and give each other medals" offered in 1816 by the world's first computer maker, Cambridge scholar Charles Babbage. Professional societies are tame, of course, by comparison with others, show-biz people in particular - most evidenced by the gagging mush of movie-landers accepting Oscar love from one another. I didn't dwell on this at the time, my attention drawn to one of the audience dignitaries, the previously mentioned co-inventor of the microprocessor, Ted Hoff. I wondered if he remembered me; remembered interviewing me so long ago, and turning me down for a job at Intel.

Joyce and I stood with many others, in the lightly falling rain, to watch the plaque's undraping. It reads:

> **The CP/M Microcomputer Operating System, 1974:**
> Dr. Gary A. Kildall demonstrated the first working prototype of CP/M (Control Program for Microcomputers) in Pacific Grove in 1974. Together with his invention of the BIOS (Basic Input Output System), Kildall's operating system allowed a microprocessor-based computer to communicate with a disk drive storage unit and provided an important foundation for the personal computer revolution.

> *Come unto me, all ye that labour and are heavy laden, and I will give you rest.*
> Matt. 11:28

Fourteen years had passed since Joan lost her breast, the last three in Aptos. The uncertainty was over; her approaching death - a month, a year - a given. Not to everyone; not to most MDs she saw who continued badgering her for not receiving treatment - not to certain friends, her housemate in particular, unable to understand why anyone could, should accept death. Joan did. Didn't welcome it as some, as Ram Dass and others, didn't avoid it as most. She became a student of death and dying, read it all, read Lāma Kazi Dawa-Samdup's translation of *The Tibetan Book of the Dead*, read death's then popular spokesman Stephen Levine's *Who Dies?*, read, studied, meditated; became in her own words "A dying celebrity." Not a celebrity, a well known person, dying, but one well-known, a celebrity because they are dying; one written of in local papers, one visited by clergy of many faiths, Anglican to Zen.

Joan's bedroom looked out at a garden dominated by a bushy, old, red-barked madrone, a tree often populated with one or more birds common to the area. All Santa Cruz County is a bird watcher's Eden, Aptos included, where Alfred Hitchcock, it's said, showed particular interest in their behavior around the city's upscale Rio Del Mar neighborhood. Joan had four favorites - a starling and three stellar jays. I brought her a television one day, entered her room and saw her watching one of the jays. I'd visited the previous day and now remarked, "That bird's always here. I saw it yesterday." She looked at me smiling, shook her head no, then laughed aloud, "No, that's Tizzy. It was Wallace you saw here yesterday." They didn't all look alike to her; a bird wasn't a jay, or a sparrow, or a hawk, it was a unique creature and if she'd seen it before, it had a name.

That close attention to detail sometimes collided with change. The TV I'd bought, a little 13" Sony Trinitron, had actually been my computer monitor. It had red, green, blue RCA inputs for that purpose and for the TV, a recently introduced accessory, a remote. I set up rabbit ears and got the set working. When we next met she handed me the remote and, with wrinkled forehead, asked, "Does this thing have a cord? I can't figure it out. If it does, it doesn't look like there's any place to attach it." It's impossible to describe her facially proclaimed disbelief when I pointed the thing at the set and clicked.

And so it went for the next year or so: good days - many of them, happily - funny days, hard, sad days. Joan continued counseling, increasingly with the dying, and made friends with a group of women organized around some cause I can't remember. The 'We're-In-Gang,' I'll call them, had offices in a beautiful estate up the hill just south of where she lived. They took uncommon interest, self-ordained support, in her ongoing process of discovery. Two gatherings scheduled toward that aim are particularly memorable. She learned of the first from Jack Kornfield, a leader in the growing Vipassanā community - a four-day retreat on a Watsonville mountaintop, Mt. Madonna Center, founded seven years earlier by the Hindu Mauna - one who has taken a vow of silence - Monk Baba Hari Dass. Although housed in different quarters - she in a tent with friends, me in a room set up as a male dorm - both Joan and I attended. I don't know what she took from the experience; for me 'chilled out' comes to mind. Also, it was there we heard of the second event. Stephen Levine would be holding a week-long 'Conscious Living/Conscious Dying' workshop in nearby Santa Cruz.

Once again, both Joan and I signed up. We paid our holding deposit and looked ahead - eagerly, when life for her began to change, and at a pace more rapid than ever before: her energy level fell, her weight plummeted, her strength waned. We searched for lighter and lighter cups, cups she would be strong enough to hold, to drink from. I went to the workshop alone. Stephen called, spoke with her on the phone, agreed to met at the seminar's conclusion. It didn't work. Demands on his time were too great. My offer to drive him from Santa Cruz to Aptos and back were declined. Everyone wanted him. He gave me a statuette, a figure about fourteen inches tall of the bodhisattva Kuan Yin, Goddess of Mercy, of Compassion. He asked me to give it to Joan for him.

I'd been having some muscle tightness, and Joan suggested I go see Michael Tierra, an acupuncturist and herbalist she'd done clean-up work for a year or two ago. I reminded her I'd been needled, had a couple of sessions with Michael's wife, Lesley, also an accomplished acupuncturist, and would give her a call. Both, it turned out, were away, but Michael's teacher, Miriam Lee, was guest practicing there, and would see me if I wanted. I was thrilled; Lesley had told me about her. First named Lee Chuan Djin, she'd been born in China's Shandong Province in the mid-twenties and was the first person ever to practice acupuncture in the United States. Miriam spent considerable time working with me. It turned out she knew

Stephen Levine. I told her of Joan and of how Levine had sent her a statue of Kuan Yin, at which point she straightened abruptly, stormed toward the door and, before slamming it shut, cocked her head toward me proclaiming in a very loud voice, "Jesus Christ, He died for our sins!"

After the workshop I rented a small travel trailer and, with permission from Joan's housemate, moved it onto her large property, down the road and out of sight behind a row of tan oaks. I walked from there to the house each night, sleeping on a pad by the side of Joan's bed. Joan wanted to say goodbye to close friends, friends not nearby, friends she might never see again, and decided on inviting them to a ritual, a ceremonial rite of farewell. All those she asked, came. I think around twenty. She sat propped up on pillows, ringed by her guests. As she had requested, each came forward and presented her with a small, no-value gift: a shell, a pebble, a twig whittled image, a thing like that. Five of us lifted her across - above and over - a bundle of tree limbs - a mock crossing - her passage into some other plane.

Joan's spirits remained high as the cancer snapped at her, stole the weight from her body, drained her energy. I felt honored to be used as gate keeper, learning and acting on who she would like to see and when. Most close friends and the quiet, listening purveyors of faith were almost always welcome. Occasionally a hospice nurse would visit, bringing a bandage to heal or a way to prevent the threat of a decubitus ulcer, a bed sore. The nurses worked under the guidance of Grace, a thoughtful, gentle, kind MD. Harold, a young doctor from the local village who'd read of Joan in the papers, also blessed us, coming by on his own, lending support, comfort and, when asked, advice. Joan and I had begun praying together, asking for her death, soon and without suffering. Grace gave us a half-gallon bottle filled with a dull, deep-green liquid, a fortune in morphine sulfate, a talisman against pain.

We spent much of our time together now, talking, watching M*A*S*H reruns, doing nothing. Joan gave me her wedding ring, told me of her disappointment in it. How the jeweler had taken away its grace, made it fat and utilitarian after I'd remarked on the fragility of its prototype. "Sell it if you ever need a good meal and can't afford it," she laughed as she handed it to me. I confessed that at this time I wanted her death for me, as well as for her. The following night she drank a little of the green liquor and went to sleep early, waking after midnight. I sat with her, she held me in a flaccid embrace, the strongest she could muster. I offered, and she drank more morphine. I awoke in the early hours, sometime between midnight and dawn to see her half out of bed, head on her pillow, feet on the floor. It was over, she was dead.

A number of previously arranged attendants came by at my call. We bathed her, dressed her in white, laid her on a clean white sheet. Harold gave us a death certificate, eliminating intrusion, the delay of a coroner, any fuss with legal matters. She lay in that bed, in state, a homestyle state, for several days. Ministers, Lamas, friends or the simply curious - a long staggered, trickling line - paid their respects, or reconciled their curiosity.

Dying catalyzes a love as nothing else ... does ... , can do. I deeply regret my inability to hang Joan's portrait here, to bring out her dimensions: softness, stillness, depth, humor, caring - high among them. A stormy past, a relationship of quarrels and uproar, should make it easy to list, as well, a negative or two. I can think of none.

The 'We're-In-Gang' planned the burial of Joan's cremains and the narrative for the gathering of commemorators that followed. Ashes were sprinkled on one of the estate's grassy, tree strewn hills, the heavier parts buried beneath a stone slab on a lawn fronting the group's office. The gently curved slope of a different hill, a hill covered with new May grass, served as bleachers for the many attendees seated on it, singly and in groups, listening to heartfelt, if sometimes esoteric, eulogies. At their conclusion, Yasin, co-leader of the Davis Sufi group, led us in welcomed, joyful dancing before we watched Joan's spirit lift, soar into the skies supported by, or supporting, dozens of frolicking, laughing balloons.

Part IV

The Crucifixion

Chapter 16

The Trial

Pilate saith unto them, What shall I do then with Jesus which is called Christ? They all say unto him, Let him be crucified.
Matt. 27:22

For a moment he sat in disbelief, all blood draining from his face, leaving a large, oval, ashen, scowling mask - topped above, in dark contrast, with a meticulously slicked cover of ink black hair, precision parted above his left eye to form a straight white line from brow to … . When - up went his right arm - abruptly - fully stretched, as he leaned forward - a carefully balanced jack-in-the-box - to bring a fist-clenched gavel down - loud and hard - over and over - against the judicial bench, the high desk shielding most of his short, stocky body. "Order, order in my court," he screamed. "Order, order, get that woman out of my court."

Two marshals raced toward the witness stand at his left where a tall, thin, wiry woman in late middle age stood pounding the back of the cringing prosecutor. With her arms parallel and directly to each side of her body, elbows bending from eighty degrees to out as far as they could reach, her clenched fists flew - alternately - striking him again and again. He made no attempt to turn around, to confront his assailant, only leaned forward toward the defendant he'd been questioning, covering his face with both hands. The marshals proved no match against her onslaught. Two more were summoned, and the four - three men, one woman - carried her out, squirming, writhing - her fury unchecked - her long hair, gray from early adulthood, parting from its pins, the motion spilling it from the carefully rolled bun at the base of her neck. Judge Kaufman, the honorable Irving R. Kaufman - the second Irving in the life of the exiting troublemaker - called for a recess, called for it shrilly, repeating a warning he'd given at a previous trial. "We will meet in the morning at 10:30 - promptly. I am quite a fussbudget about being prompt." A tear made its way down the left cheekbone of the young man, the defendant and current witness, before he was led away by yet another two marshals for the five-minute walk to his cell in the Manhattan House of Detention.

A guard poked him on his shoulder as he finished his simple institutional supper of chopped lettuce and lentil stew embellished with a few chunks of dry beef - a meal thoroughly enjoyed by the ex-soldier who had relished army chow with two notable exceptions - grease-dripping lamb from a British mess tent in Florence, Italy, and cheese-stuffed frankfurters served immediately following a mandatory sex orientation movie showing the male genitalia of gonorrhea infected comrades. "I'm taking you to the visitor's room," the guard grumbled. "A guy's waiting to see you."

"Uncle Ray!" shot from the prisoner's mouth, words expressing a mixture of excitement, surprise, delight, and confusion. "Lost your pants again, String?" came the unintentionally offending reply from a man in his mid-fifties, about the same height as his younger brother Irving, but with a girth far less attractively distributed. He'd asked his question dryly and loud, with no attempt at confidentiality, and while it evoked half its intended purpose - an involuntary grin from the guard on duty - it got nothing from his nephew - way too tight to respond - levity, humor, no part of his current mood. He sat staring, an awkward interval passing, before managing a cheerless, "No." Why, he pondered, must both his parent's brothers be comedians - one a city wise-guy, one a bumpkin clown.

String first met his uncle Ray four years earlier, a day after taking a room at the William Sloane house, a YMCA residence hotel on West 34th Street in midtown Manhattan. He'd debarked from the SS *America*, a beautiful ocean liner owned by United States Lines and pressed into service to return military personnel home from European war zones. The ship had carried him from Livorno, Italy - a place British maps show as Leghorn - to New Jersey, where he had gotten a ride to the city from the parents of an onboard friend, checked into the hotel, sent his uniform to the desk for cleaning, and went to bed. In the morning, he called his uncle with the news that he couldn't meet him at their prescheduled time and place; the hotel had lost his pants. That was it. Ever after, Ray's introduction of String went something like this: "I'd like you to meet my nephew - Irv, my brother out in California's kid - String. I've lived here in New York City more than half a century and never lost my pants. String's only here a day before he lost his."

String's jail-house reaction registered. The kid had always joined him, laughed with him; today, he was a different kid, Ray didn't know him. It wasn't because of the years they hadn't seen one another, he grasped that and he regretted his entry. "Sorry, kid," he began quietly, as softly as his gravelly voice allowed, "tough seeing Rosie hauled away like that." It would take time before String realized how lucky he was. Ray had taken leave from work. He was a carrier for the United States Postal Service. Had been for over 30 years, and Manhattan was his beat. Now he made String his job. String was family, a goy maybe but family, and he, Ray, could help him. Never the big bread winner in his immediate family - his wife Jean made the bucks - but the one who knew what went on in the world, his world; he read every local paper, talked with everyone on his midtown postal route. He'd followed the trial that ended just a few weeks earlier, the Rosenberg trial; knew all the details, read in disbelief, along with thousands of others, when they received a sentence of death, received it from that schmuck, that little Napoleon Jew, Kaufman, the hanging judge, String's judge.

"What'd they do with mom," was String's opener. Rose had flown to New York as soon as she'd learned of her son's arrest. Irv and Ray's sister, Birdie, put her up in her and her husband Jack's Flatbush apartment, and arranged to get her back and forth from the courtroom and the House of Detention. She'd visited String every day since the second day of his incarceration, and had arrived at the courthouse for his trial as promptly as the judge. "Your mom's fine, big guy," Ray told him, then lowered his voice to a whisper, "but we may have to get her a disguise to get her back into the courtroom." He continued, amping back up to conversational volume. "She's down in Greenwich Village in the Women's House of Detention where they kept Ethel. Bloch's guys'll have her out in the morning. I don't think she'll be charged. Even that prick judge has a mother, and besides ... " String interrupted, he hadn't heard anything since "House of Detention where they kept Ethel." "Who is Ethel?" he blurted. "Ethel Rosenberg, String, Julius' wife ... ," he stopped, incredulous, his nephew's face showing no sign of recognition, of having any idea who, what he was talking about. "Do you know who the Rosenberg's are?" he managed, as gently as his disbelief allowed; then watched his young adoptee move his head slowly, back and forth, side to side, before uttering the inconceivable, "No."

Now beginning to understand the importance of the role he'd assumed, Ray bit back his urge to ask, "What do they teach you kids in college out there in the west?" He had casually accepted his brother's call for help, Irv's offer of financial reimbursement - or, in his brother's own words, "any other support that might be needed. I'll come back there right away, or do anything else you think I should, Ray. Let me know. And, hey, ... , there is one question this old cop would like you to ask him, ..."

Like Rose, but more out of obligation to his brother than the zeal of his once sister-in-law, Ray hadn't missed any of String's time in court. Today, the fourth day, he realized the time to ask Irv's question had come, and after his short encounter with the lad, he also knew he had much teaching to do. It was awkward. He'd have to start from bupkes with this lovable schlemiel. To begin, he told String that like himself, the Rosenbergs were New York City Jews. "Not from out on the island like Jean and me, but from here in Manhattan. Your dad would think they had no brains because they think capitalism is rotten, and both are communists here in New York. I mean they're, ... they were members of the local communist party - pretty active members. They wouldn't admit it in court; they took the fifth." He waited for questions, got none and went on. "There's a senator from Wisconsin, a guy by the name of McCarthy, Joe's his first name, who's trying to make everybody believe communism's going to bring down the country - like the Soviet Union's going to wipe us out if the voters socialize some businesses - you know - force the government to own some of the corporations. I guess you never heard of him either." String hadn't. Ray continued, monitoring String's face for signs of recognition and, as above, adding explanations when necessary. "Probably giving Joe too much credit for that cold war scare, FBI head Hoover deserves a lot of it, and you can't leave out Harry or Ike's role either - they both went after red leaners and the Russians. I'm talking about Harry Truman, President Truman, the man your dad calls the haberdasher, and … " "I know Ike," Sting interjected.

Ray's disposition took an upturn. As his history lesson progressed it pleased him, surprised him even, to find String an apt learner. He felt his words were filling a heretofore vacuous head, filling it with real information, stuff the kid thoughtfully questioned, argued over, even echoed back insightfully when queried. So enough background already; he'd ask Irv's question and move on to String's current predicament: his crime - his alleged crime. He told String first about how and why he came to be there, about Irv's worrying, about his wondering if he too should have come to the trial - be with his son - then went straight to it, "Your dad wants me to ask you, 'Did you conspire to commit espionage against the United States of America?' " For the first time String laughed, he laughed long, he laughed loud, loud enough, long enough to make the guard fidget. "Me! Espionage!" Nothing else came out as the laughter subsided to giggles.

With visiting time nearing its limit, Ray shifted into cramming mode. "Listen, String, they're going to throw me out of here pretty soon, and there's stuff you need to know before they put you back on the stand tomorrow. First off, the cast is pretty much the same as the one I told you the Rosenberg's had - two of the same prosecutors, assistants last time; they replaced the big gun, Saypol, the chief attorney for the southern district of New York, another Irving Rosie would of had to cope with - he's the one who got Alger Hiss convicted after Chambers blew the whistle on him to the House Un-American Activities Committee." "Alger Hiss, Chambers?" String blurted. "Not important." Ray moved along quickly, "They're letting Roy Cohn take over; a real *schmuck*, and you're going to have to hold your own with him. He's a year younger than you, you know. Did you know that?" String answered with a non sequitur, "Isn't Cohn the name Jews give to a priest?" "Kohen or Cohen, maybe Cohn, I don't know, String, please stay with me for awhile," Ray pleaded. "I remember reading in 'Believe It or Not Ripley,' when I was a pretty young kid, that COHN spelled all living matter: Carbon, Oxygen, Hydrogen, and Nitrogen," String persisted. Ray, his hand pulling at the thinning hair above his right temple, pushed on. "Cohn had been reading from a note he said one of the members of your mom's woman's club had written about you, something about you being against capitalism, maybe being a communist. That's when Rosie made her move." It was also when the guard made his, "Time's up!" he yelled "Drek, הטיחש יד תצ סאל אַ," Ray muttered, "I'll be back tomorrow."

> ### *In the beginning was the Word, and the Word was*
> ### *with God, and the Word was God.*
> John 1:1

Back in his cell, a drab, dreary place, String wondered if all jails were this oppressive. It reminded him of Doug, of his friend's stay in the brig. Doug hadn't told him much of that life, a little of the affair he'd had with his therapist, nothing about his cell, the food, the guards, or his fears. Thoughts of the near zero chance for a heterosexual connection here in the Tombs almost brought him a smile. That's what Uncle Ray had called the place, the Tombs. String didn't know why. He'd also told him he was lucky to be here, that it was a city jail; why hadn't he been sent to Rikers Island or the Federal House of Detention up on West Street at Eleventh? Then the two had gotten into a funny verbal dance around turning state's evidence. "A lot of times a singer is brought here," Ray began it, "like that fink brother of Ethel's, David Greenglass." "A Singer?" "Yeah, a songbird," Ray went on, "someone who'll talk to the cops about something a person they know has done, something illegal." "I don't know anything criminal anyone's done, except maybe painting big letters on a water tower in San Diego," String ventured, taking Ray's words informationally, not feeling criticized - and adding, "Who's Greenglass?"

"He's Ethel's brother. I'm going to get some of the trial's transcripts for you, Neph. They'll show how he ratted out on his sister, probably lied about what she did, got her convicted."

"You said she's where mom is, will they get to meet … ?"

"No, they sent Ethel off to a place upstate about a week ago." Ray couldn't bring himself to tell his nephew that soon after sentencing she'd been sent to Sing Sing, the law requiring she be segregated from other inmates because of her sentence, a sentence of death.

String lay back on the hard bunk in his dark cell, dark long before life outside in the Big Apple would begin to stir, when locals would head for favorite watering holes to meet and to socialize. He wanted to just drift off … into sleep. He drifted instead between images from two worlds: the happy one he'd left ten short days ago, to this nightmare - made real only through the words of kin he barely knew. The whirlwind nature of his new reality had been behind many of his uncle's speculations, and at the root of his stoolie conjecture. Julius Rosenberg sat in a cell about eight months, his wife seven, before their trial began, while, for String, a fleeting six days lapsed between arrest and trial, an arrest made with no grand jury hearing. "The prosecutor must have thought he had enough solid evidence to convict you without one," Ray had volunteered, frowning. "I don't think they had one for Julius either; did for Ethel though. Getting a jury together's the only thing that's happened in about the same amount of time - only a couple a days. Both times Kaufman stepped in, did most of the selection himself. The Rosenberg's jury was told the trial would take a long time, but it only lasted three weeks. One good thing for you though, String, there's a Jew on your jury - he owns a garment shop like your Aunt Birdie's husband Jack. The rest of them, like before, all gentiles. Funny but everybody else in there -again like in the other trial - is a Jew: the judge, the attorneys, even the clerk and court reporter - all Jews." String wondered what difference it made. Time ran out before he had a chance to ask.

He wished Doug were with him tonight, lightening up this dark cell, sharing some of his young, old-man wisdom, telling more of what had happened in the brig, how he handled being locked up. Their last time together, they'd shared a pipe load of marijuana. Each claimed it was his first experience with the plant. String had lied. Eight years earlier, at seventeen, he'd been given a joint after a one-time gig - playing bass with Marvin's Movers at a San Diego nightspot. String couldn't remember how Doug had come by his stash, only that he'd been interviewed for a job with the California Youth Authority in central California somewhere along Highway 99, at a place they kept delinquent kids. String thought Doug told him one of the boys shoved the package in his pocket as he got into his car. Now, when he thought of it, that didn't make much sense. The story of them using it is such a trite one, so hackneyed, its telling is painful, and done only in the interest of keeping the facts as close as possible to the way they actually occurred. Lacking paper to roll a cigarette, they packed and tamped the grass into an old briar pipe, passed it back and forth for a drag - one to the other - each time shaking their heads, scowling, and announcing - first straight-faced, then with a smile - a chuckle - a giggle - a laugh - to peals of silly, unstoppable laughter - "I don't feel anything, do you?"

String could report no such mirth from his other experience, more its antithesis: paranoia, fear, terror. He sat in his car outside the nightclub, lit his gift - simple enough for a smoker - puffed it away, felt nothing, started his car, and began the drive home. After a mile or so, time began to mess with him. He wasn't moving; he drove on and on to nowhere; he wasn't moving, yet his speedometer read at the street's limit, 35 mph. A chill chased him, reached toward his throat; they were after him, they were going to get him, arrest him, put him away. For moments more he drove on - standing still - knowing he must stop, stop it all, stop while able. He talked to himself - aloud, "I'm on Pershing Drive, that's the Naval Hospital, pull into the parking lot." He did, turned off the engine, and the words came at him, began their attack. They came from everywhere - the words - cavalcading - words of every ilk and meaning - raining down - simple words, demanding words, oppressive threatening words. They flooded his mind, inundated it - relentlessly - came at him from every direction, caught him up in universes of words, worlds empty but for words, words suspending him in space, pounding him down.

*... Roy M. Cohn, the character, is based on the late
Roy M. Cohn (1927-1986) who was all too real;
for the most part the acts attributed to the character
Roy, such as his illegal conferences with Judge
Kaufmann, during the trial of Ethel Rosenberg,
are to be found in the historical record.
But this Roy is a work of dramatic fiction ...*

Tony Kushner   *Angels In AmericA*   (Playwright's Notes)

Except for congestion at the security entrance where a marshal held back the line, the courtroom would have filled quickly on Friday for the last session of the week. There Ab, the feisty old editor of the Yiddish-language paper *The Jewish Daily Forward*, then into his nineties, worked brusquely to explain why the companion he introduced as his new political reporter - a person shorter than himself and almost buried in Hasidic garb: black fedora pulled to a face covered with scraggly gray hair under twisted payot braids, a black coat falling to below the knees, black pants, too long and rolled to show small black shoes - couldn't answer any questions. "You can call by Jacob, if you want, see - like press pass here, but not answer back because promised no to talk, promised for Pesach Sheni, second Passover. ... OK?"

*Part of the transcript 9. the Court Reporter, prepared for
May 11,1951 follows:*

UNITED STATES DISTRICT COURT
SOUTHERN DISTRICT OF NEW YORK

HON. IRVING R. KAUFMAN
District Judge
New York **MAY 11, 1951**

SOUTHERN DISTRICT COURT REPORTERS
UNITED STATES COURT HOUSE
FOLEY SQUARE 7, NEW YORK
TELEPHONE; CORTLAND 7-4580

...

COHN: Now Mr. Xxxx, Let's go on from where we left off yesterday. I had read a note and was asking if you knew two of your mother's acquaintances, a Mrs. Appleby, and Mrs. Norman. Do you recall?

XXXX: A little.

COURT: Please explain what you mean by a little, Mr. Xxxx. As I see it you either recall what Mr. Cohn has asked you, or you don't.

The presiding judge is referred to as COURT. here the judge is Judge Kaufman.

XXXX: I recall a note being read, Your Honor. I don't think I know the two women.

COURT: Very well. Can you make your question more specific, Mr. Cohn?

COHN: Alright, then, Do the names Charlotte, Mona, and the Sapphire Club mean anything to you, Mr. Xxxx?

XXXX: My mother belonged to a group of women who worked together at Marston's Department Store. She always called them 'the girls,' but I think they may have called themselves the Sapphire Club, yes. Mona and Charlotte were both members.

COHN: Very well. Mona is Mona Norman, and Charlotte is Charlotte Appleby. If you'll recall, the note I read was from Mrs. Appleby, Charlotte, to Mrs. Norman, Mona, and stated, among other things, that she had heard you talking with a friend, she said you called him Guido. She said it occurred before a Sapphire Club luncheon your mother had prepared in your home at 3691 Pershing Ave. in San Diego. Is that accurate?

XXXX: Is what accurate?

COURT: I think you are being asked a general question about who you knew, names, locations, things like that. Once again, Mr. Cohn, I direct you to be more specific in your questioning.

COHN: Did you know someone named Guido back in 1943, and did you live at 3691 Pershing Ave in San Diego at that time, Mr. Xxxx?

XXXX: I've had a friend named Guido since starting high school, yes, and yes, that's where we lived.

COHN: Again, Mrs. Appleby's note reads in part: " … he told his friend he was a Communist … ." Did you tell your friend Guido, you were a Communist?

XXXX: I did not.

COHN: Why do you think Mrs. Appleby wrote that in her note to …

COURT: Specific, not speculative, Mr. Cohn.

COHN: Retract. Are you a Communist, or have you ever been a Communist, Mr. Xxxx?

XXXX: A Communist? No. I'm a registered Democrat.

COHN: Mrs. Appleby also wrote that you may be an atheist. You are an atheist, are you not?

XXXX: I am not.

The words for G-d below were not typed by this reporter.

COHN: Then you believe in God?

XXXX: I'm agnostic.

COHN: If you're an agnostic, you are an atheist. I see no difference.

XXXX: There's a world of difference. Agnostic means you don't know. You don't know if there is or there isn't a God. An atheist believes they know something, just like a deist or theist does. A theist believes there is a God and an atheist believes there isn't. You can't believe something and not know. There's no difference in the way theists and atheists take positive, sure of themselves, stands. The one who's different is the agnostic.

COHN: Did you tell your friend Guido that communism was a better form of government than democracy?

XXXX: I wouldn't have said that. You can't compare them. Communism is a way wealth is distributed. Democracy is a type of … of, you know, how a government is run. It's an apples and oranges thing.

COHN: And you believe democracy is the wrong way to, as you say, run a government?

XXXX: No, I'd have to agree with Winston Churchill, when he said "democracy is the worst form of government, except for all the others," or something like that.

COHN: Alright, but for the record, Mr. Churchill prefaced his comment to the House of Commons with, "it has been said that," before the democracy remark you attribute to him. Now, on to your second point, Mr. Xxxx, do you believe wealth should be distributed here as it is in the Soviet Union?

XXXX: Probably not like it is in the Soviet Union, but more equitably than now with capitalism alone.

COHN: We'll get back to that again later; now for now, was your mother, Mrs. Xxxx, a Republican, and did she, as Mrs. Appleby wrote, call you a Communist?

XXXX: My mother is a Republican. Has been all her life. I could never figure out why. I don't remember ever talking about politics with her.

COURT: The question was, did she ever call you or refer to you as a Communist, Mr. Xxxx. Did she?

XXXX: No.

COHN: Now I'm going to read you part of a letter sent by a soldier to his wife. A soldier you met when you first entered military service at Fort Ord, California. The letter reads:
"Darling, during lunch hour I had two discussions on political questions with some fellows. I used the utmost patience and care in the choice of words so that I could get my point across and still not be suspected of Communism, … I'll raise the red flag yet so don't worry about the future. It's ours."
That letter Mr. Xxxx, was sent by David Greenglass to his wife Ruth. Just a month ago Mr. Greenglass was sentenced to fifteen years in prison for espionage. Mr. Greenglass says he remembers you well. That he met you at the Fort on Passover, April 8th, 1944 and that you contributed to a political discussion, citing many interesting examples of the evils of capitalism. Do you remember meeting Mr. Greenglass, Mr. Xxxx, and will you please summarize your recollection of what went on that day?

XXXX: I think I know who you mean, a corporal, or maybe a T/5 - two stripes with a

T under it - who stopped and asked me how come I was eating a sandwich on, was it, pesshock?

COHN: Pesach, Passover, your sandwich may have been made with leavened bread.

XXXX: That's it, he invited me to eat with him, sayders, he said.

COHN: Seder, go on.

XXXX: I thanked him and asked what he meant. He had trouble believing I wasn't a Jew. He was quite assertive, sure of himself, he said religion didn't much matter, I should eat with him anyway. After I declined, we talked a bit about politics before two or three other guys came by, guys he knew, then we all kicked ideas around.

COHN: Did he have a lot of good things to say about the Soviet Union?

XXXX: It wasn't just some corporal saying good things about the Soviets. That'd been kind of a major theme around camp, with the army I mean. The day before - my first full day at Ord - I'd been ordered to sit through a couple of films; films put together by the army, films about how great Russia is; America's wartime ally they kept saying. They quoted praises from a lot of people about the Soviet Union's heroism against the Nazis. I remember hearing Winston Churchill and General Douglas MacArthur's names. MacArthur's kind of surprised me. The Lieutenant doing the training said Hollywood made a couple of good movies about them too: Mission to Moscow and Song of Russia. He didn't show those though, the last picture we watched was about venereal disease, mostly clap, and right before dinner when we were served weenies stuffed with cheese.

COHN: Let's stay with the political discussion you had with David Greenglass and his associates for awhile. Did you personally get into talking about the distribution of wealth?

XXXX: Yes.

COHN: OK. What did you have to say about it?

XXXX: Well - it's quite an involved subject - I think wealth is what's out there in nature: food, water, material for building housing to keep warm and dry, and for clothes to wear. Money hasn't much to do with wealth.

COHN: And capitalism is at fault when people don't get those things from nature?

XXXX: To a large extent. Everyone in the country is forced into being a cheap salesman, pounding each other constantly, day and night, to buy, buy, buy, just to keep it afloat, and what if the population stops increasing, and we make stuff to last for a lifetime, how would it work then?

COHN: Is that what you think now, or is that what you were telling Greenglass and the others?

XXXX: Both. I pretty much think now what I did then. People starve and don't have to. There's enough out there in nature to feed, clothe and house everyone, if we keep population in check. We just have to learn how to distribute it equitably, less greedily.

COHN: Like the Soviets do, Mr. Xxxx, with their Politburo?

XXXX: No, it hasn't been done very well there, so far. I'm not sure if it can, but I'd like to think it could be brought about democratically.

COHN: Just last year you went door to door campaigning against Senator Nixon, Richard Nixon, when he ran against Congresswoman Helen Gahagan Douglas. Is that correct?

XXXX: It is.

COHN: Did you know, and would it have deterred you in your support, to know that one of Congresswoman Douglas' rivals in the primary, Mr. Boddy, publisher of the Los Angeles Daily News, called her "the Pink Lady?"

XXXX: No I didn't know that. It wouldn't have made any difference, Nixon was also saying similar, very slanderous and untrue things about her. Lies … .

COHN: Did you, in fact, refer to Mr. Nixon, as "Tricky Dick," and go door to door for Mrs. Douglas, passing out her literature and singing, "Drop dead, Dicky Nixon drop dead, we need you like a hole in the head," and so on?

XXXX: I did, but I can't take credit for making up any of the song, or for the title either.

COHN: Now Mr. Xxxx, I believe you landed in Leghorn, Italy with the U.S. Army on July 7th, 1946, and were in your assigned quarters only two days before you left with an acquaintance - and without leave - that is, without permission to leave - to visit a brothel about 15 miles north in Pisa, Italy. Is that correct?

XXXX: I … We … We did land in Livorno, Italy. I don't remember the exact date. Did I go to a brothel in Pisa? … No.

COHN: Did you go to Pisa without a leave of absence shortly after arriving in Italy, Mr. Xxx?

XXXX: Ah, … yes.

BLOCH: I'm having trouble understanding how brothels, or being absent without leave, has anything to do with this espionage trial, Your Honor.

COURT: Are you objecting, Mr. Bloch?

BLOCH: I am.

COURT: Very well. Please tell the court where you're going with these questions, Mr. Cohn.

COHN: My evidence suggests that the accused we are dealing with here had far more power during his stay in Italy than can be attributed to his status. I intend to uncover the source of that power, and show how it directly relates to espionage.

COURT: Explain.

COHN: Well, on arriving in Italy Mr. Xxxx was a pfc, a private first class, one step above the very lowest rank possible in the United States Army. Yet from the very first, he seems to have had privileges even a field grade officer would have trouble receiving. On the ship taking him there, he avoided both guard duty and KP - kitchen police - cleanup for the mess - the place they serve food. He received the Good Conduct Medal even after traveling wherever he pleased, without authorization, permission of any kind; trips to Venice, Trieste, Grado, the Alps, even Paris. In fact, it appears he crossed the Morgan Line into Communist Yugoslavia, a complete violation of Allied Forces law. He was promoted to a first three grader, three stripes over a rocker in about three months, an almost unheard of short period of time. He had a close friend and subordinate leave to visit the notorious Mafia boss, Lucky Luciano, in Sicily. As I said, I want to show who pulled those strings for him, and why.

COURT: You may proceed.

COHN: Again, Mr. Xxxx, did you go to Pisa to have sex with a prostitute?

XXXX: I didn't go to Pisa to have sex. No.

COHN: Did you have sex with a prostitute, or pay for sex, on that trip to Pisa, Mr. Xxxx?

XXXX: Ah, … ,Yes, I don't know if she was a prostitute, and not in a brothel, in her home. We went to Pisa to visit the cathedral, and the tower.

COHN: Now tell us about your rapid promotions.

XXXX: I'd been in the army for a couple of years as an infantryman and had a lot of weapons training. When we got up north I was asked by a high ranking medical officer - I think he was a Colonel, a physician - if I would like to be a medic. I told him no. The next day they transferred me to Gorizia, to the Medical Headquarters of the 349th Infantry Division, and changed my MOS, my Military Occupational Specialty, to Surgical Technician.

```
COHN: OK, but the next week you were pro-
moted to corporal with a T, then quickly
had two more promotions. Why was that, and
were you given medical training?

XXXX: I was promoted because I could type,
use a typewriter. Medical training? No.

COURT: I've received a signal from the jury
that a break is needed. We will reconvene
after lunch, at 1:30 PM - promptly.
```

> ### *I despise a judge who feels God told him to impose a death sentence.*
> Felix Frankfurter, Associate Justice of the
> United States Supreme Court
> writing about Irving R. Kaufman

It's unfortunate that court reporters report only the words, not the actions, behavior, the demeanor of the subjects they quote, or of the people in the gallery. Much could be learned by noting the judge's grimace and his consternation at Mr. Cohn's ambiguous questions, at Mr. Xxxx's chuckle when he spoke of Winston Churchill, his long pause before addressing the question of wealth distribution in the Soviet Union and his squirming over the "to visit a brothel" question, or the attempt by the Hasidic reporter to stand up on several occasions, and old Ab's struggle to make sure that didn't happen.

The afternoon progressed much as it had in the morning: Mr. Cohn asking questions in seemingly random order about Mr. Xxxx's European tour of duty; Mr. Xxxx's responses - often flippant sounding, the Court's occasional interjections, and Mr. Bloch's infrequent objections. One such objection occurred after Mr. Cohn intimated that Mr. Xxxx had strayed into Yugoslavia to pass along atomic secrets. Mr. Bloch objected on the grounds that the alleged event took place two years after Mr. Greenglass had given information to the Soviet spy, Harry Gold. When Mr. Cohn observed that the Soviets hadn't detonated their first bomb until August 29, 1949, two years after the claimed Yugoslavia crossing, Judge Kaufman overruled the objection.

That night String, back on his cot after a once again hearty consumption of prison fare and working to keep his sobbing inaudible, got buoyed by a curt shout from the cellblock guard, "Move it, visitor to see you." Once inside that typically most welcomed room, he extended an unenthusiastic, "Hi," expecting, hoping to have seen his mother, not his uncle. Ray greeted him, amiably enough, but quieter than previously. "You doin' all right, buddy, long day huh? If you'd rather just get some rest, that'd be OK, let me know, I could come again tomorrow. Only a couple of things I can fill you in on anyway." String heard nothing, "Where's mom?" his single response. "She's fine, big guy, guess you know the judge won't allow her to see you here, actually thinks he's kept her away from you completely." His guffaw startled, made String uneasy. What could there be to laugh about? "Told me to say hello to you, tell you you did fine today." "How would she know how I did, Ray?" "Sometimes I can't figure you out. Yesterday I thought you were a pretty bright lad; today it's like you lost your pants again, can't even recognize your own mother." Bells went off as Ray unfolded the story of Ab and Jacob, went off like shattering ice, leaving String echoing his uncle's guffaw.

They spoke earnestly after that, Ray advising, sharing his assessment of the day; String listening, shrugging, telling how it had been for him. "No, not at all, I wasn't trying to be a wiseass. I just tried to answer his questions as honestly as I could. It does mess me up the way he jumps around. I can't guess what's coming next. And the Judge, it kind of scares me when he butts in." "I can understand that. I heard Julius Rosenberg called Kaufman 'a cross between a rabbinical student and an army sergeant.' " String straightened in his chair, a deep pall seeping over his face, "Bloch told me they, Julius and his wife, got the death sentence. Said he'd get it commuted, but even so … ." Ray reached his hand over the table, started to drop it on his nephew's, saw their guard move closer, and pulled it back. "I'm sure he will, kid," he mouthed as softly and reassuringly as he could. "Are they really guilty, Uncle Ray, of espionage?" "I don't know from espionage. I'd guess Julius did pass along some stuff to the Russians. Who cares? With Ethel it's different; probably more like she was a good housewife, supportive. Like I told you before, it's that fink brother of hers, Greenglass, that told stuff about her, I'd guess lies to save his own sorry *tuches* and to keep his own wife out of it. I've heard rumors that even FBI Chief Hoover wanted to pussy-foot with Ethel, wanted her to go on trial, but then to kind of jerk her around, you know, to get stuff out of Julius. Neither happened; she gets convicted big time, and both stay clams. Let's talk about ... "

"Ten minutes left," the guard intoned. "Feh!" Ray spurted. "There's stuff Cohn brought up he hasn't gone over with you yet. Like the travel. Is that true?" "Well, the army, itself, moved me around a lot while I was there, and I had medics attached to the troops up along the line dividing Italy and the Jugs. Guess I did take a little advantage of that sometimes. I'd tell 'em at headquarters that I'd be up on the line, and up there they'd think I was down at headquarters. Let me have a bit of free time with my two buddies, both Army Pictorial Services photographers." "Could you just get up and go places with them, String?" "Like I told Cohn, I could type. You could do most anything in the army if you could type. I'd just type up an order to go with them. Got free transportation out of it too, most of the time. Cohn was as much off as on though. My first trip to Trieste was for army business, and the trip to the Alps, Cortina it was, like the one to Paris, were both legitimate rest leaves." "In Venice did you really fall into the Grand Canal like he said you did?" "Fall in? No, no. Don went to take pictures for *Life* magazine of a celebration they have there every May, "The Marriage of Venice to the Sea." People put up little tables along the canals to sit and watch. Everybody has vino, and everybody insisted I share a glass. I may have passed out a little, but I didn't fall into the canal." String chuckles, "Probably have to have had a dozen or so vaccination shots if I had." "Oy, did your friend get his pictures for *Life*?" "Nah, he forgot to take the proper night lighting gear." Ray shook his head, having a little trouble believing what anyone said. "Just two other things, then we should spend the rest of our time talking about how you should answer the rest of Cohn's questions. First, did you get out of work on the boat coming over, and how, and why did your friend go visit the mob boss, Luciano?" "The boat thing's easy. I told the ship's chaplain I played the string bass and asked if I could start a band. It went crazy - went from band to variety show to on-board paper; a whole floating entertainment center aboard that little *Central Falls* Victory Ship. I got treated like a celeb. About Vinny going to Sicily, I never figured that out. Only that, like you, he was a life-long New Yorker. He said he had a lot of regard for the Mafia, spoke of their family values."

But they cried, saying, Crucify him, crucify him.
Luke 23:21

Uncle Ray had wished him, Mazel Tov, before leaving. It hadn't been meant that way, but it felt ominous. Their talk of Italy had brought back memories of happy times, of fun, of adventure. Now, back in his still daylit cell, he hung onto those thoughts, desperately wanting a typewriter, wanting to pour it out, tell it all, tell it especially to the man he'd admired most in that other land, that other life. Uncle Ray, the postman, would know how to get it to him. But there was no typewriter, … , he got out a pen, good paper his mother had brought him, and began:

May 11, 1951

Dear General Eisenhower,

It seemed so strange to see newspaper pictures of you in civvies after you left the army to be the president of Columbia University. I'm happy that you're back in uniform again, commanding NATO. It's like I can salute you again, stand at attention and watch you pass by during inspection. I felt so honored when you did that, went by my little unit on the Campoformido Airfield near Goriza (closer to Udine) in October of 1946 (I can't remember the exact day). I still have 10 pictures my friend Jack from Army Picto-

rial Services took of you that day. There's
one of you shaking hands with my regimental
commander, a couple of you walking the lines,
in a few a nice looking lady in the background is taking notes. I guess she must be a
reporter. The one of you in the jeep got faded.
I'm sorry about that. My favorite is the one
where you're standing up high on the wooden
platform they built for you. It's my favorite
because it was from there you motioned for us
to come near you, and we all broke ranks and
crowded around. I think you might like to
have them, so I'll have my mother send them
to you as soon as she can. I can't send them
myself because I'm in a New York City jail.
That's why I'm writing you today.

I've been put on trial for espionage. I'm
not sure exactly what that means, but I do
know I'd never do or say anything to hurt
our country. I enlisted in the army in 1944
when I was 17, but it was a couple of years
later, along the Morgan Line in Italy where
they think I did something wrong. One of the
reasons they think that is because I did talk to
a soldier by the name of David Greenglass at
Fort Ord, and agreed with some of his political ideas. They just convicted him to 15 years
in prison, also for espionage.

I know you're more conservative, more like
my parents than I am. My dad is a police

officer and was also a sergeant, but during
WW 1. My mother worked with clothes at a big
department store before quitting to raise me
and my sister. They've both been Republicans
all their lives. I'm a registered Democrat. I
guess I'd have to admit to being a kind of lib-
eral one, but I would never break any law that
would hurt this country.

I know you're very busy, sir, and I guess
I've gone on longer than I should have, but I
would appreciate it if you would pass my message along to whoever got the idea I broke the
law. If you'd like me to give you more information about my background and service, my
address at home is 3691 Pershing Ave., San
Diego, 4, California.

Sincerely and with many thanks,

Former S/Sgt _____

Chapter 17

Final Aside

*But of that day and hour knoweth no man, no, not
the angels of heaven, but my Father only.*
Matt. 24:36

I'm enough of a statistician to consider it very odd that I'm
still alive. Few obituaries in the local news eulogize anyone
older - next year I'll be a nonagenarian, yea, I had to look it
up too - and I do have health issues, notably prostate cancer, a
subject discoursed inordinately in Chapter 9, the 'First Aside.'
Old timers, it's said, are wont to talk health issues to death. I
thought myself innocent of that charge, but apparently not.
In the 'Second Aside,' I went on to praise Dwot, my urologist,
for the splendid job he did TURPing me, the operation to
better assure my ability to continue peeing once he'd frozen
my prostate in an attempt to kill the cancer. About a year-and-
a-half ago, six months after the TURP and with equivalent
caring and skill, he executed that procedure, a prostate cryoablation. Did it work? The jury's still out, but complete acquittal
is improbable. Does it matter? I can't answer that either. Like
most my age, I claim a litany of minor complaints, indignities foisted on the old, some known to be associated with the
cancer, some of questionable connection, and others, like 'dry
eyes,' definitely unrelated. 'Dry eyes' is the name given by oph-
thalmologists to a condition in which eyes tear-up and drip
continuously. I've had my say about med speak. You figure.

When someone asks about my health, how I'm doing, I
always answer, "Not too bad." If they persist, I go on with,

"Hey, I've lived a good life, a long one; what's left now is frosting on the cake. Dying's no big deal." That's what I say to people. I'm not sure it's true, but that's what I tell them. I have no post-life expectations. Life, and whatever counterpart gives that word its meaning, are great mysteries. I've had no personal contact with anyone who remembers what happened to them before they were born. If I had, I'd be skeptical. On Christmas Eve, Joyce and I went to a candlelight service at a protestant church in our new neighborhood. We'd moved during the summer, bought a small house in a friendly San Ramon retirement community not far from the libraries she once managed. While the choir excelled, leading us, the congregation, in and into a joyful, stirring nostalgia of old carols, the pastor's sermon - a tale of how the baby Jesus grew to be tortured and killed, to die in order to give us everlasting life - frightened me. If I had my druthers, I'm not sure how long I'd choose to live, but forever would be pushing it. The computer work we old engineers got caught up in, work thought to ease human labor - not simply make money - likely expedited social media and other technologies I've come to heartily dislike - the romance of letters penned on fine stationery gone, sextants and stars replaced by GPS. And of course you're never too old, while you're still alive, to be out of the jungle; shit will still happen; there'll be fender benders driving, disagreements with mechanics and handymen, suits over something or other; brushing, flossing, and the rest of daily living's boring chores will persist; nothing will go away, you'll not be treated with loving kindness, shouts of hallelujah, because you're an old fart, a bloody senior citizen.

Whoa! Slow down. Does eternal life mean everlasting orgasms and, if so, would they be the big bangs of yesteryear's popping prostate, or dreamlike, dissociated from today's post-frozen gland: quiet, gentle, like floating downstream on an inner tube with the sun beating down persuasively, sending waves of warmth to the loins. The literature on procedures of the prostate will tell you that ED, erectile dysfunction, may occur. With cryosurgery its more like EC, erectile catastrophe, a 'hard-on' deemed miraculous. I've often wondered about all the fuss over ED, except of course for the big bucks made peddling drugs like Viagra, and Cialis. I doubt women loving other women find ED much of a concern.

For health problems other than cancer, I try to see Duno, my primary care guy, only when I feel awful. I don't expect him to know what's wrong with me unless it's obvious, a poison ivy rash or a strep throat maybe, but he has a list of specialists - a number of them tops - and I can always count on him for an antibiotic or a referral. On my last visit, after I became a bit offensive over wanting to see a neurologist when he thought an endocrinologist was in order, he got testy with me - I'm guessing he'd taken an assertiveness training class from the health group he's part of. Anyway he won, I saw a very pleasant endocrinologist who gave me an order for an osteoporosis bone density scan and recommended I see a neurologist. I'll see one next month. Duno made the referral.

I no longer feel the shadow of death hovering, constantly cloaking me, as I did a couple of years ago. The reason, I believe, lies in my expectation that this story will soon be completed.

> *When I have fears that I may cease to be*
> *Before my pen has gleaned my teeming brain,*
> John Keats

Unlike Keats, my brain doesn't teem, it more trickles, and I do have fears, fears surfacing without warning, fears of not seeing what I've written, am still writing, printed out in full book glory. By honoring its commitment to publish these words as they were submitted - chapter by chapter - HeronDrivePress saved me a little ongoing anxiety. It couldn't stave off a deeper longing, a need to clutch, grasp, to hold onto them in an object of tactile perfection, a small paperback book. Nothing bests a book; nothing shortens life, robs it of time, flaunts the specter of mortality, like need - obsessive need, compulsion, having something to do that must be done: climb a mountain, sail a sea, cure a malady, write a book. The difference between want to and need to is profound. Now, here, near the end of this story, I can picture life as it might, could, should perhaps always be: day by day wonder, day by day awe.

> *The eye that mocketh at his father, and despiseth to*
> *obey his mother, the ravens of the valley shall pick it*
> *out, and the young eagles shall eat it.*
> Prov. 30:17

My parents were both kind of remarkable, each in his or her own way. Uh-oh, whoa once again - after writing that I have to wonder, doubt even, if they differed much from folks bringing up other kids. In what way were they so unique? Does every child, even an ancient one, see those who nurtured them in infancy - whose faces they associated with life, recognized before anyone else - as special people, as remarkable? Given the way I would describe my progenitors - a clinging, uncommunicative mother and a father I'd differed with on most every important life issue - I marvel at their influence on me; how - as the cliché goes - much like them I've become. I wonder, too, how many children support one parent over the other. For me, accepting my mother's role as sufferer, the offended party in every domestic dispute, likely blinded me to whatever affection my father may have offered, left me un-knowing and denied, denied with scant promise until one very special day: the day he chose to die, did die, died a remarkable death.

My mother lost her ability to live alone, to manage by herself, around the same time Joan did. The self-pledge I'd made - be available for Joan in Aptos - restricted the number of eight-hour drives I could take, made it difficult to help, to spend time with mom outside an occasional overnight trip. The burden of care fell to my sister. She found Frances, a live-in caregiver, a gruff, muscular, little woman who showed no affection for her charge and received none in return; recip-rocal disdain forming the only and ever-strengthening bond between them. Once, when Frances and I spatted over the way she fed her, mom - ever-protective of her son - flailed out, fists clenched and intent on corporal retribution.

On a weekend some time later, while walking up the stairs to mom's front porch - overnight-bag in hand - a young wom-an from the corner house across the street ran to stop me, to confide, timidly and with concern, that she had been seeing an old lady, wearing nothing but flimsy nightclothes, step onto this very porch at various late night hours and, to paraphrase liberally, regale the neighborhood, in as many decibels as she could muster, with a rendering of The Lord's Prayer. What prompted mom's excursions during the last months of her life remains unclear. Her interactions with my sister and me could, at times, be rambling or include longer than expected vacant stares, but were never completely bizarre; her oddest behavioral quirk being a persistent insistence that we be with her in a few weeks - she actually named a specific date which I don't recall - to celebrate her birthday, an event we had shared with her only a month before.

Sis told me a new medication might have been started, and our search through the house's single medicine-cabinet turned up the heavy-duty antipsychotic, Haldol, Haloperidol, a drug used for a wide range of mental conditions, mood disorders to schizophrenia. I dumped the pills into the toilet, got the prescribing doctor's name from the bottle's label, found his address in the yellow pages, located him in a shabby office a few blocks from where mom lived, and discouraged him from further playing psychiatrist. Frances, it turned out, had found him and had, on her own initiative, enlisted his support. I later learned that nursing homes often use the drug as a restraint, chemically assisting the control of uncooperative residents. A 2012 editorial by Mike Masteron, "Our Most Easily Abused," reads in part:

> "One drug of choice was Haldol, a powerful antipsychotic medication that left them continually stunned into head-drooping, drooling submission. Misusing a Haldol pill was much cheaper than paying for an adequate care staff. Just slip 'em a pill and forget about 'em."

Haldol has also been shown to greatly increase the risk of heart failure, and that's how mom died. Although I'd flushed the drug a month earlier, she died of a massive heart attack. In the early morning hours of October 13, 1985, my sister phoned me from the waiting room outside the hospital's emergency department. She'd gotten a call from a hyperventilating Frances, "Oh God, God," she heard her panting. "Mrs., your mom, dropped down on the living room floor. They just now took her away, put her in an ambulance and took her away. What they did to her before that, Oh God, Oh God. They came after I called 911, Oh God, what they did, they did to her." Sis gave me a much calmer synopsis of that call, ending with: "Don't know what she meant, what they did aside from trying to revive her. I'm still here at the hospital. I'll let you know what's happening as soon as I find out. You may want to think about coming down." It was less than half an hour when she called again. "Mom's gone," she told me quietly "They couldn't bring her back." Her death preceded Joan's by seven months; she was ninety-three. I hadn't called anyone, and there was still time to meet the day's commitment. It would be better for me to tell them in person. I took off for Aptos, for the Forest of Nisene Marks State Park, where I was to meet Joan and our children for a party we'd planned long ago, a celebration of our son's 21st birthday.

At 99 my father was still going strong: swam daily, square danced occasionally - twice a week before his third, and last surviving, wife died - and hadn't stopped driving. By then he had neither insurance nor driver's license; couldn't see well enough for the latter, and who'd insure him without a license? The last time I rode with him as passenger, he jumped his big Honda Accord out of an intersection the instant its light turned green, popped his clutch drag style, and raced ahead of the car next to him. "Got to check out my reflexes," he confided. As said, it was the last time I rode with him as a passenger.

Early in the morning of Friday, March 5, 1999, I got a phone call from Howard, my father's devoted young companion, protector, and helper with many physical tasks. I call him young in contrast to dad, the man he so often accompanied. Howard was 83 at the time, a retired navy chief warrant officer living with his wife of 56 years, herself a former WAVE, the Navy's World War II acronym for Women Accepted for Voluntary Emergency Service. He'd called to tell me to come down. Pop was always after my sister and me to visit. We hadn't seen him since the big birthday party, the one we'd hosted for him when he turned 100, nine weeks earlier. Until Howard got his voice more under control and added to the terse message: "You should come down. I'll call your sister, too, if you want me to, … unless you want to," his advice seemed strange, almost eerie. "Are you OK?" left my mouth without thought and I quickly continued with, "How come my old man isn't calling?" The prolonged pause, the faint, muffled sound of stifled tears, choked me as well, tightened my throat. What could be said to this sweet hulk of a man, this old veteran, eleven years my senior. "I'll call sis, then start down right away, Howard, … can you tell me anything about … what's happening?" His response, simple enough, took long in the telling, relief apparently freeing him from the restraint of unexpected despondency, and he chose to review every historical precursor along with the information pertinent to his call.

"Remember how your dad always sat alone to eat dinner in the Tower's dining room?" he began. I did. Pop had lived in the Laguna Hills' community of Leisure World for over thirty-five years, the past several in its stately high-rise. A commitment to not disturbing others - one of the subtle things he taught me - resulted in his extreme position on coughing at the table. We tried to convince him his company would mean more to the other diners than his cough. He remained unconvinced. How could he enjoy his meal while concerned for their comfort? Food wasn't just maintenance; no one left the dining room much before he did, savoring first, a plate piled high from the salad bar, then entrée and dessert, nothing offered by the kitchen ever declined. He ate slowly, for pleasure, the joy of eating validating a large and paradoxical part of his senior life; the more he ate, the thinner he became.

"Yesterday," Howard went on, "your dad couldn't swallow. He didn't want them to, but they took him to the hospital." A more precise accounting indicates he'd been coughing for a long while, couldn't maintain deep enough breaths to provide his oxygen needs, blanked briefly, head slumping to the table, when one of the servers rushed to attempt a Heimlich maneuver. Up popped his head, his hands flew to the front of his throat, palms facing out, and he managed to whisper, "I can breathe," through the pursed lips of a pale, damp face. Management staff acted quickly, called 911 and over pleas and desperate attempts to ward them off, the emergency medical tech and ambulance driver quickly strapped him to a gurney, rolled it to their vehicle, and sped away. The embarrassment brought him far greater agony than any he could have received from physical pain. When I told Howard I'd drive straight to the hospital, he stammered at first, objected, then confessed, "I … I kind of brought him home this morning. Your dad's at home now. He's resting." It turns out the two of them had broken every hospital rule. They'd found, in the two-person ward's hanging closet, the clothes he'd worn on arriving, dressed him, and spirited him through the halls, sneaking past everyone with any appearance of authority.

After speaking to hospital employees up and down the line - dignitaries to aides - apologizing over and over, promising to bring my father back in the morning, to sign every conceivable form releasing the hospital of responsibility, I received the necessary assurance he would be reinstated, evaluated and treated. I called my sister, then headed for Interstate 5 and the long trip south. Normally I'd go a little over halfway, spend the night in the drab, dusty little town of Buttonwillow before heading over the grapevine. This day I drove straight through, getting past a guarded Leisure World entry gate a little before four in the afternoon, right before pop's daily whiskey ritual - a ritual not to be avoided simply on the grounds of poor health. He'd always offer a second. "Another splash?" he'd ask, standing over your glass, bottle tipped ready to pour. He never shared much of his life, more over whiskey than other times, and he'd never, never spoken to me of his personal affairs, his bank account or, for that matter, his health. That afternoon, as if he'd been holding something back, something important, he announced, in a tone of delight, and with a grin falling between self-satisfied and sheepish, "I'm a millionaire."

When she arrived a couple of hours later, my sister and I decided against going down for dinner. Dad still had trouble breathing, even the whiskey kept him coughing for awhile. At the time of our imbibing, a cupboard check of his munchies larder came up empty. Annoyed, he declared, "I'm going to run down to Trader Joe's and pick up a few snacks." It took effort to convince him I didn't need any nibbles, and if they were for him, he probably wouldn't be able to swallow them. Now, after my sister settled in, it was my turn. I announced my intent, then went off to Trader Joe's to buy snacks and sandwiches for the two of us, leaving sis to ply pop with Ensure, the brand name for a thick, pasty, milk-like drink, marketed as a nutritional supplement by Abbott Laboratories, the only thing we thought he might get down.

The next morning, by the time we got past admissions and to the correct hospital wing, the big round clock on the wall across from the nursing station read 10:12. From there, pop was led to his room - this time a single-bed ward - and helped into a regulation, butt-exposing gown, another indignity bordering on torture for a hundred-year-old shouldering a lifetime of self-pride.

A medical doctor, I'll call him Dsuk, specialty unknown, began his examination a short time later. The nurse accompanying him drew the curtain around pop's bed - I don't know why in that private room - shutting me and my sister from the action. We listened to pop saying "aaah," and answering questions. Soon the physician made his solemn pronouncement, "You have dysphagia," prompting the obvious response, "What does that mean?" "It means swallowing is difficult." I feel fortunate in being unable to see the apoplectic face from which came the censorious words I did hear, "… of course … stupid … that's why I'm here … what should be done … of course … of course … ." The sharpness of an old man, sharp in tongue, sharp in mind, made no impact on the man of medicine; he proceeded to pontificate, slowly, loudly - his antagonist might be hard of hearing - and in detail. "The most common swallowing symptom is the sensation that swallowed food is sticking, either in the lower neck or the chest. If food sticks in the throat, there may be coughing or choking with expectoration - spitting that is - of the swallowed food. If food enters the larynx, even more severe coughing and choking will happen. Loss of weight can be a sign of either severe dysphagia or a malignant tumor. We'll know for sure when we look down your throat. More often than losing weight, people describe a change in their eating pattern … … … ."

After lunch, the three of us, pop, sis, and me, overheard Dsuk - in the hall near our ward door - hold forth pretentiously on his findings. I didn't know - and never found out - if his two colleagues were gastroenterologists, otolaryngologists, residents or just buddies. He was saying, "… If I find strictures or Schatzki's rings, I'll treat him with endoscopic dilation." Then in response to questions, "Yeah, yeah, we can stretch it with a long, semi-rigid tube through the mouth, or blow up a balloon inside the esophagus," and, "No, no, it depends upon whether it's above the esophagus-stomach junction, or in the lower esophagus at the squamocolumnar junction." In a drawn out, mournful drone - an appeal impossible to disregard - pop commanded, "Call the nurse."

He looked up at the attentive young woman we'd summoned and, without explanation, announced, "I just want to go to sleep." Her puzzled reaction, knit brow, hunched shoulders, evoked a repeat, a more plaintive declaration, an appeal, "I just want to go to sleep." Still unsure his wishes were known, he said it once again, this time in a low, pleading, whistled voice, just short of a whine, "I just want to go to sleep."

After that, events moved quickly. The nurse had heard him. On her own, she called a local hospice and within an hour, one of their nurses joined us, went over all options, got sis and my assurance we'd not contest pop's choice, and provided us with a much smaller, nonetheless adequate supply of morphine sulfate, the same magic elixir Dr. Grace had given Joan. The knowledge he'd soon be leaving the hospital buoyed pop's spirits, lifted him like nothing else could have; lifted him until new information slammed him right back down; an ambulance had been ordered. I thought he might cry. "I won't let them strap me onto a stretcher again," he blustered defiantly yet beseeching. This new hurdle caught all of us off guard. We knew the hospital wouldn't let him walk out on his own; we had no idea they would object to my wheeling him to my car for the two minute, six block ride down the street to the long term care facility. The impasse resolved itself through the wisdom of the ambulance driver. "I can't let him ride in front," he pondered aloud, rubbing his left temple, "Oh wait," he scratched his head again. "If you get him down here I may be able to strap the chair to the supports in back, where I usually tie down the cart." We did, and he could. Pop was pleased.

Late in the afternoon, attendants at the nursing home saw to Dad's comfort in a clean, bright room before leaving us to ourselves on that still sunny, pre-spring day. Dad chose not to dawdle, asking for and cheerfully drinking the hospice-provided bright green fluid. He said it tasted pretty good, and immediately had us drag chairs to either side of the bed - sis to his right, me on the left - and after a long, quiet period - minutes, hours, I can't recall - stretched out his arms, side to side, grasping our hands, her left, my right, and, before closing his eyes, looked first at his daughter, his princess, squeezed her hand while saying her name, softly, lovingly, then turned to me, squeezed mine, and I thought I saw the trace of a smile, before his drifting, fading words, "Bye, String."

Epilogue

I have heard the check of my reproach and the spirit
of my understanding causeth me to answer.
Job 20:3

Much as Samuel Clemens needed Mark Twain to get his stories sold, the author of this tale needed anonymity to get his told. Thus the emergence of Guri P Essen, a creation who cannot be put aside until he attempts to reduce the head-scratching, or at least dampen curiosity concerning the people and events portrayed. Here then, in his words, are some gap fillers, both forward and backwards in time, from the date String wrote General Eisenhower.

On June 19, 1953, two years after String's trial, Ethel and Julius Rosenberg were electrocuted at Sing Sing, New York State's Correctional Facility in Ossining, New York - the only American citizens to be executed for the crime of conspiracy to commit espionage. String's trial ended in a hung jury, eleven to one, or one to eleven, for acquittal; he never bothered to find out which, and the government chose not to retry him. He had no interest in genealogy either, would never have thought to trace the possibility of a family link between himself and his courtroom tormentor.

This story would not be much enriched by detailing every event in String's life between the trial and his life as a married man. In a nutshell then, he returned to California, left San Diego for Los Angeles, received an AB degree from Chapman College, became distraught over a rejection from the first major love of his life, followed her across the country on an ex-army, Indian motorcycle - those were beatnik days - abandoned his search for her after arriving in New York City, and ended up working for Vinny at Taffy's - later called the Village Burger - a Mafia-owned restaurant in Greenwich Village. He met Joan at the home of a patron, a sky-lighted artist's studio on nearby Macdougal Alley, the city's last gas-lamp lit street. At the time, she worked in a lower east side settlement house, The Church of All Nations, and lived in a fifth floor, cold-water-flat walk-up above it, a place where taxis wouldn't stop. A short time after their wedding, Vinny went back to Italy, met the woman he would marry, earned a doctor of medicine degree at the University of Padua, and returned to do his internship at Atlanti-Care Regional Medical Center in Atlantic City, where String last saw him after arriving by train from California to give a talk titled "Digitized photographs for illustrated computer output," at the 1967 Spring Joint Computer Conference.

String's father Irving drove to Florida where he'd traced his own father - the man who had deserted his family 64 years earlier - and confronted him with, "I'm your son." The old man brightened, thrust out his hand for a shake, and replied, "Great to see you, Ray!"

Marine hero Chet surprised everyone by living to the age of 82, 14 years longer - sadly - than his wife, navy nurse and fellow WWII vet, Jean. They share a military gravesite at the Fort Rosecrans National Cemetery in the Point Loma peninsula hills of southwest San Diego.

After college, String lost all contact with George Talbott. It turns out he first studied philosophy, then received a Doctor of Science degree in physics. Coincidentally, he also lived 82 years, part of them spent writing eleven published books - books largely incomprehensible to the average reader. Among them: *Fermat's Last Theorem*, an acclaimed two-volume *Philosophy and Unified Science*, *A Twelfth Dynasty Egyptian Papyrus*, and *Sir Arthur & Gravity*.

Four former Kings popped, now and then, into String's life. Doug, the closest to him and the only other King not to remain in, or close to, San Diego, took his own life in a Fresno garage when in his late thirties and a field representative for the California Youth Authority. Robbie spent his life with Thelma and his working years as a mathematician with a department of the Navy. He died of a heart attack at 69.

Max died of cancer at 74. String last saw him at their 40th high school reunion. Max pointed out everyone to String he thought he had known. No one remembered String, not even his rival for junior class president. Guido lived to be 75 and, as would be expected, died with the greatest theatricality. He went down in flames just short of the Jacumba airport, seventy miles east of San Diego, solo flying in a two-seater Van's RV-4 aircraft.

Last year String made it to the only other high school reunion he'd ever attended, his 70th. Of the group there - larger and cheerier than expected and not at all behaving as grim survivors - he knew only three. One was written of here, the vocalist singing for the Marvin's Movers band.

Retreating further into the past, back to the warm fuzzy, fading days of grammar school and before; thumbing photographs of friends turning brown on curling print-paper: the Beans, Lima, Pinto; recalling others, people and things not recorded: the Goon retreat, a round tailed dog, Mitzi and other loves - all dance around in cloudy time for him, orange and washed-out teddy bears, lost to history, to memory's sharpness.

String sits now in his newly furnished retirement house, in denial, immortal, looking forward to meeting old-timers like himself, folks to talk with, to get to know, to compensate, never to replace, those he's lost. For him life's mysteries persist. "No one really knows shit," he'll tell you. "Just breathe slowly and ... look around."

3 1901 05897 5527

CPSIA information can be obtained
at www.ICGtesting.com
Printed in the USA
FSOW01n0401230915
11379FS

9 780692 420867